MBA FUNDAMENTALS
STRATEGY

MBA
FUNDAMENTALS
STRATEGY

Thomas P. Ference, PhD
Paul W. Thurman, MBA

This publication is designed to provide accurate and authoritative information in regard to the subject matter covered. It is sold with the understanding that the publisher is not engaged in rendering legal, accounting, or other professional service. If legal advice or other expert assistance is required, the services of a competent professional should be sought.

© 2009-2016 by Thomas P. Ference and Paul W. Thurman

All rights reserved. The text of this publication, or any part thereof, may not be reproduced in any manner whatsoever without written permission from the publisher.

Printed in the United States of America

ISBN-13: 978-1-5412-4019-3

For Ellie, as always
—Tom

For Crissa and our ladies, Tahlia, Vanessa, Stella, and Lisa.
And in loving memory of my father, Clovis
—Paul

Table of Contents

Introduction ix

Part I: The Concept of Strategy and of Strategic Thinking 1
    1. What Is Strategy and Why? 3
    2. Thinking Strategically and Preparing for Action 23
    3. The *Strategos* and the Three Levels of Strategic Thinking 49

Part II: Strategy: Mission, Vision, and Values 69
    4. Developing a Strategic Perspective: The Conceptual Level 71
    5. Developing the Strategic Concept—The Fundamental Questions 89
    6. Building on the Mission—Identifying Values and Vision 119

Part III: Strategy: Analytical and Operational Considerations 139
    7. Developing Strategic Perspectives: Macro-Market Analytical Frameworks 141
    8. Developing Strategic Perspectives: Micro-Market Analytical Frameworks 165
    9. Developing Strategic Perspectives: Operational Considerations 185

Part IV: Putting it All Together: Implementing a Strategy 221
    10. Completing the Process—Developing the Strategy 223

Acknowledgments 255
Test Yourself "Answers" 261
Endnotes 301
Index 311
About the Authors 317

Introduction

IS THIS BOOK RIGHT FOR ME?

Strategy, in a business context, is perhaps the most used—and sadly, the most abused—term in firms today. Even worse, MBA programs around the world—and executive education courses, corporate retreats, and the ever-popular "strategic planning off-site"—are replete with the use (and misuse) of this term. *Strategy, strategic planning, strategic management,* and *strategic thinking* are all terms that have become synonymous not only among themselves but with basically any type of organizational thinking, planning, or operations. In many business schools—and in schools of public affairs and administration, schools of public health, and others that teach organization and management—a *Strategy* course is unfortunately all-too-often used as a catchall for concepts that may not have been covered in other core courses. Even worse, the course is often perceived by students—and by many of our clients—as a course focused on buzzwords, creative writing, and "fuzzy" management skills.

We are on a mission (see the first chapter!) to change this perception! The concept and indeed the *process* of strategic thinking is a demanding one *conceptually* (what is our real purpose?), *analytically* (can we do what we say we will do and will the "market" support/accept it?), and *operationally* (how will we organize ourselves and use our resources to do what we said we would?). As any operations management student will attest, anything that is a process can be *mapped, planned, measured, and optimized (or improved).* This is precisely the approach we take to strategic thinking—we will illustrate a process that for our thousands of students and clients is process-driven, mapped out, and planned with specific goals and visions in mind, analytically justified, and operationally implemented and measured. Ā is is not to say that the process of thinking about or of creating a strategy is an assembly-line operation. Quite the contrary, since the "raw materials" change every time and the machine parts—your firm, people, marketplace competitors, and so on—also are in constant flux. However, like an assembly line, if a process can be followed repetitively, we fully believe that it can be measured and made better. And like an assembly line, some things can be process-oriented while others require real "workmanship" in the form of good judgment, ethics, and a sense of values that are irrefutable for you, personally, and for your firm.

Instead of a buzzword, catchall framework, this text (and this course) will be read *after* completion of critical core management courses such as marketing, finance, accounting, operations, and data analysis. Ā en, *strategic thinking* will become an exercise in *synthesis* whereby these core tools and learnings will be applied in concert to devise, justify, implement, and measure any new idea, product, service, or concept. It may be true that with more experience comes increased strategic success. We firmly believe, however, that students and new general managers can increase their own probabilities of strategic success from their very first strategy formulation or planning effort.

As such, this text is intended to introduce managers, executives, and graduate students, particularly those in MBA, MPH, and MPA degree programs with some core course requirements behind them, to the thought processes, development toolkits, and measurement frameworks critical to strategic success. Ā ankfully, we have developed these lessons, cases, and real-world examples from our careers, which span over 60 collective years of for-profit and not-for-profit consulting and executive and other graduate-level training in the private, not-for-profit, and public sectors. We have drawn our cases and examples from all three sectors - private, not-for-profit, and public—because we believe that the concepts and tools apply equally well in all organizational settings. We sincerely hope you find this book useful for not only a one-time course but also as a constant companion on your bookshelves throughout the remainders of your professional careers.

THE CONCEPT OF STRATEGY AND OF STRATEGIC THINKING

CHAPTER 1

What Is Strategy and Why?

INTRODUCTION

> Alice was a little startled by seeing the Cheshire Cat sitting on the bough of a tree a few yards off.
>
> The Cat only grinned when it saw Alice. It looked good-natured, she thought: still it had <u>very</u> long claws and a great many teeth, so she felt it ought to be treated with respect.
>
> "Cheshire Puss," she began, rather timidly, as she did not at all know whether it would like the name; however, it only grinned a little wider. "Come, it's pleased so far," thought Alice, and she went on, "Would you tell me, please, which way I ought to walk from here?"
>
> "That depends a good deal on where you want to get to," said the Cat.
>
> "I don't much care where -----," said Alice.
>
> "Then it doesn't matter which way you walk," said the Cat.[1]

This familiar scene from our childhood is at the heart of what <u>strategy</u>—and more importantly, *strategic thinking*—is all about and of why we need to *think and act strategically* if we are to succeed, organizationally and personally. The Cheshire Cat—the archetypical consultant—asks exactly the right question: "Where do you want to get to?" When Alice cannot answer, he gives exactly the right guidance: "Then it doesn't matter which path you take."

This is the essence of strategic thinking (and the purpose of this book): knowing, deciding, choosing where you want to get to and then crafting the set of decisions, plans, and actions—the strategy—needed to get you there.

Thus, strategy starts with a clear sense of purpose, proceeds to assess what has to be done to achieve that purpose, and then develops and executes plans of action. More precisely, strategy, as we will use it, refers to *the overall process of consciously choosing and achieving a desired future—for our organization, our unit, our career, our life—that would not otherwise occur in the natural flow of events absent intervention on our part to make it so.* When we engage in strategic thinking, we begin by conceiving of a future state of affairs—for our firm, our industry, our society and our place in it—that we find more desirable than the present state, but that we also know will not come into being if we continue with "business as usual."

> **WHAT'S AHEAD**
>
> In this chapter, you will learn:
> - Why Strategy is important both to managing the organization internally and to competing externally.
> - What Strategy "looks like" in terms of relating desired futures to current realities.
> - The first KEY to Strategic Thinking and how to use the Strategic Perspective as a learning process.
> - How *scarcity* and *competition* define Strategy.
> - The importance of creating specific *value propositions* for products, services, and offerings.

IN THE REAL WORLD

You have just been appointed executive director of an afterschool homework assistance program for high school students. The program is largely supported by funds from the State Department of Education. Funding for your program, along with many others in your city and in other cities across the state, is renewable on an annual basis upon review of your performance against contract requirements and objectives. Your program is conducted by your staff onsite in local high schools using regular classrooms after the teachers who use the rooms during the regular school day have departed. You have to contract, again on an annual basis, with the high school principals for permission to use the classrooms.

You received your position when the previous executive director had been let go because student participation in the program had fallen below the norm for afterschool programs in the city and was in danger of losing its funding. Your board of directors, which hired you, has asked you to submit a strategy for "turning this wonderful program around." The program has been consistently rated sound academically but has trouble meeting its enrollment targets. Sounds like a great opportunity. What do you propose?

THE KEY CONCEPTS

Strategy begins with an expression of human *aspiration*, either collective or individual, and is inherently emotional and subjective—it is what "we" want or hope to do. It then asks how to fulfill that aspiration given current internal capabilities, resources, external constraints, and competition. "How can we, consciously and deliberately, change ourselves and the external context or environment to make room for our aspirations?" Strategy, therefore, is the process by which organizations—and people in organizations—achieve significant human purpose together in a resource-constrained, competitive reality. The challenge for the strategist—for the strategic thinker—is to turn *soft*, subjective aspiration into *hard*, objective achievement.

In this context, it is also important to realize that strategic thinking—thinking as a strategist—is not something that we would do only occasionally or ceremonially. "It's time once again to do a five-year strategic plan." It is, rather, the way that we should approach all decisions and actions in our organizational roles. If we are serious about our purposes, our aspirations—whether they are to maximize sales of our automobiles, find a cure for cancer, promote a particular political philosophy, or corner the market in chicken futures—then every choice that we make among alternative actions is, in effect, a strategic one. Which decision or action, if implemented effectively, has the highest probability, as best we can judge given our current state of information, of achieving our purpose? Our purpose in this book is to help you develop the competences of thinking strategically at all times—of being a strategic decision-maker.

A Few Words about Language, Jargon, and Rhetoric

Strategy is one of the more malleable words in the English language, and we shall explore its origins and place in the study of organizations later in this chapter. It is a noun, a verb, an adjective, an adverb, and so on, and can be used to refer to something as complex and comprehensive as "placing a man on the moon by the end of the decade" (President Kennedy's strategic mandate to NASA in the early '60s) or to something as simple and straightforward as making a luncheon reservation ("Call these three restaurants and see who has a quiet corner table for five available at noon"). Given its breadth of potential usage and the modern tendency to refer to every organizational action as a "strategy" no matter how it was developed or chosen, the term can become so plastic as to be almost devoid of meaning—or to be little more than a buzzword dropped indiscriminately at cocktail parties and in *Dilbert*.

We are going to seek to give the term precision in this book by limiting it to two usages. **First,** as a noun, we shall use "strategy" to refer to the major thrusts or directions that an organization adopts, consciously and deliberately, in the pursuit of its primary purposes. Thus, Team A has chosen to pursue a home-grown, farm system strategy to winning the championship while its competitor, Team B, has opted instead to rebuild itself annually through free agency in its pursuit of the same end purpose. Or, Firm A is following an intensive, high-investment research strategy in seeking industry dominance while Firm B, in the same industry, has dropped its research program and is pursuing market leadership through mergers and acquisitions.

Second, and more frequently, we will use the adjective (strategic) or adverb (strategically) forms to modify other terms in the overall strategic process. Thus, we will use the following terms:

- **Strategic thinking:** the overall process of consciously choosing, pursuing, and achieving desired futures through a deliberate, designed, disciplined process
- **Strategic conceptualization:** the way we think about our purposes and aspirations in terms of such notions as mission, values, and vision
- **Strategic analysis:** the application of the array of tools for assessing the challenges and probabilities of achieving our strategic purposes
- **Strategic planning:** the process by which we use the results of our analyses to identify high probability approaches for transforming our aspirations into achievement in the context of the realities that we have identified
- **Strategic plans:** the specific sets of actions, steps, and sequences that follow from the prior steps in the strategic process
- **Strategic implementation and operation:** the execution and monitoring of strategic plans in "real-time" in order to test

achievement against expectation and intention and to provide feedback and guidance to the ongoing strategic process

We will also use the terms *the strategist* and *the strategic team* to identify those persons who engage in strategic thinking on behalf of the organization.

In this chapter, we will develop fully this notion of strategy—or, more properly, of strategic thinking, of adopting a strategic perspective—as a comprehensive process. We will also discuss the importance of strategy in organizational and personal effectiveness and set the stage for developing the essential concepts and tools of strategy in later chapters. Now, let us follow the advice of another of Alice's strategic guides, the King of Hearts, who said:

Begin at the beginning and go on until you come to the end: then stop.[2]

SO WHY IS STRATEGY SO IMPORTANT?

Why, you might ask, all the fuss about strategy? If we have a great product, dedicated people, and a respected name, why do we need to worry about strategy? Why can't we just keep on keeping on—doing what we're already doing? After all, wasn't the catch phrase: "if it ain't broke, don't fix it"?

Let's step back and take a look at what drives the need for strategy. While the terminology of strategy is drawn from combat and the military, as we shall see later, the fundamental argument for the importance of strategy in managing organizations comes from basic economics. As shown in exhibit I, strategy is defined by two related economic concepts: *scarcity* and *competition*.

Scarcity refers to the availability of the *resources* any organization needs to pursue its strategic aspirations. Resources include not only the tangible: money, materials, knowledge, people, information, space, time, facilities; but also the intangible: commitment, passion, reputation, access. All of these are essential to building and sustaining an effective organization and all are scarce, both absolutely—there are only so many hours in the day—and relatively—we can secure or acquire only so much of a given resource.

The objective reality of scarcity, therefore, leads directly to *competition*, where competitors are defined as those who seek to draw on the same resources, even though they may use those resources to pursue different purposes. This differs from the everyday understanding of *competitor*, which is typically used to refer to others seeking to provide the same products or services to the same customers. Taken together, these two aspects of economic reality define the need for strategy in the pursuit of purpose.

Exhibit I—Why Strategy?

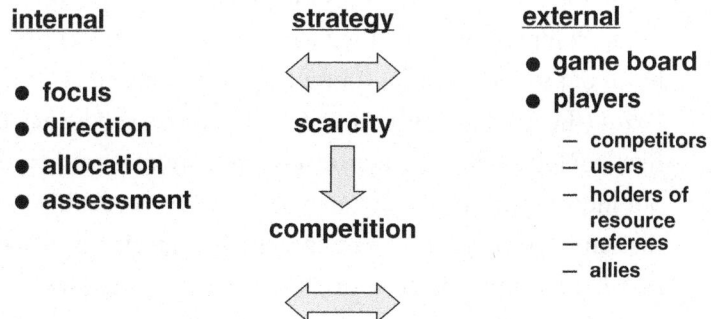

Internally, the reality of resource scarcity—we never have all the resources that we want—requires that we husband and deploy the resources that we do have consciously and deliberately. We need a clear sense of strategy—of where we want to go and how we are going to try to get there—in order to provide guidance to four key processes:

1. **Focus:** Strategy is essential to focusing the efforts of all of the members and components of the organization—to ensuring

that we are all "on the same page." Without a clearly articulated and communicated strategy, everyone would be free to pursue his or her own sense of what is important and how to do it.

2. **Direction:** Once focus is attained, it remains to aim that focus in a chosen direction—we are all going to go this, not that way, and not some of us this way and some of us that way.

3. **Allocation:** To pursue our chosen direction, we will need a comprehensive strategic analysis and plan in order to apply our scarce resources effectively and efficiently.

4. **Assessment:** Finally, our sense of strategic purpose and of our desired future will provide us with the criteria needed to monitor and assess our performance on an ongoing basis so that we can learn from our efforts and make adjustments as needed.

Externally, the need for strategy is even more apparent. Defining competition in terms of resources (inputs) rather than in terms of products or sales (outputs) significantly enlarges the *game board* (the playing field) on which our efforts will be acted out. It now contains a large group of diverse *players*—not just those in our industry or market, but all of those who are seeking to acquire the same resources to pursue their own strategic purposes, which may have nothing to do with ours. The key sets of players include the following:

- **Competitors** are all parties seeking to acquire the same resources we are, whether they are seeking to sell the same products and services to the same customers or not.
- **Users** are the eventual targets of our products and services, whether we call them customers, clients, audience, patients, students, or whatever.
- **Holders of Resources** are the parties who presently hold the resources that we seeking; they may include investors, funders, suppliers, or even potential employees—who have the skills we

need. Users are, of course, a special case of holders of resource which is sufficiently important to be included as a class in itself.

- **Referees** are the parties who make and enforce the rules of play. They may include legislators, regulators, accreditors, professional associations, licensing bodies, and so on.
- **Allies** may be defined *not* as those parties whose goals and needs are identical to ours—they may be our most severe direct competitors. Instead, potential allies are those parties whose goals and needs are congruent with ours for a time for a purpose. Thus, allies may be drawn from any of the above sets of players depending on the situation. We may form an alliance with competitors to seek regulatory change while we strive to take market share away from them.

We must take the potential strategies of all these players into account if we are to be successful. Further, their identities are not always obvious. A few examples, particularly with regard to customers and competitors, may help to underscore this point:

> Remember our newly appointed executive director running the afterschool homework assistance program for high school students? Who are the competitors our executive needs to consider in formulating a strategy?
>
> Well, first you might say other afterschool assistance programs, which are competing for the same students and the same financial support from charitable and public funds. Then, since many of these programs use school facilities, you might include other types of afterschool programs such as sports and band—and maybe even teachers who do not want their classrooms disturbed.
>
> But what about hanging out with friends on the corner or riding the subways? What about an afterschool job, or the need to go home to care for younger siblings? And then there is the Wii™, Xbox®, and Playstation® . . . . The list goes on.

Why? Because the key resource that our executive is competing for is the student's discretionary time—and our executive's strategy must be able to persuade the students that they will be able to derive more of what they value from spending their time in the afterschool program than in any of the competing activities.

This last point in our example is crucial. How does the potential user (in this case, the student) decide how to allocate his or her resource (discretionary time)? The answer is clear—the student, as with any potential user or holder of any other resource, will allocate his or her resource to that activity that is perceived to provide the greatest *value* in return. Moreover, value itself is a subjective concept and is defined in terms of what the user or holder of resource most values: financial return, status, power, satisfaction of basic needs, and so on. This is referred to in the field of marketing as a value proposition and may be defined as follows:

> A *winning value proposition* creates and sustains the user's perception that our product, service, or program will provide greater value than would competing uses—in terms of what the user values—in exchange for the user's resources.

We will return to this concept of a value proposition in later chapters when we consider the challenge of developing market- or customer-specific strategies. Our second example deals with the challenge of defining who our real customer is.

Consider the familiar children's toy business. You are responsible for your firm's marketing strategy, particularly the focus and placement of your TV and print advertising. To do so, you must decide who your primary customer is in order to direct and target your message most effectively. What could be more obvious? It's the child—or is it the parent? And does it matter if you make the wrong choice?

In the simple world of conventional, Adam Smith economics, there are producers and consumers. Company A makes soap and Customer B wants soap. When they reach an agreed-upon transfer price—a shared value—an exchange occurs and a market is created. In practice, it is not so simple. In our example, Customer B **decides** to buy Company A's soap, **pays** for it, **uses** it, **and benefits** from it by feeling clean.

In practice, different parties may provide these four aspects of "customerness." We must ask:

1. Who **decides** or chooses the product or service?
2. Who **pays** for the chosen product or service?
3. Who **uses** the acquired product or service?
4. Who **benefits** from the use of the product or service?

In the case of children's toys, the best market research, and common sense, says that the child decides, the grandparents pays, the child uses, and the parents benefit—presumably from the peace that comes when the child is absorbed in play!

Thus, most advertising in the toy business is highly visual and active, featuring children playing, and is placed primarily on children's TV networks and shows, and in children's magazines.

Having demonstrated need for strategy in pursuing aspiration and purpose in the context of a resource-constrained, competitive reality that requires internal discipline and a mastery of the Game Board, we can next consider what strategy "looks like" and what is involved in thinking strategically.

BUSINESS STRATEGY IN ACTION

In the case below, Norm Putnam, the corporate director of administration, faces a tricky situation that has dropped in his lap unexpectedly late on a Friday afternoon. Fred Troy, one of his analysts, is being pressured by Art Farber, a very senior sales executive, to cut corners in the review of a proposed "deal" in order to secure a major contract. The review procedures have been designed to ensure the profitability of such deals, which are risky, and were established in the aftermath of some deals that had gone bad. The Firm has, therefore, a deliberately chosen strategic approach to reviewing business opportunities—but Art Farber is one of the Firm's most experienced and most successful producers and is convinced that the deal is sound and that timing is critical.

Norm is facing a classic dilemma—how should he balance strategic discipline with short-term expedience? He could, for example, tell Troy to comply with Art's request—after all, Art has earned some special consideration. He could tell Art that "rules are rules," and that he shouldn't be putting pressure on junior staffers. He could ask David Wells what to do. But he is concerned that, no matter which of these short-term actions he might take, there will be repercussions and bad feelings—and the possibility of either lost revenue or a bad deal. Also, he realizes that, no matter how he handles the situation, he will be setting precedents and that David Wells, all the sales reps, and his analysts are watching.

Norm clearly needs to develop a strategic response to this potentially explosive situation—and yet his time is limited. How might the Purpose of the Firm, as stated by Joseph Burton, help him? How can he make both a sound business decision and also maintain the commitment and support of all of the involved parties? How would you advise him to proceed?

TEST YOURSELF

Read and analyze the case, Burton, Wells & Co., below. Be prepared to respond to and discuss the following questions:

1. What should Putnam do to resolve the current situation?
2. What consequences might follow and what should he do to manage these consequences?

3. What changes should be made at Burton, Wells as a result of this experience?

BURTON, WELLS & CO [3]

It was a typical late October afternoon, clear, crisp, with just a hint of potential frost. Norm Putnam had little enthusiasm for the panorama of autumn colors outside his office window, however, as he mulled over the meeting that he had just finished with Fred Troy. Putnam, the Director of Administration for Burton, Wells & Co., a medium-sized but rapidly growing equipment-leasing company, was greatly disturbed by the problem that Troy, one of four senior analysts who reported to him, had presented.

Troy, who had requested the meeting, had reported that he was being pressured by Art Farber, the Company's Eastern Regional Vice President, to alter drastically the normal review procedures for a computer network package that Farber had put together in order to meet a November 1 contract deadline. Troy was certain that the Company's review procedures, which had been in effect for less than one year, could not be completed in time and also felt that the package in its present form could not satisfy all of the short- and long-run financial criteria.

As he told Putnam, "I explained all of this to Farber and indicated that I was just following Company policy. He said that there was no way that he was going to allow an administrative staff procedure to sabotage a major piece of business and ordered me to complete the review favorably by November 1. He said that he was determined to 'get the deal off the street before someone else grabbed it' and that, if there were problems with scheduling residuals and meeting yield requirements, it was our job to 'clean them up later.'"

After they had talked through a number of options, Putnam said, "Let's just be grateful that it's Friday. You go ahead and enjoy your weekend, Troy, and let me sort this out. We'll get together Monday morning and decide how we will handle it."

BURTON, WELLS & CO

Burton, Wells & Co. was formed over 20 years ago by Joseph Burton and Jack Wells, an office equipment distributor and a financial analyst, respectively, who foresaw a growing demand for leased office equipment, particularly on the part of small- to medium-sized firms who could not keep pace with the rapid advances in office information-handling technology. Over the years, the company had developed a considerable reputation for reliability and customer service. The company was particularly well-known for its ability to spot and package emerging technology improvements and for aiding customers in assembling and implementing new equipment and systems. The company had also maintained an excellent profit performance and had chosen to remain independent and privately held despite overtures from several potential acquirers.

The Company prided itself on the high degree of professionalism that it brought to its work, a tradition that stemmed largely from the personal philosophy of Joseph Burton. As he wrote in his first annual message to the company's employees, "The purpose of Burton, Wells & Co. is to provide our customers with professional leasing services that will satisfy the most demanding standards of product quality and availability, that will take full advantage of the most favorable financial arrangements and instruments for the company and its customers, and that are closely and consistently managed."

The company had grown rapidly, particularly in the last eight years, and now included four regional vice presidents with business development and relationship management responsibilities and a sales force of seventeen account representatives. The company had also developed a full complement of administrative support or back-office functions including Norm Putnam's Section. While both Mr. Burton and Mr. Wells had retired, the company is still strongly influenced by their philosophy and methods. David Wells, Jack Wells's younger brother, is president and CEO. Putnam reports to Wells on a day-to-day basis.

COMPUTER NETWORK SYSTEMS

The computer network package put together by Art Farber represents a fairly new development in the evolution of the type of programs that the company has assembled for its customers. Traditionally, the company had focused on specific pieces of office equipment (word processors, copiers, desktops, etc.) but had recently been responding to the market development and demand for integrated office systems by building packages that included hardware, networking equipment and software, and licensed proprietary software applications. In general, the company found itself moving from low-ticket, high-volume, and low-risk transactions to increasingly bigger ticket, lower volume, and higher risk deals. This evolution of the business has been paralleled by a movement away from informal and toward more formal relations with clients and a greater need for proper documentation and analysis of the implications of each deal.

Farber, the packager of the deal in question, has been with Burton, Wells for eleven years and a vice president for the last three. As is typical in putting such a deal together, Farber has taken the lead with the customer in designing the package (equipment, software, licenses, professional services, etc.). Before the deal can be closed, the equipment acquired and committed, and the financing put in place, the entire package (acquisition costs, equipment availabilities, credit scoring, clocking of residuals, yield analysis, possible cost exposures, and so on) must be subjected to a series of demanding reviews by the appropriate support groups. The effective responsibility for review vested with the administration section.

As Norm Putnam described his section's work:

> We review all deals above a certain dollar level for completeness; satisfaction of various financial and legal policies and requirements regarding licenses, tax implications, and the like; and overall consistency with established company objectives and procedures. We are not account representatives and we

don't claim that we can do the work of the field. All the same, I think my section, particularly my senior analysts, knows more about all the pieces that have to go into a good deal than do many of the sales and marketing people. Our job is to police the application of various policies and decision criteria and to make sure that every deal has covered all the bases: availability, cash flow and yield, residuals, and so on. I sometimes think that the account reps and even the RVPs in their anxiety to close a deal forget how complex a leasing program can be. They also tend to minimize the potential danger to the company from doing a sloppy job.

The normal procedure for the administration section is to assign responsibility for the complete review of a program such as Farber's package to one of the four senior analysts. Until two years ago, the review process had been fairly informal with the steps and procedures left largely to the discretion and experience of the analyst in consultation with the account rep who had put the deal together and his/her RVP. At that time some major problems with a few complex deals had led to a reconsideration of the review procedures. Significant miscalculations with both acquisition costs in the software area and residual performance of rapidly evolving technology had damaged profitability and, in at least one instance, the relationship with a major customer. As a result, David Wells had insisted that the review processes be tightened up and standardized.

As Putnam recalled the situation, "Mr. Wells felt that the review process had become too idiosyncratic, too dependent upon the methods chosen by the particular analyst. There was no sense that anyone was cheating or deliberately doing sloppy work, but we had to face up to the reality that everyone in the company is always working under enormous time and competitive pressures. Everything always needs to be done yesterday. The RVPs especially tend to bring deals in late and to want them reviewed overnight. This puts a lot of stress on the senior analysts, all four of whom have been with us ten years or more, because they feel that they have been entrusted with preserving the integrity of the Company."

At Wells's insistence, administration did a major study of the review procedures and established a standard review process that defined the sequence of steps to be taken, the criteria to be applied at each stage, and the contingent actions to be taken as a result of application of these criteria. At the end of the study, a procedures manual was prepared and approved for implementation beginning with the current year. Putnam felt things had been going smoothly with the new procedures until Fred Troy brought in his problems with Farber's deal to today's meeting. As Troy described the situation:

> I think we are going to have major problems with Art Farber on this deal. He brought it to me today and told me that he needed it ready to go by November 1 in order to hold on to the customer. He said he was concerned that, if we couldn't provide what was needed, then they would take their business elsewhere. I looked over the package that he had put together and a number of red flags went off. I went to see Farber yesterday and told him that I seriously doubted that I could get it through review in the time that he had allowed. I pointed out that the sequence of review steps required by the procedures took time and that each step had to fall in the proper order. Quite frankly, Putnam, even if his deal passes muster at each stage, we can't meet the deadline. Worse yet, while I didn't say so to Farber, my preliminary run though the package has convinced me that it won't pass review as it presently stands.
>
> Farber was extremely angry when I told him about the schedule problems. He insisted that the deal was absolutely critical to his business and said that he had already lined up several potential additional deals along the same lines if this first one was closed on time. When I ran him through the

sequence again, pointing out the time needed at each step, he suggested—actually insisted—that I alter the sequence of steps. He mentioned several other deals of his that he felt were comparable that had been reviewed by a different set of steps and that were successful. I agreed with him that, if we did it his way—the way that we used to do things before the new procedures—we could get it out on time, but to do so would violate procedures.

He replied that I better get it done or else and, while he didn't fill all the blanks, his message was clear. He insisted that the procedures were meant only as guidelines. He said, "Don't worry; you won't get into any trouble. Just do it the way I told you and, if anyone questions you, just say that I authorized it." What should I do, Norm?

After talking through several options, Putnam suggested that they think about it over the weekend and meet again on Monday. Later, as he prepared to leave the office, Putnam reviewed his options. He could tell Troy to go ahead and do as Farber had asked, he could try to deal with Farber himself, or he could go to David Wells and ask him to resolve the matter. He mused:

If I let Troy go ahead and something goes sour, I wouldn't want to bet that Farber's authorization would save us from getting the blame. Besides, I think it would really damage present morale if I told him it was all right to set aside the procedures. He chaired the task force that put them together, and I think that he has a lot invested personally in the credibility of the process. On the other hand, Troy's got as good a relation with Farber as anyone in Administration—Farber was on the task force!—and, if he can't get anywhere with him, it's not clear that I'll be able to.

If I go to David, he would probably support me, but I'm not sure that I want to play that card. He has commented on a number of occasions that he expects the Administration Sections to provide discipline and consistency to the Company and that he has full confidence in us. This could be a real mess. Farber is one of the top producers in the Company, and it won't do us any good to have him as an enemy.

KEY POINTS TO REMEMBER

- Strategy is a comprehensive *process*, not just an outcome or a "document."
- *Strategic thinking* is the process or complex of concepts by which we transform *soft aspiration* into *hard performance*.
- *Scarcity* and *competition* drive the need for Strategy.
- Well-crafted Strategies combine *winning value propositions* with purposeful allocations of scarce resources to operate effectively internally and compete successfully externally.

CHAPTER 2

Thinking Strategically and Preparing for Action

INTRODUCTION

In a field one summer's day a Grasshopper was hopping about, chirping and singing to its heart's content. An Ant passed by, bearing along with great toil an ear of corn he was taking to the nest.

"Why not come and chat with me," said the Grasshopper, "instead of toiling and moiling in that way?"

"I am helping to lay up food for the winter," said the Ant, "and recommend you to do the same."

"Why bother about winter," said the Grasshopper; "we have got plenty of food at present." But the Ant went on its way and continued its toil. When the winter came the Grasshopper had no food, and found itself dying of hunger, while it saw the ants distributing every day corn and grain from the stores they had collected in the summer.[1]

"Well, of course," you might say. "Everybody knows that you have put up stores for the winter. What's the big deal?" Let's take a closer look at what our two characters are saying.

The Ant, our strategist, is saying, "I know that things will change, that they will not always be as they are today, and that I have the choice of anticipating and managing that change or waiting to see what happens and hoping to be able to react. When winter comes, I want to be warm and well-fed—with extra food. This tells me what I must do today to ensure that the winter will happen as I intend."

The Grasshopper, who is like so many of us when things are going well, is saying, "Everything is fine today; it was great yesterday; and it will be fine tomorrow. If things change, I'll deal with it then." If the winter is mild, the Grasshopper will be fine. The Ant simply isn't willing to leave the future to chance—and so the Ant develops and implements a strategy!

Now that we have defined thinking strategically as a process that balances aspirations with the purposeful allocation of scarce resources to compete effectively, we need to delve further into this thought process to help us develop and execute a strategy successfully. For now, let's focus on the essential nature of the strategic thought process.

WHAT'S AHEAD

In this chapter, you will learn:
- What it means to think strategically from a process point-of-view
- The process of "folding back" and mapping out a plan to achieve critical milestones and to surmount obstacles
- The importance of "folding back" and the key skills exhibited by best-in-class strategic thinkers

IN THE REAL WORLD

As part of an overall strategy, a Manager has been charged with opening an additional satellite office of her firm by 12 months from today. In thinking about how to get this done on time, and the deadline is absolute because of commitments that senior management has made, she realizes that she will have to buy furniture, find the space, employ and train a new staff, engage a contractor to do the necessary renovations, hire a mover to transfer equipment, get building permits, work with a realtor, satisfy various inspections, choose a site, and get senior management approval—all while doing her regular job.

She clears her calendar, writes a to-do list, and reaches for the phone; she knows prime commercial real estate is scarce, contractors seldom bring projects in on schedule, there is no spare space to house new staff before the satellite opens, and the city inspection processes are notoriously slow and capricious—so there is no time to waste! But whom to call first? What would you do?

THE KEY CONCEPTS
What Does It Mean to Think Strategically?

We have defined thinking strategically as engaging in the process of consciously choosing and achieving a desired future that would not occur without our intervention in the natural flow of events. What is suggested by this is shown graphically in exhibit II.

At any given point in time—t_p—our organization exists with whatever configuration of resources and attributes we have achieved to date; this is shown in the exhibit as a square. Our aspirations—our mission and values—at that point in time **envision** a future state of affairs at a specific future point in time—t_{p+x}—that is more desirable than our present state; this is shown in the exhibit as a triangle, which is also the Greek letter *delta*, the mathematical symbol for change. As shown by the diagonal line connecting the square and triangle, the task or the purpose of our strategic process is to transform our organization from the square to the triangle in the selected timeframe, defined here as x.[2]

Thus, we may think of the strategic process as that of deliberately chosen change, of transforming our present reality into a more desirable future by conscious effort on our part. To make this notion of deliberate effort or intervention clear, consider the lower half of the exhibit. Here a dotted line is shown connecting two squares in the same timeframe. The second square represents what our organization would look like at t_{p+x} if, instead of pursuing a conscious strategy, we had been content to continue with 'business as usual', to go along with the **natural flow of events [nfe]**.

Exhibit II—The Strategic Process

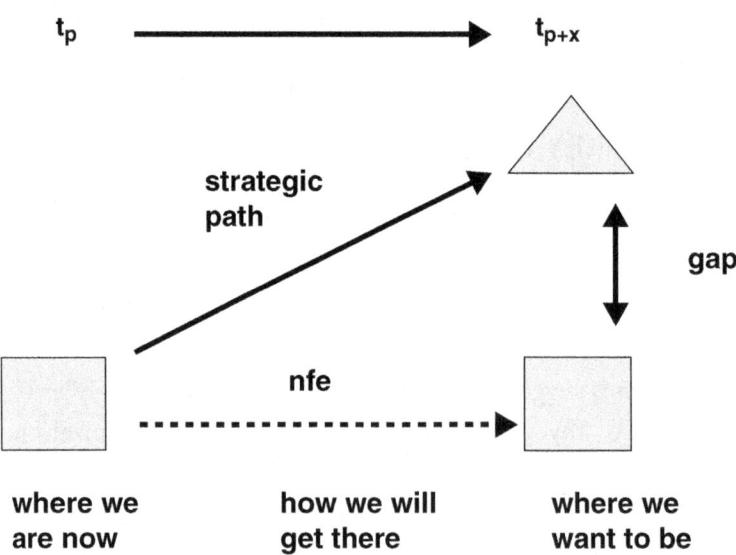

We may think of the natural flow of events as a baseline or trend line for our strategic thinking. It is what we would reasonably forecast or project to occur, using the best analytical data and forecasting tools available, if we did nothing more than continue with our current efforts. Thus, the **gap** between what we would expect given the natural flow of events and our desired future state of affairs—our vision—is the expression of our aspirations and the objective of our strategic efforts: to close the gap in the desired time frame.

Thus, at its most basic level, the strategy process asks three fundamental questions:

1. Where do we want to be at a specific point of time in the future?
2. Where are we now relative to that desired future point?
3. How are we going to close the gap between the present and the desired future?

We will take up each of these questions in detail in subsequent chapters. For now, let's focus on the essential nature of strategic thinking.

THINKING LIKE A STRATEGIST – THE MINDSET

"Ok," you might say, "we know where we are and we know where we want to go. The rest should be easy. With the target—the endpoint—in view, or at least clearly in mind, we can just start moving forward and keep going until we get there."

This is where life gets complicated. Just because we can "see" or envision where we want to go does not mean that the path is clear or that there will not be numerous obstacles, potholes, roadblocks, and other obstructions along the way. These might come from unanticipated actions of competitors (a price change or a new product launch), from changes in the larger environment (a change in regulatory requirements, an economic downturn, an advance in science, a major natural disaster, and on and on), from the impact of emerging information not available to us at the time we set off on our journey, or from the immediate consequences of our own actions.[3]

In other words, while we may initially have a clear sense of our actual starting point and our desired end point, the world around us will not hold still until we complete our strategic journey. The world around us—the environment and all the players noted earlier—is dynamic and constantly evolving on its own momentum, influenced by our actions and those of all the other players. As one wit once put it:

> Strategy is like shooting at a moving target from a moving platform with everything in between in flux.

The implication of this is that the pursuit of a strategic vision—a desired future—takes place over a timeframe in which the initial attributes and forecasts (of the marketplace, the other players, and our own organizational realities) on which our strategy is based are changing constantly *in part in reaction and as a result of our strategic efforts!* Thus, strategy is more properly the study of **dynamics** rather than of **statics**. This implies that our strategic efforts will require constant monitoring to determine if they are working as intended and are staying on target. We will also have to make periodic adjustments and adaptations in response to the experience and new information that our efforts are generating.

This iterative process of targeting, acting, monitoring, and adapting is shown visually in exhibit III, which adds two essential new concepts to our original simple map. The first is that of **milestones** or **checkpoints**, which represent markers along the path to our target where we might stop to take stock of what has happened so far and to determine what, if any, adjustments we might need to make in our current path. As shown, this might even include shifting to a different path if events and new information suggest that our initial choice no longer provides the highest probability of reaching our target. The second concept is that of **folding back**, as shown by the arrows moving from right to left. This represents the fundamental perspective or mindset of strategic thinking—of the strategist—that of consciously choosing the future and using that future as the basis for choosing actions in the present. This mindset is the first KEY to becoming an excellent strategist.

CHAPTER 2 • THINKING STRATEGICALLY & PREPARING FOR ACTION

Exhibit III—Folding Back

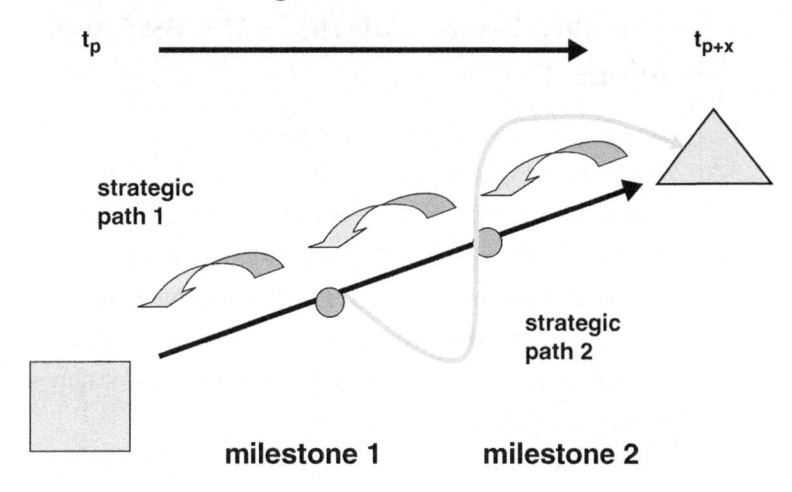

t_p → t_{p+x}

strategic path 1

strategic path 2

milestone 1   milestone 2

As shown in the exhibit, we begin in the present by defining a desired future at some point in time that seems meaningful to us—it is "as far as we can reasonably see into the future"—and then using that vision of the future as our frame of reference for choosing our strategic path. By folding or walking back from that imagined future, we can identify what has be achieved or in place by certain key points along the way—our milestones or phases. These in turn enable us, using all the available information that we have from our analyses and forecasts, to identify what seems to be the most likely path to follow by avoiding or overcoming the various obstacles noted. Once we start out along our chosen path, we can check our progress periodically against plan to determine what, if any, midcourse adjustments might have to be made.

In the example shown in the exhibit, new information on progress and changing conditions at **milestone 1** has led to a shift from **strategic path 1** (the straight line) to **strategic path 2** (the curve). Further adjustments might have to be made when we reach **milestone/checkpoint 2**. The strategist's mindset that lies behind this process is spelled out in the accompanying box.

Thinking like a strategist – the essential mindset

Let's follow the Strategist's thought process:

Standing on the platform of the present we can see some meaningful period of time into the future, say, three years from today, the state of affairs (for our organization, for ourselves) that we intend to commit to bringing about through our efforts and that would not occur absent conscious intervention on our part to make it so. This is our vision—our strategic intent.

To determine the best path, the highest probability strategy given our current state of knowledge about the environment and ourselves, to achieving that vision, we must "walk" in our mind's eye out to that future point (three years from now) for it is from there that we get the clearest view of possible paths connecting the present and the future—with all of the roadblocks, detours, blind alleys, and the like out of the way.

We can then walk back to the present, noting key milestones or potential checkpoints along the way. Thus, if we want to have achieved this by three years from today, we had better have this in place by two years from today, and this under control by one year from today, and, therefore, we'd better do this by tomorrow.

It is our image of a desired future (our vision) that enables us to select the current best path, to identify the key milestones or phases, and to prioritize our current actions.

Once we launch those actions, or begin to implement our chosen strategy, we of necessity alter the very conditions that led us to choose the strategy in the first place. We begin to act on and change the natural flow of events and, therefore,

> we have to assess periodically the effect of our actions. Our milestones (our targeted phases of the rolling out of our strategy) become our checkpoints for determining how and in what ways we may need to modify and change both our targets and our strategy.
>
> Thus, our strategic thinking is a dynamic and ongoing process—a dialogue between the present and the future where the future leads the discussion. It is an informed dialectic where at each checkpoint we have the opportunity and the necessity to incorporate new information generated since the previous checkpoint and to go through the entire strategic thought process again.
>
> In this perspective, all decisions are strategic in that our clear sense of the future, of where we are going, enables us to ask ourselves, "Of all the things we might do at this moment or to which we might allocate scarce resources, which most contributes, as best we can tell given current information, to achieving our vision?" Each checkpoint becomes the new starting point for the next thought cycle. We are always, in effect, in the first day or the first phase of our next three-year or five-year or whatever strategic plan.
>
> Note that this approach has the added benefit of providing guidance on what to stop doing or of when to stop allocating resources.

A simple example of this thought process might be the following;

Let's go back to our Manager who is responsible for opening a satellite office for her firm by 12 months from today. In thinking about how to get this done on time—and to determine whether her target is realistic—she walks through the following process:

> *If I want to be certain to be able to open my doors at the new office 12 months from today, I had better have all of the necessary furnishings, equipment, utilities, and inventory in place no later than 11 months from today in order to allow for slippage and other emergencies. To get all of that in place by 11 months, I had better have my Certificate of Occupancy (C of O) in hand by 10 months from today. To do everything needed to get the C of O from the municipality, I had better have all of my renovations done by nine months from today. Given the special needs of my business, in order to get the renovations done by nine months, I had better have the lease signed and be able to take possession of the new site no later than five months from today. In order to take possession in no later than five months, I had better have chosen the site no later than three months from today. In order to have chosen the site by three months out, given the current tightness in the commercial real estate market, I had better engage a realtor this afternoon to start searching—and even then it might be too late to hit my target!*

Why call this a *strategic* thought process? If our manager had simply decided that she wanted to expand, and then engaged a realtor (who might take three or four or even more months to find a satisfactory site), and proceeded to lease with the owner (which might take some time), and then had to find and engage a contractor (because she couldn't lock one in until she had access), and so on, she might easily miss her target by several months—and, perhaps, never get there. By having a clear concept of the office she wanted to create, the unique requirements of her business, the timeframe for renovations, and the tightness of the real estate market, she is able to assess the likelihood that she will hit her target and to define a controllable process going forward—after she calls the realtor this afternoon!

Further, she has now laid out a series of checkpoints for monitoring progress and for making adjustments—perhaps by engaging a new realtor, or paying the contractor extra to work evenings and weekends, or even preparing to open the new office earlier than intended if her timeline proved conservative.

To summarize, the first KEY to strategic thinking is that of *folding back*, of using a clear and detailed definition of the desired future as the platform for developing a comprehensive timeline containing milestones and checkpoints to select, monitor, and dynamically adapt the strategic path.[4] At each checkpoint, even at each major decision, there are three critical adaptations that are possible and that can significantly improve the probability of successfully implementing our strategy; these are:

1. We can use our experience in getting to the checkpoint to reassess and sharpen our image of the desired future—our vision. When we began, our sense of the future stretched as far forward in time as we could comfortably "see," say, three years from the present. We are now closer and should be able to see more clearly specifically what we want;

2. We can use the results of our efforts to date—what worked as we thought it would, what didn't, and why—and what new information we now have on the environment and the other players to fine-tune or change our current strategy, our actions, our plans, our sequence and timing, and;

3. We can extend our image of the desired future out in time. While the range of our vision may still be three years, we can now "see" three years from the checkpoint. This, in effect, makes our original target a checkpoint or milestone for our new or extended target and makes our strategic thought process a continuous learning process.

This last point demonstrates the value of strategic thinking as a dynamic organizational or personal learning process or system. Strategic thinking involves a continuing conscious, deliberate cycle, grounded in purpose and aspiration, of visioning, analyzing, planning, executing, monitoring, and adapting where the adaptations based in experience from the previous cycle become the bases for re-visioning and informing the next cycle.

These ideas are captured in exhibit IV, which summarizes the process in the fundamental mantra of the Strategist:

If we want to be . . . . by . . . ., then we better be . . . . by . . . .

Exhibit IV—The First Key—The Strategist's Mantra

strategic thinking is
- consciously choosing the future
- using the chosen future to direct/guide choices/actions in the present
- using the results of these choices/actions to
  — reassess and refine the chosen future,
  — fine-tune the next set of choices/actions, and
  — extend the chosen future

If we want to be ... by ..., then we better be ... by ...

A Few Summary Comments on Strategic Thinking

In developing the strategic process above, we have noted the importance of milestones or checkpoints—terms that we have used interchangeably. A reasonable question might be, "How many milestones or checkpoints should be included on our strategy map, and where or when should they occur?" There are two guidelines that are appropriate here, one drawing from the notion of milestones, and one from that of checkpoints:

- **Milestones**: these would be a function of the intrinsic nature of the strategic effort itself. In the example of Manager P seeking to open a new branch, the nature of finding, acquiring, and preparing a facility for a new use suggests that there would be five milestones or major phases of the effort plus an initial step (get a realtor!). Thus, the number of milestones would be determined by the number of major phases or decision points in the effort, and it would be appropriate to do a full checkpoint review at each of these;

- **Checkpoints:** these would be determined in part by the number of intrinsic milestones and in part by the degree of volatility in the external environment as it affects our efforts. Annual reviews of strategies, or five-year plans renewed every five years, done from a "calendar" logic may not suit either the nature of the business or the dynamism of the market. In a highly volatile market with many competitors or with a high rate of technology evolution, we may want to checkpoint our own strategy quarterly or even more frequently. In a more stable market, with few competitors or stable technology, annually may be sufficient. In a new enterprise, we may need to checkpoint continuously in the start-up phase.

The essential point is that checkpointing at intrinsic milestones and at regular market-driven intervals provides us with an opportunity to learn and adapt and, therefore, to increase our chances of success.

Another positive benefit of strategic thinking and the strategic process as presented here is that it increases the flexibility of the organization in responding to changing conditions. If we use the desired future as the criteria for setting priorities, allocating resources, and guiding actions, we are, in effect, opening ourselves to the possibility of reordering the priority of existing programs and activities, of withdrawing and reallocating resources, and of redirecting or terminating current efforts. In other words, the strategic process provides us with the rationale for *stopping* currently committed programs and activities, something organizations often find very difficult to do. Note that this does not necessarily imply criticism of past decisions and actions or an assessment that something has no value. It simply suggests that, given our current vision, that activity or product may have outlived its usefulness, even though it was essential to getting us to where we are today, or may no longer fit in our priorities given our resources. The value of this antidote to the force of habit should not be underestimated.[5]

This last point underscores the fundamental difference between Strategic Thinking as presented here and more traditional approaches to Strategic Planning as often experienced in many organizations. Rather than *folding back* from a vision of the future, planning as practiced in many situations is based on working forward from the present conditioned by the decisions of the past. In conventional approaches, we start with the current array of activities, products, programs, and so on, contained, for example, in the current chart of accounts. We then forecast the natural flow of these entities forward into the future—we extend the trend lines and cost them out—against the forecasted trend lines. Finally, we test the total cost of our current bundle of commitments—our budget—against expected revenues and only if there is a surplus do we normally consider new activities and allocations. Thus, many efforts at planning are really exercises in budgeting and result in the enshrining of the past.

By treating much of what has been seen as fixed as potentially variable, the approach to strategy presented here opens the organization to a much wider range of options moving forward and, not incidentally, places more pressure on existing efforts to prove their continuing worth.

BUSINESS STRATEGY IN ACTION

In the case below, Maria Caterina Oliviera has to sort out a series of complex and potentially conflicting signals from her superiors—and, apparently, do so in a very short time. In essence, she is being asked to transform Human Resources, which has been a discrete "real time" functional unit in a siloed organization, into a full business partner on a senior strategic team, and in the process, create a strategic HR capability. At the same time, she is being pressed to make key personnel selections from candidate lists generated by others and affirm major decisions regarding information systems programs that will involve major expenses and long-term commitments.

She is also caught between what seem to be differing expectations from her two direct "bosses"—to be strategic and innovative and to be certain to hit all short-term targets. Cat knows that this is not unusual in her firm. In fact, a frequently heard complaint from field managers, especially in Sales, was that there was a disconnect between the official corporate philosophy, aggressively reinforced in seminars and training programs, and actual practice. To quote one regional sales manager from Consumer Products, "They tell us that the new realities of our industry will require innovation and strategic leadership on the part of managers at every level, but what they really want is for us to hit the numbers and be implementers of programs and plans handed down from above. That's what determines bonuses and promotions."

Cat needs to develop a strategy that will organize and balance this complex set of issues—strategic, behavioral, organizational, and operational—and, at the same time, serve her own career objectives and opportunities. Can you help her?

TEST YOURSELF

Read and analyze the case, Ivtak Americas Group, below. Be prepared to respond to and discuss the following questions:

1. As Cat, how would you define the major elements of your new responsibilities?
2. How do you understand your mandate? From Pierre? From Roberto?
3. What information will you need to set your priorities? How will you obtain it?
4. What is your agenda for the next 90 days?
5. What should your calendar look like for the next two to three days?

IVTAK AMERICAS GROUP: THE HR CHALLENGE [6]

As her plane passed over the sprawling lights of Buenos Aires on its final approach, Maria Caterina Oliviera tried to organize her thoughts. She reflected on the whirlwind series of meetings she had just experienced in Brussels. When she had left a week earlier for the annual Corporate HR conference, she had expected the usual round of speeches and workshops capped by the usual "pep talk" from Pierre Balmains, the Global HR Head and Managing Board member, exhorting country and business unit HR managers such as herself to become true "business partners" of their country and business unit CEOs. Cat, as she was known to friends and foes alike, had to smile as she thought of her reaction to Pierre's talk; she remembered thinking:

> Here he goes again. I'm sure that Pierre believes that this is the necessary role for HR in this company going forward—and I agree with him! I think that I can provide considerable value as an HR professional *and* as a business manager. But I'm not confident that the rest of the company, especially the country CEOs and the BU heads, are really ready for this. Even my boss, who is very open to new management approaches, tends to see me and my people as record-keepers and trainers, as firefighters. They have mastered the rhetoric of HR, but their mindset is still old-fashioned personnel operations. Pierre may be accepted as a business partner at the Corporate Board, but for the rest of us in the field there is still a long way to go.

These considerations of the potential changing role of HR and of the challenge to HR executives to forge new working relationships with their functional and business leadership took on a much more urgent and compelling tone for Cat when

Pierre asked her to meet with him at the end of the second day of the conference. Pierre wasted no time in laying out his agenda:

> Cat, I want you to take on the position of Senior HR Head for the Americas Group beginning immediately. I've watched your performance as the country HR manager for Argentina, and I think that you are ready.
>
> This is a real opportunity and a real challenge. I don't want to understate the difficulties that you will be facing. This has been a "revolving door" position—the last two individuals lasted less than a year each —and the reason that I want you to start immediately is that Jose Vasconeles (the current Head) has already left. We haven't made the announcement yet, but Roberto Cuevas (Region Head for the Americas) wanted him out.
>
> We'll still retain a matrixed relationship, but you will be reporting directly to Roberto. As you know, he is a brilliant executive with a strong drive. I think that he believes in principle with the strategic importance of HR, but in practice, he is often impatient and frustrated with details and demands quick solutions to current problems no matter how complex. He was dissatisfied with your two immediate predecessors for different reasons—Walther because he was "too much of a technician, too inflexible" and Jose because "he was all charm and personality but was always reacting."
>
> With your broad experience, particularly with the fact that you have been out in the field on the business side, which Roberto values, I think that you can show him that HR is critical to the future success of the business. The marketplace is changing and the workplace is changing. We need to take the lead in developing the organizational systems and processes required to compete in the market and in finding and nurturing the talent needed to staff and operate in the emerging work environment. We need to prepare our business leaders, including our senior executives, for the future.

Cat smiled as she reviewed Pierre's charge to her. Pierre was a visionary, and she shared his enthusiasm and convictions. But she also sensed that abstract visions of an HR function optimally integrated as a full partner into an ongoing strategic business operation were easier to conceive at the corporate level than they were to realize on the ground in the field.

She also thought a bit about Pierre's comments regarding the difficulties that her predecessors had experienced. Walther Freihoff, with whom she had worked when she first joined Ivtak, was known throughout the industry as a consummate personnel systems professional. He had designed and implemented a compensation/incentive process for non-sales professionals that was considered to be a model for the industry. He was also known to be particularly adept at working with consultants and vendors to develop or adapt packaged generic HR records systems software to Ivtak's unique needs. He had seemed to be an ideal appointment to the Group HR position given the diversity of legacy and idiosyncratic systems in the several counties in the Americas and the desire to bring them into alignment with Ivtak global product line and corporate systems. After less than a year in the position, however, he had left the company for a position with a systems consulting firm. The word had been that he "wasn't good with people, that he wasn't sensitive to or didn't seem to grasp the unique needs of individual units."

His successor, Jose Vasconeles, seemed like the perfect antidote. An old-timer who had come up through the ranks, Jose had spent most of his career in operations as a plant HR manager and then as a labor negotiator in his native Chile and in several other locations. Jose's negotiations and conflict management skills went beyond formal contract discussions to mediation and crisis management. As one business unit executive had stated, "He was the kind of person that every management team needs. Jose knew everybody, and everybody knew him and trusted him. When we were having major conflicts with our logistics and warehousing workforce—when they had locked the doors and things threatened to get ugly—Jose went in alone and after a few hours had everything resolved without giving up any principles."

Cat was surprised that he was leaving the Senior HR Head post after only eight months, but had heard talk that he had done little to pursue the implementation of the systems that Walther had initiated and was content to wait for problems to arise. This was consistent with her own dealings with him. Jose had been very responsive and helpful on some specific problems that had arisen at one of her plants but had not replied after several months to some questions regarding developing a staffing table and set of job descriptions for a new institutional sales organization.

Cat realized that she would have to sort out these issues and reach some decisions about how to approach her new position in a very short time—all with the challenge of moving her household from Buenos Aires to Group headquarters in Sao Paolo. During the final days of the conference, she had been able to hold a brief phone conversation with Roberto Cuervas, her new boss. He had closed their conversation by reiterating his perspective on what he needs from his HR Head:

> The business is changing and we need to change with it—and we don't have lots of time or resources for experiments. We have had HR-driven and HR-initiated programs coming out our ears. We need to find and develop people with the talent to run real businesses in real time. We need to shape up our organizations to get ahead and stay ahead of tough competitors. And we need to anticipate problems and resolve them before they occur. We don't need specialists; we don't need consultants; we don't need firefighters. We need people, like you, who have been in the field and have the instincts and the ability to put principles into practice.
>
> It would be nice if you could have a bit of time to get your feet on the ground and get settled in, but we have too much going on. I'm sending you reports on some matters that need

immediate resolution, including picking your replacement in Argentina. Let's sit down and discuss your solutions as soon as you get back.

Cat wondered whether her experience and education to date had really prepared her for the challenge of finding the right rhythm and structure for the HR function in the Americas Group. She had completed her studies at the University in Human Resource Management and Accounting and had joined Ivtak as a compensation and benefits specialist. Seeing being a personnel "techie" as a potential dead-end, she sought a transfer to an operating unit and spent two years in the field as a consumer products rep calling on retailers and distributors. She followed this with a stint in sales training and then became part of a regional organization behavior (OB) group that functioned as internal consultants on professional recruiting, counseling, and team development. She spent two years on the campus recruiting circuit, followed by a posting to the corporate Talent Management project. Three years ago, she had assumed her last position as HR Manager for Argentina. Certainly a lot of different perspectives, she thought, but, perhaps her volunteer career as a salsa instructor would stand her in better stead.

THE COMPANY

Ivtak was founded in Brussels at the turn of 20th century. Its growth as an electronics giant had accelerated in the 70s with the advent of microchip technology. Entering the 21st century, Ivtak Electronics was a world leader in high-tech industrial electronics and in sophisticated consumer products, competing head-to-head with such giants as GE, Sony, and Apple.

The industrial division (IPD) has three core franchises: Medical Systems, Robotics, and Process Controls. The consumer products division (ICP)' originated as a vehicle for the transfer of industrial applications into at-home products. Over time, the Division has taken on a life of its own as Ivtak developed a line of personal care products and introduced a home entertainment line. In some markets, ICP provides a larger share of total revenue than does the industrial unit.

Ivtak is known throughout the industry for its scientific excellence. On the operations and commercial sides of the business, Ivtak's record is somewhat less impressive. The company has had difficulties in coordinating its production processes and has generally experienced higher than average manufacturing costs for its major products. This has translated into pricing strategies that the market has not always seen as justified by the superiority of Ivtak products.

On the consumer products side, Ivtak has sought to protect its margins by marketing itself as a premium line. Ivtak products are sold under a variety of different brand names and at different price points in different countries. Even senior Ivtak managers are occasionally heard to remark that, "Oh, I didn't know that we made that!" or "I didn't realize that this was the same cell phone that I bought in Europe (for twice the price!)!"

In addition, Ivtak has gone through a number of reorganizations of its sales and marketing efforts. The recent "Quality, not Quantity" sales initiative was seen by many in the field as an effort on the part of the corporate office to smooth over the fact that Ivtak was being outspent in some of its key product/market areas by its major competitors by as much as two or three to one. Industrial and consumer sales forces are separate and, although incentives are generous on the consumer side, there is clearly a perceived status or class system, with consumer reps often seeking to step "up" to one of the industrial forces.

In its HR approach, Ivtak has been seen as relatively traditional, with an emphasis on individual performance and a reliance on formal systems for recruitment, advancement, compensation, and so on. The company has had a strong management culture and has typically taken a hard line on labor negotiations; its relations with its unions could be described as chilly at best. Despite this tough approach to bargaining, wage rates at the plant level are higher than industry averages, contributing in part to the manufacturing cost problems noted above.

Ivtak had been slow to embrace organization development (OD) and organizational behavior (OB) approaches. However, the increasing costs of recruiting and retaining the levels of quality personnel needed to staff a growing global organization and the challenges of maintaining a flexible, mobile pool of qualified professionals and managers has forced the company to focus directly on its HR strategies. Ivtak moved five years ago to initiate a talent management effort to identify, develop, and retain the needed cadre of future leaders. This was seen as the first step in having HR fulfill a strategic function in addition to its traditional operational support role.

At its core, Ivtak senior executives are a collection of researchers and academics who value science and research more than marketing of the product. This corporate culture, with its emphasis on leading-edge science and clinical excellence, clearly drives management thinking at Ivtak. As one senior executive put it, "We are a company of scientists. We are committed to technical advance, and we believe that the intrinsic merit (of our products) will win the day. Marketing and Sales have to realize that their job is to get this winning message to the market."

THE IMMEDIATE ISSUES

As her plane taxied up to the gate, Maria Caterina Oliviera tucked the two folders that she had been reviewing back into her attaché case. Her new boss, Roberto Cuevas, had sent them to her in Brussels immediately after she had accepted her new position, indicating that he expected her to be prepared to present her solutions at their first meeting upon her return. "No rest for the wicked," she thought to herself as she hurried on to the baggage claim area, realizing that the meeting would probably take place tomorrow or the next day at the latest.

The Replacement

Cat had been surprised when Roberto told her that he wanted her to name her successor as HR Manager for Argentina immediately and that he and Pierre Balmain had already conducted a preliminary review and settled on three finalists. Apparently, the changes in HR leadership for the Americas had been in the works for some time, and now management was ready to move ahead at full speed. She reviewed the three finalists in her mind as the limo sped through the early Buenos Aires evening. She knew each of the three from HR conferences and various projects but could not say that she knew any of them well. As she went over their qualifications, she realized that none of the three was a perfect fit:

> Osvaldo Mercier joined Ivtak in North America about five years ago after a 10-year career in management consulting with an international firm that specialized in global management systems. Oz, as he was known, had been on the consulting team brought in to create the global R&D strategy team for Ivtak's Robotics franchise. Known as an expert on self-directed teams, he had been offered a position with the R&D headquarters staff to serve as an internal team development co consultant. His current position is as HR Manager, Organization Development, Global R&D. His noted strengths include good project and process management skills, knowledge of the R&D process, and team orientation. His development needs include awareness of the total business process, line management experience, and exposure to formal personnel systems;
>
> Sonya Fuentes-*Drazin* had her MBA from Northwestern University and joined Ivtak immediately after graduation

12 years ago. She had begun as a market research specialist in the consumer products group, working initially on the company's line of personal entertainment products. She moved into the leadership development area and spent several years developing and delivering internal training programs for the Marketing Group in such areas as managing change, brand development, and so on. In her present position as HR manager, leadership development, consumer products, she has two main responsibilities: global staffing for the division and liaison with Columbia University Executive Education, which conducts the division's senior leadership development course. She is known as an excellent co-ordinator and facilitator with good conceptual abilities and communications skills. She is seen as needing more operations experience and more exposure to business and financial management;

Edison DeJesus is presently a regional sales manager for Ivtak Process Controls Mexico and is responsible for the northern sector of the country. He has been identified through the talent management program as a key resource within the sales function and a potential future general manager. He began his career as a field rep in Juarez and moved rapidly up through sales. Now 33, he has been a consistently high performer as an individual contributor and, in his five years as a territory or regional sales manager, his group ranked in the top five globally every year. A hard-driver who leads by example, he is tough and impatient. With one of the highest turnover rates in the company among his reps, he is seen, as one senior manager put it, "needing some of the rough edges smoothed off," before he is ready for a senior line position. His TM plan suggests that a 12–28 month stint in a country-level staff position might provide the necessary seasoning.

As she arrived home, Cat was still unsure as to how to choose from among the three and wondered whether she shouldn't push to reopen the search to find her own candidate.

Outsourcing the Personnel Database

The other matter for which Roberto wanted an immediate decision seemed deceptively simple. The Group Information Systems & Processes (ISP) unit had been pushing for some time to place the task of maintaining and managing the group's HR database with an outside provider. Their proposal was to turn over such functions as basic personnel records, payroll, pension and retirement funding, and the like to a specialty vendor. ISP had been arguing that the above were basically commodity "warehousing" functions that could be performed more effectively by an expert specialist rather than as part of the portfolio of internal systems that ISP had to maintain. The provider could guarantee full protection of corporate and individual privacy. A single interface with HR for transmitting updates and changes was all that would be needed.

ISP argued that there would be considerable savings on current operating costs and on the recurring capital expenses needed to maintain state-of-the-art technology (hardware and software) on Ivtak's own equipment. The provider would be responsible for all of this, and Ivtak would pay only a single negotiated fee, freeing up ISP resources to pursue other projects. ISP also argued that the move would lay the basis for a global Ivtak database management system that would facilitate such things as inter-country and inter-regional transfers that often were delayed while issues of pension, salary, and so on were worked out on a case-by-case basis.

Cat found the proposals intriguing but wondered if the Group was ready for this, even if it could deliver all that it promised. As a country HR manager, she was aware that there were considerable differences among the countries in the group as to how they handled many of these matters in their record systems, and in fact, there were even differences among the business units within countries, particularly where there had been acquisitions.

"Never a dull moment," she thought as she opened her front door.

> **KEY POINTS TO REMEMBER**
>
> - Strategy is a *process* that involves not only articulating desired end-states but also all possible paths to get to them.
> - Creating these paths is accomplished through "folding back"—a process that takes us from the desired state back to our current state.
> - A key element of "folding back" is the establishment of checkpoints and milestones. Strategy is never static; it constantly changes and evolves in response to market movements, competitors, internal capabilities, etc.
> - Thus, the strategist has to constantly plan and re-plan to meet milestones and to clear any planned or unexpected hurdles or constraints that may occur over time.

CHAPTER 3

The *Strategos* and the Three Levels of Strategic Thinking

INTRODUCTION

Then I chopped down a Truffula Tree with one chop. And with great skillful skill and great speedy speed, I took the soft tuft. And I knitted a Threed!

The instant I'd finished, I heard a ga-Zump! . . . I saw something pop out of the stump of the tree I'd chopped down. . . He was shortish. And oldish. And brownish. And mossy. And he spoke with a voice that was sharpish and bossy. . .

"I am the Lorax. I speak for the trees. I speak for the trees, for the trees have no tongues. And I'm asking you, sir, at the top of my lungs . . . What's that THING you have made out of my Truffula tuft?" . . .

"I am the Lorax who speaks for the trees which you seem to be chopping as fast as you please." . . .

Then we heard the tree fall. **The very last Truffula Tree of them all!** [1]

We are all familiar with Dr. Seuss' cautionary tale of self-interest, of expedience, of failing to think beyond the present or to anticipate consequences. While it may be true that "Threeds [are what] everyone, *everyone*, **everyone** needs," when we chop down the last Truffula Tree, there will be no more Threeds. A children's tale?

An environmental parable? To be sure, but, from our perspective, a wonderful reminder of the importance of strategic thinking—of the need to be clear on our aspirations for the future and to use those aspirations to guide and discipline our actions in the present. And let's not forget the Lorax, our strategic thinker, who speaks for the trees and reminds us that the role of strategy is to turn aspiration into reality.

To this point, we have presented strategic thinking as a particular approach to leading and managing complex organizations in a resource-constrained and dynamic world. We have assumed the existence of a special player—the strategic thinker or the strategist (the Lorax)—who is actually doing this thinking and producing these dynamic approaches to organizational and individual behavior.[2] But, you may ask, how special is this individual? Is this a mindset, a competence, that is limited to a small number of unique characters or can anybody, especially me, learn to do it?

WHAT'S AHEAD

In this chapter, you will learn:
- The mindset and concept of the *Strategos*
- How to identify the three levels of strategic thinking
- Key elements of the *conceptual* level of strategic thinking
- Tools and techniques that comprise the *analytical* level of strategic thinking
- How to identify components of *operational* strategic thinking and planning

IN THE REAL WORLD

You have just been appointed as the head of one of the key regional offices of your company—a complex, highly competitive market that figures prominently in the company's future plans. Within a few days, you are told by your corporate superior that your new unit is not performing up to expectations and that you will need to turn things around quickly. Also, your predecessor in the unit has been moved to a senior product manager role with responsibility for a major strategic product initiative and you will be expected to work closely with him—and your new team was hired and trained by him!

Your immediate superior at the group level has reviewed with you a number of staffing, relationship, and current product issues that need attention and has indicated that she will be expecting to review your strategy in two weeks—and you just received a call from a colleague proposing a meeting of regional heads to "discuss" the implications of the global strategic products strategy for "our jobs."

So what do you attack first? How do you keep from getting pulled in several directions at once? What is your real job and how can you proceed to do it?

THE KEY CONCEPTS

On Being a Strategic Thinker—The Competences of the *Strategos*

The answer to the question posed in the introduction (is strategic thinking a skill that only some people possess or can it be learned) is "yes"—some (perhaps many more than we might think) come to it naturally and others have to learn (or relearn) it. To sort out this seeming contradiction, let's first consider the roots of the concept. The term *strategy* has its linguistic roots in ancient Greece in the days of the city-states. The Greek word is *Strategos* and is militaristic in its focus and meaning. It draws from the frequent wars among the city-states and refers not to the conceptual apparatus that we have developed above but instead to a particular individual.

The *Strategos* was that individual chosen to lead this year's campaign in the field. He or she was chosen not because of seniority or bloodline or prowess. Rather, he was perceived as having a bent of mind, a perspective, a way of thinking that allowed him to see, as we might say, "the big picture"—the desired results to be achieved at the close of the campaign and all of the possible paths through which those results might be achieved. Moreover, the *Strategos* had the ability to monitor events as they transpired and to move from one path to another when appropriate. The *Strategos* oversaw the battlefield—the game board—and directed the efforts of the generals in the field—the tacticians and operators—in an organized and coordinated manner.

To put it more formally, we may define the *Strategos* as shown in exhibit V.

The **STRATEGOS** has the ability to:

Exhibit V—The Strategos

- hold the <u>actual</u> present and the <u>desired</u> future simultaneously in mind
- see all possible paths connecting the present and the future
- move flexibly from one path to another as events require

So, to be a strategic thinker—to function as a *Strategos*—is to engage in nonlinear thinking, to think simultaneously in time and space, to be visionary about the future and rigorously analytical about the present. The *Strategos* is both a right-brain and a left-brain thinker who is able to move fluidly back and forth between the desired future and the actual present, constantly using the stream of information provided by ongoing events to monitor and adapt his/her strategic actions in pursuit of his/her evolving vision. (Note that the *Strategos* may well be a strategic team.)

This is the competence (the mindset) that we hope to develop and hone throughout this book. We believe that it does come naturally to some (more than we might think) and that it can be learned (or relearned) by the rest of us. We say "relearn" because we observe that what we consider strategic thinking (the ability to link desired outcomes dynamically and flexibly with alternative behaviors and lines of attack) to be common to the very young yet often rooted out by our educational systems, which tend to value statics and standardization over dynamics and creativity. Witness the three-year-old who moves easily between mother and father and grandparents looking for a compliant response, never losing sight of the objective and carefully keeping the various respondents unaware of each others' positions. Our educational processes, however, tend to reward an emphasis on a linear causality that moves relentlessly forward in time. Thus, A leads to B leads to C because it always has and, therefore, D must follow.

Compare this mode of thinking to the youngster with a video game, which places a premium on nonlinear thinking, strategic planning, and flexibility and adaptability, who is both able to "see" and to describe a strategy of play that cuts across levels and time and that conditions current moves by a clear sense of what will be required to reach the desired endgame.

We are not suggesting that corporations should adopt Xbox® or PlayStation® as their core planning tools. However we are suggesting that successful strategies will require a mindset that can deal simultaneously with the present and the future, with aspiration and execution, with discipline and flexibility, and that uses the focusing power of a desired future to guide actions in the present.

So, whether you are a born *Strategos* or a strategic thinker in the making, let us proceed to develop the competences, skills, and tools necessary for leading and managing strategically—for successfully choosing and achieving the future. The Cheshire Cat would be proud.

IN SUMMARY—THE THREE LEVELS OF STRATEGIC THINKING

In this chapter, we have presented **strategic thinking** as a dynamic learning process for the individual strategist and for organizational strategic teams. This process is best summarized as having three distinct levels that are shown in Exhibit VI and described below.

Exhibit VI—There Are 3 Levels of Strategic Thinking

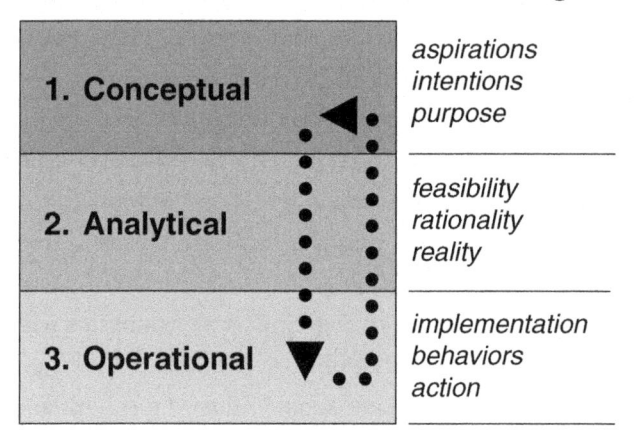

1. Conceptual	aspirations, intentions, purpose
2. Analytical	feasibility, rationality, reality
3. Operational	implementation, behaviors, action

1. **Level One: Conceptual**

    The Conceptual Level is concerned with our basic understanding of our enterprise—our organization, our product or service, our career. It starts with purpose—with human aspiration and emotion—and envisions a future when that purpose is fulfilled. At this level, we are concerned with our basic reasons for existence and the beliefs and values in which those reasons are rooted. We define what is important to us, what is worth pursuing, and what we hope or expect will transpire as a result of our efforts. It is here where we seek to identify and choose our intended future—the future that would not occur in the natural flow of events absent our conscious efforts to make it so.

This chosen future is much more than the analytical extrapolation of current activities and processes, and uses conventional forecasting models and methods as means for setting baselines. In effect, at this level, we are saying, much as the scientist does, "All others things being equal, this is where current trends are taking us. How do we feel about it? What do we aspire to do, to achieve, that goes beyond what we would get beyond continuing with business as usual?"

The conceptual level is inherently subjective in nature. It deals with aspirations and intentions, with hopes and dreams, and is likely to involve dreams and fantasies more so than it is forecasts and trend lines. Its focus is on the value that we intend to add through our efforts and provides the rallying points around which we seek to attract resources and secure the commitments of others to join with us in the effort.

Thus, the conceptual level is the starting point (the catalyst) for strategic thinking. It provides the organizing framework for collecting and analyzing data, for generating and selecting among options, and for guiding and assessing actions. Its key elements include the concepts of *Mission, Values,* and *Vision.* These are developed fully in the next three chapters.

2. **Level Two: Analytical**

The Analytical Level is concerned with the determination of whether the future envisioned at the conceptual level is possible. Now that we have defined our aspirations and intentions, we can turn to the tools of rational analysis to identify the challenges, the obstacles, and the possible barriers that may prevent us from achieving our purposes within the timeframe we have chosen. We also use those same tools to look for the resources, the supports, and the potential factors that may assist us in our efforts.

At this level, we are testing our dreams against the cold, hard facts of reality. We are asking, "Given the best data available, the most reliable forecasts and analyses of environmental trends, and the likely strategies of competitors and potential customers, is there a finite probability of reaching our desired future? Is our vision within the bounds of reason? Is it feasible and, if so, which of the possible paths that we might pursue has the highest probability of getting us there?"

The analytical level is inherently objective in nature. It involves the consistent application of rigorous, science- and experienced-based models and tools in collecting, processing, and interpreting data in order to identify problems, make forecasts, and compare competing possible strategies. It provides the left-brain balance to the right-brain freedom of the conceptual level.

Thus, the analytical level is the necessary balance wheel of rationality and objectivity applied to the subjective and emotional perspective of the conceptual level. It uses the conceptual to determine what questions must be asked of the market, of the industry, of the behavior of the other players in order to identify the problems and challenges to which our strategy must speak. Its key elements include such powerful models and tools as *Industry Analysis, Environmental Scanning, and Competitor and Customer Analyses* at the macro level and *SWOT* and other internal assessment tools at the micro level. These are developed fully in chapters 7 and 8.

3. **Level Three: Operational**

   The Operational Level provides the essential synthesis between the conceptual and the analytical and also drives the learning process. Its first task is to transform the results of the analytical phase into detailed plans of action that will effect the changes in the external environment (the marketplace) and in our organization needed to "make room" for the effective pursuit of our desired future. Designed to advance strategic purpose or intent within the context of strategic analyses, these are properly referred to as *strategic plans*; that is, these are plans that derive directly from strategic thinking. They are the product of the strategic process.

It should be apparent, however, that it is not enough to have a great strategic concept (a vision) supported by a rigorous, comprehensive strategic analysis that yields a coherent strategic action plan. That strategic plan must also be executed and implemented effectively. This is the second major task of the operational level—to identify and perform effectively the actions and behaviors called for by the chosen strategy.

Finally, the third task of this level is to monitor and assess performance to determine if things are working as planned, to identify the need and opportunity for both fine-tuning and major directional changes, and to discern what is being learned in order to stimulate and inform the next cycle of strategic thinking.

At this level, we are asking, "What actions must we successfully execute, in what order and with what intensity, in order to overcome the obstacles and challenges we have identified in order to achieve our purposes? As we reach each milestone, what is working and what is not working and how can we use our ongoing experience to improve our efforts? What are we learning and how can we use this to advance our thinking at the conceptual and analytical levels?"

Thus, the Operational Level is not distinct from strategic thinking but is the essential test and validation of the entire process. Its key elements include such powerful tools and models as *Project Planning and Management, Benchmarking,* and *The Balanced Scorecard.* These are developed fully in chapter 9.

BUSINESS STRATEGY IN ACTION

In the case below, Bill Harrigan is faced with the challenge of producing major change in the way Fidelity Corporation, a traditional investment banking house, does business. Some change is clearly required and unavoidable because the competitive landscape of the industry has shifted dramatically and most observers expect even more to follow. Bill has found it difficult, however, to gain much acceptance among his colleagues of the need for change and had even less success in achieving a consensus of any sort as to the direction the Firm should take going forward. As a result, Fidelity, one of the premier Houses, is losing ground to more aggressive competitors and runs the risk of becoming a minor player—or even of being taken over! His problems are compounded by a Firm culture that is deeply grounded in and reveres a treasured past when young executives apprenticed to the senior partners and eventually inherited their portfolios, where firms considered it "unethical" to raid other firms' clients, and where personal relationships were the keys to success. Fidelity is, moreover, a partnership and while Bill has in principle the authority to command, his success will be determined by his ability to lead.

Bill will have to find a way to balance the enthusiasm and energy of younger, newer partners who believe that aggressive selling, "like the insurance companies," or technical wizardry and sophisticated modeling are the wave of the future with the conviction of more senior partners that the above are simply fads and that the "old ways" will, and should, prevail.

It will take all of Bill's skills—professional, managerial, leadership—to craft with his colleagues a strategy that will honor the history and culture of Fidelity, compete effectively in the evolving investment banking marketplace, and mold these warring groups of strong-minded individuals into a winning team. How can Sam Heinz, or you, help him?

TEST YOURSELF

Read and analyze the case, Fidelity Corporation, below. Be prepared to respond to and discuss the following questions:

1. What are the most significant strengths and vulnerabilities of the Fidelity culture?
2. How will the culture help or hinder Bill Harrigan in developing the corporate finance practice at Fidelity?

FIDELITY CORPORATION[3]

INTRODUCTION

Fidelity Corporation is an established, highly respected financial services firm located in New York. Although not the largest in the industry, it consistently appears as one of the top three or four firms in the ranking of financial services firms. It is an old-line Yankee firm that gradually went from unquestioned preeminence in the 80s and 90s through a severe slump at the end of the dot-com boom to indications of a recovery in the mid-00s.

Fidelity is recognized for its strengths in corporate finance. Bill Harrigan, 44, has headed the Corporate Finance Department as partner-in-charge for the past four years. Harrigan came to Fidelity from the US Treasury Department in 2000 to manage the International Department. Prior to that, Harrigan had been a senior corporate lending officer of a major commercial bank. Shortly after arriving at Fidelity, he was placed in charge of corporate finance.

THE SITUATION

Harrigan had just returned from a meeting of the 25 corporate finance partners where the department's latest earning performance had been discussed. He settled down to answer some questions from Sam Heinz, a friend who was with a firm that specialized in the problems of professional firms. He had asked Sam to come in to look at some of Fidelity's problems:

> You know that our numbers so far this year are phenomenal. Leasing volume is way up; our advisory fees have held strong; our new business efforts are starting to bear some fruit. Everyone feels good, and it certainly is an improvement over recent years, but frankly I am disturbed. We are not where we should be, and I fear that our recent minor successes will lead us back into the complacency that started our problems.
>
> Even though our business is way up, our strongest competitors have done even better. The industry seems to be entering a consolidation phase, with customers flocking to a handful of the big houses, perhaps looking for some stability after the turmoil of the last few years. Our market share is getting larger, but our competition is really cleaning up. All have done some fairly wholesale housecleaning in recent years, even forcing a few partners out. I understand that Wildham, Bigelow called in all of its present accounts and reassigned them on an industry basis to specialist groups—even when it meant taking some partners off accounts that they had worked on for 10 or 15 years! We hired some fairly senior people from there who were offended by the change. They each brought a few clients with them but don't seem to be driven to seek new business.
>
> Over the last four years, we have tried everything under the sun to improve our new business efforts. First, we assigned all of the corporate finance partners new business targets in terms of specific potential clients whom they were responsible for approaching. The results were miserable. The partners resented being assigned names. Not only did we not get any new clients, we found that fewer than half of the companies designated were approached. But it is hard to come down on

these people. The whole culture runs against it. It is not that they are lazy, they all work to 7:00 or 8:00 at night. It is just that in this business, you've got to be all over your own clients or they will get taken away.

Our experienced partners seemed to be fully occupied watching their own clients. Some of them came from smaller firms that we absorbed five, even ten years ago, and they are still operating as if they were local boutiques.

When the calling program failed, we decided that we needed to teach selling skills, so we sent all the officers in corporate finance (which includes vice presidents and assistant vice presidents in addition to the partners) to a GE sales course to teach them basic sales techniques. I don't know if any of it sank in.

Our latest attempt has been to set up regional offices in the US outside of New York (Chicago, Los Angeles, San Francisco, Dallas) with two corporate finance partners and a small staff in each office. This is in its early stages and there have been no major successes. This approach worked well with our global offices in London, Zurich, and Tokyo. Too many of our partners, however, seem to see the international activity as a new line of business not related to their ongoing relations with their clients.

CORPORATE FINANCE AT FIDELITY

The Corporate Finance Department at Fidelity is composed of 150 professionals: 25 partners, 40 vice presidents; 65 associates; and 20 analysts. During the last five years, specialty groups have been evolving by both function and industry. These specialty groups tend to be a vertical slice of the department, composed of one or two partners, three or four vice presidents, and five or six analysts and associates.

The specialty groups are: Mergers and Acquisitions, Niche Financing, Venture Leasing, and International Financing (this unit is concerned with providing services for US corporations dealing with non-US suppliers and is not involved directly with International Department). The largest group of people in corporate Finance are called "Generalists." This group includes most of the Partners and Vice Presidents and is the prime focus of Harrigan's concerns.

THE BUSINESS ENVIRONMENT

Jim Dedham, 36, an MBA from Michigan, is one of the younger, more aggressive partners. He has been made responsible for the latest new business effort—the development of regional offices. Dedham took on this assignment against the advice of the senior Partner with whom he had worked for several years, who felt that Dedham would be better advised to continue to tend to his established accounts. Heinz arranged to speak with him; Dedham began:

> Look, we have to match the way selling is being done by the sophisticated firms in our industry. We have to have people who are willing to call on potential clients when they do not already have an established relationship. Today's clients simply do not buy financial services the way they used to. In the old days, the partner-in-charge would know the treasurer of the client firm for 20 or 30 years, belong to the same clubs, perhaps, or have gone to the same schools. Their relationship was personal and professional and that was great. They shared a high level of unspoken communication and understanding. It was a wonderful way to do business, but it just does not fit present circumstances.
>
> In the new businesses we are approaching and in many of our existing clients, the client personnel we are dealing with are younger, highly trained, highly mobile individuals on the way up. The same person will not be in the job for five or ten

years, and they want facts, evidence of performance, and precise cost analyses to justify our fees. Trust is still important, but it now comes from professional performance and not personal relations.

Moreover, potential new clients and many of our old accounts are no longer clustered in a little enclave in New York, nor are they willing to fly in at our convenience. We have to go out to the regions, match the clients' competence in our own staffs, and put real pressure on the regional offices to perform. If that means more structure where partners-in-charge of regions are given objectives and removed if they do not achieve them, so be it.

The problem that Fidelity has had is that it gets wound up in the complexities and fails to realize that financial services is a relatively simple business. We have a product to sell that is very difficult for clients to differentiate.

The firms that get new business have organized calling programs where people keep knocking on doors asking for the order. We would do better with experienced insurance salesmen who know how to "ask" instead of a bunch of bright technocrats who are more comfortable discussing the 11 possible ways of structuring a leasing deal than meeting new people who probably are not as smart as they are.

The investment banking business has changed. In the past, companies never changed financial services firms. It was like law firms or accounting firms used to be before they began to stumble. A company made a change once every 15 or 20 years, and, in some circles, it was considered unethical to call on another company's client. When the other major financial services firms began investing heavily in hiring talented people, they also began calling on companies, including a heavy effort directed at our clients.

We simply did not respond quickly to this change. When the shakeout began, the big got bigger and the small merged or disappeared. The firms that grew during that period were those that developed a system for getting new business. They did not rely on individuals but created a system, picked their markets, and attacked.

Fidelity has not yet developed a clear focus or system. We spend much more time in a defensive posture, worrying about our own client base instead of seeking new clients. I think the solution is to split the department into "new-business-getters" and "processors." Have the new-business-getters work out of regional offices and when they land an account call in the processors from New York. A formal organization with clear division of labor and responsibility is essential. You need individuals to focus on specific aspects of the total business in order to develop the expertise needed to match the competition. Sales is a dirty word to some, but we need "salesmen" to bring in the business. Then they can call in the processors, the implementers with the technical systems, forms, computer printouts and so on, to work with the client's technical people. And for God's sake, let's keep our theoreticians away from the clients.

Another view was expressed to Heinz by John L. C. White, who had grown up at Fidelity working on certain major accounts, including some of the largest and best known companies in the US. White, 53, joined the firm upon completion of his studies at Yale, and enjoyed regaling his juniors about his "apprenticeship" under Perkins Bosely, who had been a legend in the firm. As White matured, and as Bosely's interests turned to national affairs, he inherited Bosely's major accounts, historically been among the largest and most profitable for Fidelity:

Fidelity has a fine franchise. We have as good a set of clients as any firm, and we should focus on providing triple-A service to these clients. If we never get another client, Fidelity can be profitable by milking its existing client base. Furthermore, I believe that the best way to get business is to maintain a reputation for quality work, and companies will seek us out. If we start working with every company we can dig up, our quality image will be tarnished, and we will risk losing what we already have.

I think we run the danger of demeaning ourselves by hustling aggressively after new business. The clients look to us for mature, established competence and confidence, not for glad-handing or technical wizardry. Yet we seem to be increasingly populated, on the one hand, with sales types who ignore longstanding clients in favor of dazzling "prospects" with fancy PowerPoint presentations, and, on the other, by technocrats who delight in models and elaborate statements of obtuse, theoretical performance indicators. Neither type seems to realize that success in this profession comes from nurturing long-term relations with a few clients who will not be dazzled by showmanship and who have neither the interest nor the ability to understand abstract theory.

I know my clients—their business, their markets, their attitudes and values. I learned by observing Perk Bosely over the years, and my juniors will learn from me in the same way.

Joe Warburg, another partner, heads the Mergers and Acquisitions Group. Warburg, 39, holds a Ph.D. in economics and taught at the university level for several years; he continues to publish theoretical research articles in the trade and scholarly journals and occasionally teaches a course in financial analysis at a major business school. Warburg's group specializes in giving clients advice relating to buying and selling companies. After the market topped, when most of Fidelity's business was under attack from more aggressive competitors, the M & A group provided the bulk of the profits of the firm. Warburg was quite willing to express his views to Heinz:

> A company is like a tree—when it stops growing, it dies. The history of Fidelity has been that, where we have specialized and invested the resources, we have succeeded. Harrigan should create industry specialty groups and make partners focus on a given industry. If we grow the business, the partner should be compensated. If we do not, no added comp!
>
> Expertise by industry is the issue. We have to know the client's business inside and out—the technology, the marketplace, the competition, the economic prospects for the industry, and for the client's firm—so we can develop proposals that are keyed to likely future needs.
>
> The industry specialists would draw up plans for approaching target companies. They would also be responsible for retaining Fidelity's clients in a given industry. This puts a manageable piece under the responsibility of a given partner. Our best new business tool is getting smart people who know what they are talking about into the field. We should have a slew of new business people out in the field, but they need to be able to call on industry experts with high levels of technical sophistication to close the business.
>
> The key thing is to create an organized approach. Partners should be given management responsibility for targeting an area, requesting resources, and managing a group of people. It is about time that we ran this place like a business and not like a club.

Harrigan was asked about Warburg's ideas:

Joe's ideas are academically sound and might make sense in some areas, such as energy. Frankly, however, if I have a partner who has spent years building up a relationship with one steel company, two banks, one retailer, and two manufacturers of industrial equipment, how do I convince him to focus on retailing and give up his other accounts? A partner is a partner is a partner—forever, in some minds. Is the partner-in-charge of a regional office the boss of the other partners in the office? Is a partner who cannot or will not sell and is transferred to New York to do technical work on someone else's deal, or to nurse an established account, a second-class citizen? The simple ideas are not all that simple, Sam. What should I do?

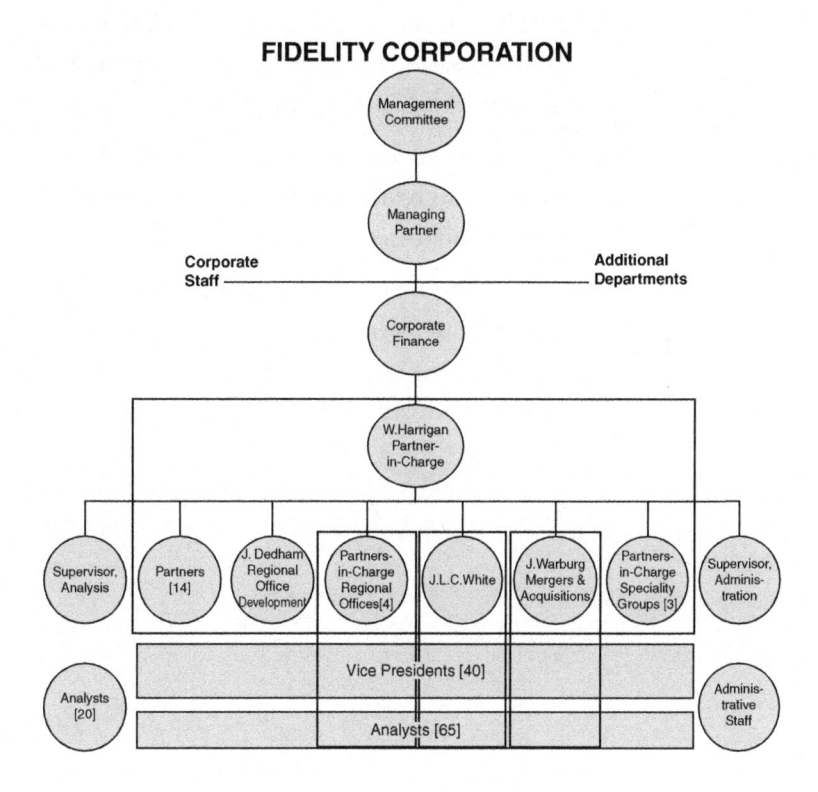

FIDELITY CORPORATION

Management Committee

Managing Partner

Corporate Staff —————————————— Additional Departments

Corporate Finance

W. Harrigan Partner-in-Charge

- Supervisor, Analysis
- Partners [14]
- J. Dedham Regional Office Development
- Partners-in-Charge Regional Offices [4]
- J.L.C. White
- J. Warburg Mergers & Acquisitions
- Partners-in-Charge Speciality Groups [3]
- Supervisor, Administration

Analysts [20]

Vice Presidents [40]

Analysts [65]

Administrative Staff

KEY POINTS TO REMEMBER

- The *Strategos* is an individual who can keep the present state and future/desired state in mind simultaneously while envisioning and moving among multiple pathways to get from now to the future.
- Strategic thinking comprises three levels of skills, toolkits, and analyses.
    - The *conceptual* level emphasizes clarification of aspirations, intentions, and purposes and also provides insights on leadership styles and skills.
    - The *analytical* level of strategic thinking helps us answer questions related to feasibility, rationality, or "do-ability" of our aspirations, etc.
    - In the *operational* level of strategy, we focus on how to implement our intentions—after being vetted by analysis—and how to shape our actions and behaviors to support our implementation plans.

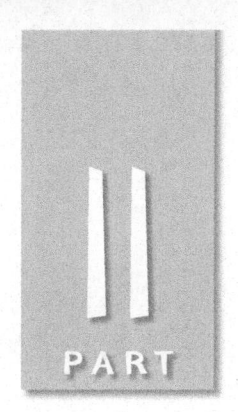

STRATEGY: MISSION, VISION, AND VALUES

CHAPTER 4

Developing a Strategic Perspective: The Conceptual Level

INTRODUCTION

An American consultant was based in Japan for a considerable time. He was invited to visit the home of a Japanese colleague—an unusual gesture in a culture where most entertaining is done in restaurants and other public facilities. During his visit, his colleague proudly showed him his Zen garden, a beautiful and restful, and incredibly complex, configuration of rocks, sand, and bonsai plants.

After admiring the garden, the consultant, in typical Western fashion, asked his executive friend, "But don't you ever get tired of it and want to change it?"

His colleague responded, "Oh, yes, I do from time to time."

"But how?" asked the consultant. "Wouldn't it be terribly complicated and time-consuming? And once you start, how do you know that it will turn out right?"

His friend relied, "First, I imagine what it will look like when I am finished—and then every day I turn over one rock."

The Japanese executive would certainly understand and appreciate the Cheshire Cat, and vice versa. The strategic thought process begins with the ability to conceptualize the future, to conceive of a clear, explicit image of a future in which one's aspirations are achieved, and then to use that image to identify the steps that must be taken—day to day—to bring that future about. Our executive takes the Cat one step further, however. He clearly understands that, while strategy is conceived of in terms of a grand, sweeping vision, it is achieved day-by-day, step-by-step, through a carefully developed sequence of specific, concrete actions.

WHAT'S AHEAD

In this chapter, you will learn:
- Key skills needed to understand how to strategically think and plan at a conceptual level.
- The second key to Strategic Thinking—becoming an excellent Diagnostician.
- The differences between Leadership and Management in a strategic context.
- How to build an effective strategic team using position (authority), relationships, and competence (experience).
- The importance of *facilitation* in the context of leading and managing your strategic team.

IN THE REAL WORLD

A patient comes into Doctor Jones's office complaining of severe pains on his lower right side just below the ribcage and above the waistline. Although the office is crowded, the patient rushes by the staff and enters the doctor's office. "Doctor," he says, "it hurts me here. The pain is awful—you've got to do something right away!" Doctor Jones, who is with another patient, looks up at the man and immediately begins weighing her options.

She could, with due respect to the more appropriate scientific terminology, consider the following responses:

- "Here, take some of these blue pills. If they don't work, come back in a couple of hours and we'll try some purple ones."
- "Let's get you on the operating table, open you up, and take a look."
- "What did you have for lunch? Here, have a drink of seltzer."
- Or...???

What would you do if you were Doctor Jones? What would you have your staff do? What would you want your doctor to do?

THE KEY CONCEPTS
Conceptual Strategy and Leadership

Thus, the success of any endeavor—personal, organizational, societal—depends first, on a clear sense of purpose and belief and second, on a guiding image of the future that we are seeking to bring into being by our conscious and deliberate effort. As noted in the previous chapter, our "concept" of our enterprise—provides the catalyst for strategic thinking. The ability, therefore, to develop a comprehensive, explicit conceptualization that will serve as a guide to analyzing possibilities, making strategic and tactical choices, implementing strategic plans, and assessing and measuring actual performance is fundamental to the strategic process.

We have termed this ability—this perspective—the Conceptual Level of strategic thinking. It requires that we define our aspirations, our intentions, and our purposes clearly and concisely. How we conceive of our enterprise, our sense of *Mission, Values,* and *Vision*—what have been called the atomic elements of strategy—drives our analyses of what is feasible and directs our operations to what can be achieved.[1]

This can be a formidable task. Developing a mission statement that effectively sets the criteria for analytical and operational decision-making, a sense of shared values that defines an organizational culture and guides individual behavior, and a vision that focuses effort and binds the organization together will require considerable effort and energy. We believe, however, that this effort will be well spent and that individuals and organizations that are willing to make the necessary investment in time and energy will reap considerable rewards. When we have fully satisfied the Conceptual Level of strategic thinking, we will have built the foundation for analysis and action, for resolving conflict, and for knowing which stone to turn over in what order so that we can create our Zen garden.

"Fine," you might say. "You have convinced me that I have to think strategically in order to turn my dreams (my Big Ideas) into reality. I get that resources are scarce, that I have to be disciplined internally, and that the game board is crowded and dynamic. I understand that strategy is central to dealing with all of this effectively. So, how do I do it? How do I know when I have done a good job of developing the concept of my organization?"

Let's be clear on what we want to accomplish when we think conceptually about our organization:

- We want to craft a "good" Mission statement that will inspire our members and attract new members, and that will give them clear guidance in allocating scarce resources—most importantly, their own time, energy, and passion.
- We want to identify a "good" set of shared Values: the root premises that define our sense of what is right and what is wrong, of what is acceptable practice and what is not—so that we can consistently and consciously make choices of which we can be proud and that we can live with.
- We want to articulate a "good" Vision statement: a description of our desired future that will focus our energies and give us a sound, explicit basis for monitoring our progress and assessing

our achievements, and for which we are willing to be held accountable and judged.

But what constitutes a "good" mission statement? Is it simply a catchy slogan?

Better things for better living... through chemistry.[2]

When it absolutely, positively has to get there overnight.[3]

We bring good thing to life.[4]

Are "good" statements of shared values simply that, reiterations of eternal verities and platitudes, the conventional wisdom of what constitutes 'goodness'?

Our customers come first.

We stand behind our products.

Our employees are our most valuable asset.

Is a "good" vision statement nothing more than the assertion of an organizational or societal ideal?

To be the industry leader in the areas in which we choose to compete.

To make the world safe for democracy.

We have chosen here to use historically familiar or hypothetical statements. It is not our intention to criticize or judge the current efforts of organizations or institutions to describe themselves to their members and to the world. What we would like you to consider is whether these examples "do the job." Do they, in fact, fulfill the functions and perform the tasks that we have assigned to "good" statements of mission, values, and vision as the conceptual foundations of strategic thinking? As we said, this is no easy t ask and there is a lot of work to be done.

Learning to craft "good" statements of mission, values, and vision will allow us to complete the first stage of the journey that will take us from conceptualization (aspiring and dreaming), to analysis (testing the feasibility of our dreams), to operationalization (turning our dreams into reality). When we have completed this stage of the process, we will be able to move on to the Analytical Level in chapters 7 and 8 and the Operational Level in chapter 9.

This is the point of this chapter—to begin our strategic journey by defining fully the principal elements of the Conceptual Level of strategy and by developing a step-by-step approach to articulating each of these elements. By understanding how to achieve consensus within our organization on the core concepts of *Mission*, *Values*, and *Vision*, we will be laying the necessary groundwork for making the crucial decisions that we will face at every point along the way as we seek to define the best path for fulfilling our aspirations. In the words of the noted raconteur and philosopher, Yogi Berra, we need a touchstone for confronting the tough choices:

> *When you come to a fork in the road, take it!*[5]

LAUNCHING THE PROCESS

So how do we get the process off the ground? What does it take to become an excellent strategic thinker—a World Class *Strategos*? We have suggested repeatedly that effective strategic thinking requires both a conscious, comprehensive process and also the skills and attitudes needed to implement that process effectively. Let's start with the skill and with a strong assertion:

> **The most essential skill of the strategist is that he/she is first and foremost an excellent diagnostician.**

If the first KEY to strategic thinking is a matter of attitude or mindset, as captured in the Strategist's Mantra:

> *If we want to be . . . . by. . ., then we had better be . . . . by. . . .*

then the second KEY is just as clearly a matter of skill—that of diagnosis.

We use diagnosis or diagnostic skill here in the same sense as that of the physician, the crime scene investigator, the scientist, or the journalist. It is *the ability to ask the right questions in the right order and to listen carefully to the answers.* It is based on the integration of knowledge, experience, and insight. Our diagnostic approach, therefore, is composed of a set of heuristics that provide us with the ability to reduce the seemingly overwhelming complexity of the organization and its environment to a workable model through a series of carefully chosen and sequenced questions. Depending on the answers to these questions, and to the further probing that the answer to each question suggests, we are able to form hypotheses, assess probabilities, and make choices for action.

Let's take an example that we all have experienced—a trip to the doctor's office:

> *A patient comes into Doctor Jones's office complaining of severe pains on his lower right side just below the ribcage and above the waistline. Although he asks to see the doctor instantly, the office staff has him fill out a lengthy questionnaire on a clipboard that asks numerous questions about his personal habits, his medical history, and that of his family, in addition to securing his insurance information.*
>
> *When he is taken into to see Dr. Jones, he says, "Doc, it hurts me here (pointing to the region noted). You've got to do something." Rather than immediately prescribing a medication or prepping the man for surgery, Dr. Jones reads the questionnaire, and then proceeds to ask the man additional questions, perhaps even occasionally turning to his computer and looking something up. The man gets increasingly agitated, "Doc, can't we do all this chit-chat later? It hurts me here and it's getting worse. Give me something for the pain."*

> Dr. Jones instead does a brief physical examination and then suggests some tests, saying, "I want to see the results of these before I draw any conclusions." Despite the man's desire for a quick fix for his pain, Dr. Jones is proceeding in this systematic manner because she knows from her medical training, her experience as a practitioner, and the man's history, comments, and current signs, that the symptom expressed as "it hurts me here" might have numerous causes ranging from indigestion to an inflamed appendix to a possible cardiac infarction, and that the proper treatment for one of these possible causes might, in fact, be harmful or even deadly if the symptom is coming from a different cause.
>
> Dr. Jones's diagnostic approach, however, allows her to explore and reduce these alternate explanations, thus helping her to pinpoint the cause and select the treatment option that has the highest probability of eliminating the pain without further harm.

We will be applying this diagnostic approach to the strategic thought process in much the same manner as Dr. Jones did to the treatment of her patient. We will be developing our conceptual analysis through an explicit diagnostic approach based on our experience in guiding organizations through the strategic process. Our diagnostic model will involve a series of carefully ordered questions, each intended to further reduce the complexity of our situation, to eliminate possibilities and alternatives, and to focus our attention on the critical issues and choices that we face in transforming our soft, subjective aspirations into hard, objective performance.

Note also that by "asking the right questions in the right order and listening carefully to the answers" we not only sharpen our sense of where to probe deeper and what question to ask next, but we also may gain information or insight that leads back to an earlier stage in the process to reconsider an earlier answer or choice.

Thus, the diagnostic approach is dynamic and iterative rather than simply linear and reflects the essential mindset of the strategist as developed in chapter 1.

A Few Thoughts about the Diagnostic Approach and Buzzwords

If diagnosis involves asking the right questions in the right order and listening to the answers, it stands to reason that:

(a) The questions have to strike at the heart of the fundamental issues of human aspiration, whether individual or collective.

(b) They must apply with equal force to all forms and levels of human endeavor—from societies and cultures to formal organizations (whether public or private, for-profit or not-for-profit and their component departments and units) to tribes and families to individuals.

(c) They should be stated in language that is unambiguous and understandable to both the diagnostician and the respondent so that there is no misunderstanding and so that interaction and dialogue can occur.

This, again, is easier said than done. We know that it is in the nature of human endeavor to develop special language and terminology to facilitate communication among insiders and, often, to exclude outsiders. Thus, most professions and fields, whether in medicine or law, high-tech or retailing, social service or education, and so on, have developed their own jargon, often by using ordinary English in special ways, by creating unique and nonobvious acronyms, or by appropriating phrases from Latin or Greek. We acknowledge this by referring to buzzwords or jargon or the catchall, semantics, that both facilitate and impede effective communication.

In fact, we have freely employed special language, often referred to as business lingo or MBA jargon. We have freely used a raft of everyday words: leader, manager, mission, values, vision, strategy, and so on as if they had special meaning within the context of this book that would be understandable to all readers.[6] We have defined some terms carefully, notably, *Strategos* and the various uses of *strategic* as an adjective, but have left most others open to interpretation. While we acknowledge the value of buzzwords and jargon in facilitating communication among the *cognoscenti*, we feel too much is at stake in the strategic process not to take steps to ensure against misunderstanding.

We are concerned that the strategic process be open and available to all within and outside of the given organization whose input might be sought and who might seek to contribute. We want our diagnostic model to be as transparent and protected from ambiguity or misunderstanding as possible. Therefore, we will develop our diagnostic model in the most basic terminology possible so as to allow for full participation without confusion of organizational members from different fields and disciplines, from all levels from executive to custodian, from different cultures and locations, and even of those without MBAs!

Once we have developed this model, we will reintroduce and discuss special language and buzzwords as ways to facilitate communication within a given organization once there is consensual agreement as to meaning.

BUILDING THE STRATEGIC TEAM

Having developed our diagnostic model and honed our diagnostic skills, we should now be ready to assemble our strategic team and get to work. But who should be on that team? Who should be in the room as we proceed to choose and pursue our organization's future? Rather than trying to define team membership by specific titles or positions within the organization, which will vary from organization to organization, let's consider the makeup of the team in terms of the competencies and roles or functions that will be necessary to inform a comprehensive strategic process.

Note that we are presuming here that we are pursuing the strategic process on behalf of an organization and that the issues and choices that we will be considering will go beyond the capacity of any single individual and will necessitate the participation of a number of persons, a team, if it is to be meaningful. We believe that strategy is an organizational property and that the successful implementation of a chosen strategy necessarily involves a sense of ownership and commitment on the part of the entire organization.[7] Thus, organizational strategy extends beyond the purview of any given individual, even the CEO or the head strategist.[8] This implies, moreover, that successful strategies will be those developed by those persons who are fully cognizant of and embody the organization's aspirations and culture, who possess the skills to guide and assess the feasibility of possible strategic options (even though the detailed analyses may be done by others), and who own the responsibility and accountability for the implementation of the strategy once adopted. In our experience, strategic plans written by others, outside consultants or in-house specialists, no matter how professionally done are less effective and have less actual impact than do the strategic plans developed and implemented by an internal strategic team.[9]

So, what should be the composition of our strategic team? It is fair to say that the ultimate purpose of our strategic efforts is the creation of an *effective organization*. Let us begin, therefore, by defining these two seemingly innocuous every day terms:

> **Organization:** *an entity that persists over time independent of the identities of its individual members.*[10]
>
> **Effective organization:** *an organization that consistently, over time, achieves more and more of its stated purposes.*

Now, we may ask, what is required to create and sustain an effective organization? As the definitions suggest, it is not a matter of specific persons or personalities. Rather, it is a matter of acquiring and balancing a number of key functions or skills. One useful model of the essential functions or skills is shown below in exhibit I.

Exhibit I—Balancing the Essential Functions

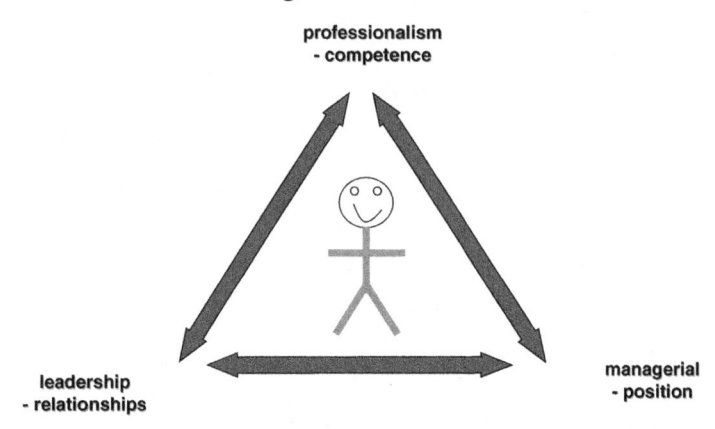

```
              professionalism
               - competence


                    (figure)


  leadership                        managerial
  - relationships                    - position
```

In this model, there are three broad sets of skills or functions that must be maintained in dynamic balance in order to sustain organizational effectiveness over time. These are:

- **Professionalism**: These are the skills and competences that are essential to performing the tasks required to produce the organization's product, services, and activities. They are represented by the functions or disciplines that individuals bring to the job and that they apply on behalf of the organization in doing the actual work of the organization. We think of professionalism in terms of the competencies of individuals, which may move from organization to organization with the particular individual.

- **Managerial**: These are the skills or functions that are concerned with designing and monitoring the systems, the processes, plans, programs, and procedures that constitute the infrastructure of the organization and provide the necessary direction for integrating and coordinating the work of the professionals. We think of the managerial function in terms of positions within the organization's overall structure, with the powers and responsibilities adhering to the position rather than to the individuals who hold those positions at any given time.

- **Leadership**: These are the functions and perspectives that are central to the purposes and aspirations of the organization, that give meaning and motivation to the activities of managers and professionals. We think of leadership in terms of the catalytic ideas and emotions that bind organizations together, of the ability to create and sustain a shared sense of purpose and aspiration, and in terms of relationships between leaders and followers that may be independent of competence or position at that may take on different form and direction from situation to situation.

When we want to talk about or describe the *effective organization*, we inevitably find ourselves employing all three of these constructs, these buckets of skill and function, in some way. We need all three: professional substance and competence; managerial systems and disciplines; and leadership visions and inspiration. Thus, for example, the effective organization is one where the skills of professionals are directed and integrated by the systems developed by managers to express and implement the vision of leaders. Or, an effective organization is one where managerial systems and processes optimally link shared leadership visions with appropriate professional competencies.

In thinking about these three essential functions or roles, there are several important observations to keep in mind:

- Excellence as a professional does not necessarily predict excellence as a manager—the best sales rep may not make the best sales manager; the best athlete may not make the best coach. Excellence as a manager may not make one a leader. Nor does excellence as a leader necessarily guarantee that the manager will take his/her followers in a professionally sound direction. These are separate functions and draw upon different skill sets.

- All three functions involve relationships with others in and out of the organization, but the nature of these relationships is quite different:
    - Professionals have peers and clients as a function of comparable or differential *competences*. "Follow my directions because, in this matter, I have more relevant knowledge than you."
    - Managers have superiors and subordinates as a function of relative *position* in the organizational hierarchy. "Follow my directives because I have the positional power to command you."
    - Leaders have followers as a function of the *relationship*, which, ironically, is defined by the follower. "Follow my lead because you are persuaded by my ideas or drawn to my person."
- Making someone a manager provides an empowered platform from which to lead. It creates the potential to exercise leadership but it is how that individual uses that platform, how he/she behaves and "connects" with others, that will determine whether or not others will accept him/her as a leader.

Strategic thinking is essentially a leadership function. Strategic analysis and operationalization are managerial functions and strategic execution is a professional function.[11] In forming our strategic team, we will clearly need persons at the table who represent one or more of these buckets of skills and perspectives, and we need to be certain that all three are adequately represented. We need individuals who will maintain focus on the organization's core aspiration and purposes—on **why** we do what we do, who will provide *strategic leadership*. We need individuals who will analyze the challenges and build the operating systems, so we know **how** we will do what we want to do, who will provide *strategic management*. We need individuals who will be able to do the required tasks effectively, who do can **what** we have to do, who will provide *strategic professionalism*.

The last question we have to resolve before beginning our strategic review is: Who will lead the team through the process? We will be challenging our team to think long and hard about our organization—about the wisdom and attractiveness of our aspirations, the quality and adequacy of our resources, our competences, our performance to date, and the potential of our plans. These are all matters about which members of the team might feel quite strongly. Advocates for a particular perspective, a preferred vision or a favorite strategy, might well be prone to stress the virtues of their viewpoint while minimizing possible deficiencies or resisting analyses that might raise doubts or objections.

While we have said that strategy starts with human aspiration, which can vary across members of the team, it is essential that our strategic process lead to an effective consensus among team members at the conceptual level. This conceptual consensus then provides us with a foundation and a reference point to which we can refer conflicts that might arise later in the process. Thus, while we expect team members to bring multiple viewpoints to the table and to argue them vigorously, our team needs a firm grasp on objectivity and process in order to draw these perspectives together and achieve the necessary balance.

Our team needs a firm hand at the helm to guide or facilitate the process, ensuring open discussion and a willingness to question and challenge dearly held views and practices. Someone has to "own" the process, to keep the team focused on substance and content, to sustain the contention of ideas and avoid the conflict of personalities. Thus, the final member of the team should be someone who will act as a *facilitator*.

The facilitator could be a member of the organization—someone with expert knowledge of the strategic process and good group facilitation skills—or an outsider—a consultant whose focus would be on forcing objectivity and driving process. Experience shows that this is a difficult role or function for a team member who has a strong stake in the specific decisions, which vision, which strategy, that the team will make. It is asking a lot to expect an advocate of a given viewpoint to serve as a process facilitator.[12] We have argued forcefully earlier against strategic plans prepared by in-house specialists or outside consultants and in favor of plans developed by the strategic team that will be responsible for implementation. However, we do feel that such outsiders or specialists can and may be the best choice to serve as *facilitators* of the process.

In the next chapter, we will turn our focus to key questions and critical skills that we need to examine in order to set the proper conceptual context.

BUSINESS STRATEGY IN ACTION

When we introduced the Fidelity case in the previous chapter, we focused on the major challenges that the changing competitive marketplace was presenting to the firm. Bill Harrigan was confronted with the need to decide upon Fidelity's future direction: Should it stick with its history and tradition, should it follow the lead of one or more of its "innovative" competitors, or should it strike out in some undefined new direction? And he realized that whatever choice he might make, he was literally "betting the business." Fidelity would either return to its place of prominence or fade into irrelevance.

Bill also realized that making a choice was only the beginning of his overall strategic challenge. He would still have to "sell" his decision to his partners, several of whom were strong advocates of seemingly contradictory approaches. Thus, Bill's internal strategy, how he secures support for his vision, will be crucial to his success as a strategic leader. How can you help him?

TEST YOURSELF

Please review the Fidelity case in chapter 3 again and consider the following questions:

1. Once Bill Harrigan, with Sam Heinz's assistance, has developed his vision and strategic direction for Fidelity, how should he proceed to get everyone, particularly his three vocal partners—White, Dedham, and Warburg—on board?
2. Conduct a thorough analysis of the pros and cons of the strategic options proposed by White, Dedham, and Warburg. How can Bill draw on the best of each of these and gain the "buy-in" of his key partners?

KEY POINTS TO REMEMBER

- *Diagnosis*, not treatment, is fundamentally what drives the concept (or conceptual level) of strategy.
- Conceptual strategy development focuses on three core ideas: *mission, vision,* and *values.* Being able to develop these succinctly and precisely is critical to further analytical and operational considerations.
- Strategy is not one person's job! Strategy—and strategic thinking—must be a shared competence across a *strategic team.*
- *Leadership* and *management* are often used interchangeably. However, each is different from the other. Leadership is more about motivation and relationships. Management focuses on position and competence. Not all managers can be great leaders . . . and the reverse is also true!
- Thus, our focus will be on strategy and strategic thinking as a *leadership* function that focuses on aspirations, motivating others to see them, and encouraging a team to "get it done" in order to achieve longer-range visions.
- However, a strategy team is incomplete if all its members only lead. *Facilitators* are key components of any strategy exercise (and, in fact, of any leadership team).

CHAPTER 5

Developing the Strategic Concept—The Fundamental Questions

INTRODUCTION

Founded in 1938 by President Franklin Delano Roosevelt, himself a victim of polio, the National Foundation for Infantile Paralysis took as its mission—its unifying purpose—the challenge of finding a solution to this dreaded disease. The spokesperson for this effort, the noted entertainer Eddie Cantor, defined the strategy for this effort when he dubbed the campaign "The March of Dimes" and said on the radio:

> The March of Dimes will enable all persons, even the children, to show our President that they are with him in this battle against this disease. Nearly everyone can send in a dime, or several dimes. However, it takes only ten dimes to make a dollar and if a million people send only one dime, the total will be $100,000.

Thanks largely to the millions upon millions of dimes donated by millions of individuals and collected by generations of school children, the scourge of polio was eliminated in the US through the vaccines developed by Dr. Jonas Salk in 1955 and Dr. Albert Sabin in 1962.

Emboldened by its success in the battle against polio, the Board of Directors of the March of Dimes in 1958 committed to the continuing application of its strategy in an enhanced mission, now stated as:

> Our mission is to improve the health of babies by preventing birth defects, premature birth, and infant mortality.[1]

The role of *strategic thinking* is to unify human purpose and values in the pursuit of a specific vision in order to define and identify the mostly likely and effective means for achieving that vision in the challenging context of the "real world." We believe that the story of the March of Dimes is a compelling example of the power of a clear mission and a compelling vision to catalyze and guide the formulation and implementation of winning strategies. It demonstrates the central role of a clear *strategic concept* in laying the foundation for action.

In this chapter, we will develop the Conceptual Level of strategic thinking by applying our diagnostic skills, by asking the right questions in the right order. Remember, we'll start with everyday language and return to jargon and buzzwords later.

We will present the questions as if we were facilitating the process with the strategic team of an organization. The process would work equally well, however, if it were being employed by an individual—a single strategist. It also works equally well if the strategic team represents the most senior level of the organization, a unit within the organization, or a cross-section, either horizontal or vertical, of the organization.

Notice also that we would follow the same process whether we were working with the particular strategic team for the first time or if we were facilitating a periodic review with a team with which we had been working for some time. The central point is that the questions, in the order asked, are intended to capture our understanding of the essential nature of our organization—our concept—and that this concept is itself dynamic. As we pursue the strategic priorities that we agreed upon at our last review in our own part of the organization, our understanding of the overall strategy and our concept of the organization will naturally be influenced shaped by our experiences within our own units or functions. This is why as a strategic team—as an organization—we need to come together periodically to share our experiences and learnings and to affirm that which we hold in common: our living, dynamic concept of our enterprise.

WHAT'S AHEAD

In this chapter, you will learn:
- How to define, state, and refocus your *mission, vision, and values* for your strategy (including key questions that need to be answered to develop them).
- How to be concrete—in terms of *timeframes*—with respect to your mission and vision (and how these time frames tie into the "folding back" process discussed earlier).
- *Criteria* for successful mission statements.
- Key *elements* of successful mission statements.

IN THE REAL WORLD

A noted national health organization, let's call it Alpha, was engaged in a strategic planning effort and had appointed a five-person task force to drive the process. An outside consultant, who had been engaged to facilitate the process, began by asking each of the task force members to write the mission of the organization on a sheet of paper without reference to any previously prepared documents or reports.

The facilitator collected and read their responses:

- The mission of Alpha is to treat the victims of the disease.
- The mission of Alpha is to cure the disease.
- The mission of Alpha is to prevent the disease.
- The mission of Alpha is to educate the public to the dangers of the disease.
- The mission of Alpha is to advocate and lobby in the legislatures and professional societies for the elimination of the conditions causing the disease.

The facilitator then commented that, "you all appear to be roughly in the same line of work. There is really no direct conflict here but there certainly are major differences in emphasis and focus that could and undoubtedly do lead to problems of internal coordination and external clarity of message."

Would you be concerned if you were on the Task Force? On the Board of Directors? On the professional staff? If you were a donor? What can the facilitator do to resolve these differences?

THE KEY CONCEPTS

I. Who are we? Why do we exist?

Our first question goes to the very heart of our shared enterprise. What is it? What do we understand our purpose, our *raison d'être*, our very reason for existence to be? Where did we come from, in concept, in history, in initiative, and how did we get to where we are today?

We find that individuals at all levels of an organization or a society enjoy discussing these issues and often have unique insights to add to the common pool of knowledge and understanding. Also, we are looking for "natural" or spontaneous responses and insist that the members of the team resist retrieving or reading from past statements. What we want is the current "living" response that reflects how each person is presently thinking and the basis on which that person is presently acting. Imagine you are at a reception or on an airplane; the person next to you asks:

What do you do?
I am with Organization X.
Oh! What's that?

It is your answer to this last question, your "gut" response, that we are seeking.

If we continue to probe the responses, if we continue to ask, "Why?" we will provoke a rich discussion and, eventually, a moving consensus on the answer to our original question. We will have articulated our common sense of purpose and aspiration. We will also lay the groundwork for our next question.

II. **What do we believe in? What do we hold dear?**

If we ask "why?" in all its various forms and variations often enough, we will eventually provoke the answer, "Because." This is what philosophers refer to as a *primitive*. If we trace the reasons, the logic, the emotions supporting a particular purpose or aspiration down to its roots, we will eventually ask the primitive question to which the answer is, "Because it just is. It is what we believe on its own merits. It neither needs nor has any further explanation or justification. It just is. This is where we draw the line in the sand, where we take our stand."

Our intention here is to identify and articulate the beliefs and reasons that are basic and foundational to the organization's sense of purpose and rationale for existence. When we have reached a moving consensus here, we are ready to move forward to the next question.

So what?

This may seem a bit abrupt and argumentative—even impolite (and we have omitted it from our exhibit). This is, realistically, where our first two questions logically and naturally lead us. The first two questions are abstract and philosophical. They can clearly end up as lofty, pious statements of ideals that bear little or no tangible relation to the world of affairs. Frankly, we often experience an organization's assertions of purposes and beliefs in this way—as empty platitudes to which we give lip service but pay little attention to in practice.

It is our position that the conceptual level of our strategic thought process provides the fundamental guide and discipline to the overall strategic effort. Therefore, it cannot simply be composed of slogans and fluff. It must have "teeth" if it is to drive the process meaningfully. Here is where we first look for those teeth. The proper phrasing of our question might be:

> *Isn't that nice? You have purpose and belief, and they certainly sound wonderful. But what are you going to do about them? How are they evidenced in your current structure, operations, and performance? Where are you going with them? How will they be manifested in your ongoing behavior and achievements?*

Having made the "so what" point, we are now ready for our next question.

III. Where do we want to be? What do we want to look like at a specific future point in time?

Here is where we answer the "so what?" question. If we have an essential consensus on purpose and belief, we should be able to describe in some detail what we intend to bring about for our organization, our customers and our market, our community, our society by our efforts within a given timeframe. Our concern here is to define in explicit observable terms how much of any given aspect of our aspirations and purpose we hope to accomplish or attain by a certain date.

We understand that our ultimate purposes and aspirations may be stated in absolute or ideal terms that would have to be pursued continuously over an indefinite period time: *to maximize shareholder value, to advance medical knowledge, to make the world safe for democracy*. We also acknowledge that such lofty ambitions are powerful tools for attracting adherents and resources and for binding and sustaining organizational cultures over time and in the face of adversity.[2] Our concern here is more pragmatic and prosaic and, we believe, essential to transforming these ideals into actual achievements. In effect, we are asking:

> *If these are your purposes and beliefs, and if you pursue them efficiently and effectively over the next period of time, how much of your aspiration do you hope to fulfill by the end of that period? Starting today, how far down the road to your intended destination do you plan to get by a week from today, a month from today, a year from today? If I left today and came back to visit two years from today, what should I look for to show me that you have been here and that you have made a difference?*

With reference to the images shown in Exhibit II on the next page, we are asking, "What is the shape of your triangle, what will you look like, when will you get there, and what is the value of x?"[3] Note that when we define our triangle in terms of how much or how far we are committing to progress in pursuit of our aspirations in the next chunk of time, we are also defining the outcomes to which we are willing to be held accountable. We are not only translating our dreams into indicators of performance, we are also defining the terms on which our results will be evaluated. In the words of the great visionary, Wimpy:

I will gladly pay you Tuesday for a hamburger today.

Once we have described our triangle to our satisfaction, we are ready to proceed to the last conceptual question.

IV. What do we have to do to get there?

Here we begin to move from concept to action. Knowing where we want to be conceptually at a given moment, we can use that moment as an anchor or focus for determining the path that we will have to follow to get there. Using the ideas that we developed in chapter 1, we can fold back in our mind's eye from our triangle (our intended future) to identify the path with milestones and checkpoints that we will have to follow on our journey.

More importantly, by clearly defining the future in terms of explicit, time-based outcomes to which we will be held accountable, we are determining the parameters for the Analytical and Operational levels of our strategic process. We can ask such questions as, "Where are we now relative to where we want to be? How big is the gap? How far will we

Exhibit II—The Conceptual Level

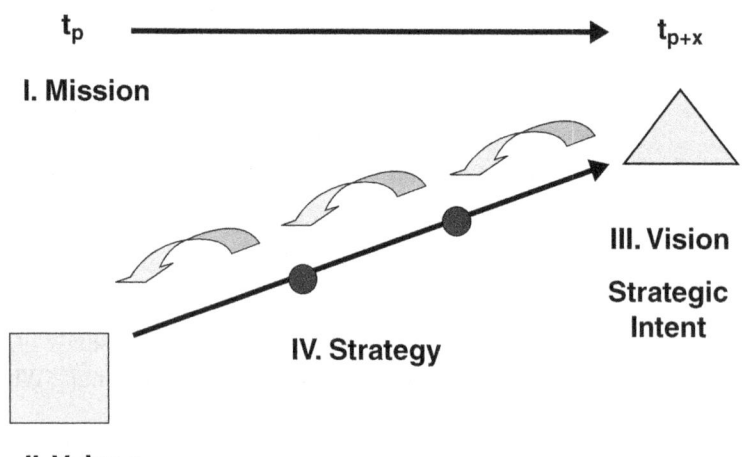

$t_p \longrightarrow t_{p+x}$

I. Mission

III. Vision

Strategic Intent

IV. Strategy

II. Values

have to travel? What might help or hinder us along the way? What will we have to do, in what order?" We will ask and seek to answer these questions when we proceed to the discussion of the Analytical and Operational levels in Part III.

For the present, however, we have completed the diagnostic process at the Conceptual Level; we have asked the right questions in the right order. The relationship among these questions in terms of our basic image of the strategic process is shown in exhibit II.

A Further Note on Language

We discussed earlier our concern for the possible confusion caused by buzzwords and jargon and our intention to present our diagnostic questions in basic, unambiguous language. We believe that we have done so, but we also believe that special terminology has its place in adding precision and facilitating communication within the group that shares that language. Thus, in Exhibit II, we have chosen to identify our four key questions by their Roman numeral and by a common buzzword as follows:

I. Our first questions, **Who are we? Why do we exist?** are what most strategists would term their organization's *Mission*. Some organizations refer to it as their vision, others as their values, others as their charter, still others as their statement of purpose, and so on. In all of these cases, they are seeking to answer the same basic question: *Who are we?* It doesn't matter what we call it, as long as we agree to call it the same thing. We will use the term *Mission*" throughout this book with the understanding that this is what we mean by it.

II. Similarly, our second questions, **What do we believe in? What do we hold dear?** are what most organizations would refer to as its *Values*. Others, however, might call this their mission or their guiding principles or their vision and then spend time debating whether a particular item is a mission element or a value. Again, the important point is that we identify and agree upon these fundamental elements of our organizational concept. We will use the term *Values* for this question.[4]

III. The term *Vision* is what most strategic thinkers would understand by our third questions: **Where do we want to be? What do we want to look like at a specific future point in time?** However, again, others make reference to their stretch goals, their targets, even their Big Hairy Audacious Goals (BHAG). We prefer the term *Vision* because it seems to us to capture the notion of tangible endpoints that we can "see," that are within eyesight in a meaningful timeframe. We also like, and have shown, the term "Strategic Intent," which is being used more commonly. *Strategic Intent* carries a clear message: This is what we intend to accomplish in this time period. We will use *Vision* and *Strategic Intent* interchangeably;

IV. Finally, our fourth question, **What do we have to do to get there?** is the best operational definition we can find for the term *Strategy* and we will use it accordingly.

For ease of reference, we have summarized the diagnostic approach to the Conceptual Level, along with the conventions in terminology that we have adopted, in exhibit III. In the next three

Exhibit III—The Fundamental Questions

- **MISSION**
    - Who are we?
    - Why do we exist?

- **VALUES**
    - What do we believe in?
    - What do we hold dear?

- **VISION**
    - Where do we want to be?
    - What do we want to look like at a specific future point in time?

- **STRATEGY**
    - What do we have to do to get there?

sections, we will provide guidelines for ensuring that our strategic team has developed 'good' statements of our Mission, our Values, and our Vision.

ARTICULATING THE MISSION— *WHO ARE WE? WHY DO WE EXIST?*

Let us return to a question that we asked earlier: W*hat constitutes a "good" mission statement?* How will we know if we have crafted a "good" statement that will inspire our members and give guidance for allocating resources and making decisions?

As you might expect, there is no clear answer or simple formula for this task.[5] We can, however, provide a basis for critiquing existing statements or for drafting new ones. We find it useful to examine mission statements—existing or proposed—in terms of whether they satisfy five essential criteria and whether they contain five fundamental elements.[6] These are shown in exhibit IV and discussed below.

DEFINING THE CRITERIA

The five criteria that allow us to judge whether the mission statement crafted by our strategic team is both comprehensive and effective may be defined as follows:

1. ***The Incremental Criterion:*** A mission statement satisfies the incremental criterion if it provides clear and unequivocal guidance to any organizational member as to how to allocate scarce resource *at the margin.* If you are down to your last hour of time, your last dollar of budget, your last erg of energy, the organization (and society) wants and expects you to spend it on that activity that most advances the core mission of the organization. The mission is, therefore, not simply a slogan or a rallying cry. It is the fundamental decision-making criterion of the organization and the essential point of reference for resolving subsequent conflict

over tactics or operations. Let us return to the example of the national health organization that was undertaking a strategic effort:

> The consultant who had been engaged to facilitate the effort had asked the members of the strategic task force, consisting of the CEO, the COO, the chair of the board, the chair-elect of the board, and the immediate past chair of the board, to write down their individual sense of the mission of the organization.[7] They were to do this without reference to any previously prepared documents or reports. The facilitator put the question as follows:
>
> > *Assume you are on an airplane or at a reception and someone asks you, "What do you do?" You reply, "I'm with Alpha." They respond, "Oh! What's that?" How would you answer, in your own words?*
>
> The facilitator framed the question this way on the perception that our current living understanding of the mission, as we would express it off the cuff, is what, in fact, guides and shapes our daily behavior on behalf of the organization.
>
> As you will recall, their responses were:
> - The mission of Alpha is to treat the victims of the disease.
> - The mission of Alpha is to cure the disease.
> - The mission of Alpha is to prevent the disease.
> - The mission of Alpha is to educate the public to the dangers of the disease.
> - The mission of Alpha is to advocate and lobby in the legislatures and professional societies for the elimination of the conditions causing the disease.
>
> The facilitator then commented that each of these were worthy and important activities and that one would hope that someone was dealing with each of them—and that Alpha could

conceivably deal with all five—but that each was fundamentally and significantly different in its direction and focus, its draw on resources, and so forth. Moreover, their responses suggested that each of the task force members would choose to apply scarce or marginal resources differently.

The task force realized that it could not move forward on its mandate until it resolved and reached a consensus on the priority and weighting of these possible mission elements. Once they had done so, they were able to develop a comprehensive strategic analysis and plan using this consensus to allocate resources and resolve conflict.

This example demonstrates the pivotal role of the mission in making priority or incremental decisions "at the margin." It also underscores the importance of a periodic review of the mission by the key decision-makers in any organization in order to reaffirm the shared purposes and priorities of the organization. As noted above, our sense of the mission of the organization is influenced strongly by our ongoing experiences in our own units. We can easily come to see what we do, our activity or program or function, as **the** mission—the center of the organization—rather than as one of the component elements that supports the mission.[8] In the task force in the example, one of the members was a research scientist, one was a physician in practice, and a third was a former Member of Congress. We can easily speculate on who made which statement regarding the overall mission!

2. *The Existential Criterion:* A mission statement satisfies the existential criterion if it allows any member of the organization to answer the question, "Why do you, why does your position, role, or function, exist?" in clear and unequivocal terms that trace back logically and directly to the core purposes of the organization. The mission should inform, guide, and inspire individual members and departments in the performance of

their duties. Well-articulated and disseminated throughout the organization, the mission is one of the most powerful tools of leadership. It provides the motivation to bridge the gap between compliance and commitment, between doing just enough to get by and going the extra mile. Consider the following example:

> A young man, let's call him "Willie," who had no formal education and few job skills was hired by the executive education division of a major business school to operate its photocopier. The division had a large number of programs and executive participants and generated high volumes of reproduced articles and other materials that had to be prepared and distributed each week. Willie was kept quite busy and proved to be a responsible employee, learning to operate more sophisticated equipment as copier technology evolved, but still remaining in a low-skill position in the organizational ladder.
>
> One day, the director of the division overheard Willie, who was well-known and popular with the participants, speaking with a group of executives at a coffee break. One participant asked, "So, Willie, what is your job?"
>
> The director expected to hear a response along the lines of "I'm the copier operator" or "I handle the logistics." Instead, he heard Willie reply: "I produce the materials that enable the participants to learn."
>
> That simple response demonstrated clearly that Willie fully understood the core mission of the division and his place in the overall scheme of things. Moreover, it was evident that he took pride in his contribution. This was evident in how he went about his work. He would confront individual faculty members with materials that they would submit for copying that he felt were not of sufficient quality and would not reproduce properly, telling them, "You will have to provide me with a better source copy. The participants will not be able to read copies made from this!"
>
> As confirmation of the value of having every member own his or her piece of the mission in this way, the director

asked a senior faculty member how he reacted when Willie confronted him with a fuzzy original. The faculty member said, "I'm getting him a better copy. I don't want to get on Willie's bad side!"

Under the existential criterion, each member, such as Willie, is able to "own" his or her part of the mission and to gain both purpose and pride. Taken together, the incremental and existential criteria are how an organization describes itself to itself. The remaining three criteria focus on how an organization describes itself to others.

3. *The Economic Criterion:* A mission statement satisfies the economic criterion if it is effective in attracting and securing resources. The mission statement must function as a tool of strategy in positioning the organization to compete effectively for scarce resources. When presented to the holders of essential resources, the mission statement, if well-articulated and communicated, should produce the response:

> If that is what you are all about, then I will invest in you, or come to work for you, or partner with you. I will risk my deployable resource to the pursuit of your purposes because I am convinced that this will provide fair return to me.

In presenting the core purposes of the enterprise to the world at large, the mission provides the basis for enhancing the organization's resources. Note that this interaction is substantively different from a simple economic transaction. In such an event, I may buy your product or sell you mine at an agreed-upon exchange rate or price without any concern for the use to which you will put my product or my currency. In the instance of the economic criterion, we are talking about the securing and committing of additional or incremental new resources drawn to us by the mission rather than acquired through the exchange of resources. The mission, thus, should create a "market" for the acquisition of resources through the attraction of purpose.

4. **The Identity Criterion:** A mission statement satisfies the identity criterion if, upon presenting it autonomously, the reader or listener is able to identify the organization. The mission should capture those essential attributes that differentiate us from others in our field or industry or society and that make us unique. Consider the following examples:

> (Our) mission is to organize the world's information and make it universally accessible and useful.[9]
>
> (We are) responsible for protecting the public health by assuring the safety, efficacy, and security of human and veterinary drugs, biological products, medical devices, our nation's food supply, cosmetics, and products that emit radiation.[10]
>
> Establish (us) as the premier purveyor of the finest coffee in the world while maintaining our uncompromising principles as we grow.[11]
>
> We want to discover, develop, and successfully market **innovative products** to prevent and cure diseases, to ease suffering and to enhance the quality of life.[12]

We either know who each of these organizations is as soon as we read the statements or we have an instant flash of recognition as soon as we check the footnote: "Oh, of course! Who else?"

The issue is not that of having a familiar slogan or tagline, which may be memorable and trigger the desired associations. It is, rather, that of having within the mission statement information that conveys directly the unique and special purpose and nature of our organization.

5. **The Action Criterion:** A mission statement satisfies the action criterion if its very statement commands response and compels behavior. Is it motivational and inspirational? Does its statement make the listener or the reader feel the need to

act upon its message? Does it command attention and guide response?

The simple test is to consider the verbs—the "action" words. Are they active or passive? Proactive or reactive? Look at the four examples above:

Google: organize, make

FDA: protect, assure

Starbucks: establish, purvey, maintain, grow

Novartis: discover, develop, market, prevent, cure, ease, enhance

How do these words compare in their impact and strength with such terms as *enable, support, provide,* and others frequently found in mission statements? Are these statements compelling? Do they provide a call to action?

Compare these to this sample output from the Dilbert Mission Statement Generator:

> It is our job to seamlessly fashion parallel materials in order that we may continually negotiate long-term high-impact leadership skills [13]

Done properly, the mission statement is truly the catalyst that launches the enterprise.

IDENTIFYING THE ELEMENTS

In translating the above criteria into a mission, we find it useful to craft the statement to include the following five elements:

1. *Rationale:* An effective mission will begin with, or have clearly imbedded in it, a "because' statement, a rationale that anchors the mission in core values and takes such forms as:

   > Given our basic belief in …; Grounded in the premise that …; Following the principles of …; we therefore …

2. ***Resources:*** An effective mission identifies the basic components of the organization's work—knowledge, technology, human resource, land, and so on:

> We will use the most advanced technology and scientific knowledge to …

3. ***Processes:*** An effective mission identifies the core methodologies and/or technologies that we will apply:

> We will employ team-based, environmentally-sensitive approaches in our operating systems …

4. ***Products:*** An effective mission identifies the essential attributes of the products, services, or activities that constitute the organization's outputs:[14]

> That will serve the following needs; that will develop the following potentials, that will support society in the following ways …

5. ***Markets:*** An effective mission identifies the broad markets that the organization's efforts will serve or support:

> That will serve the general public; the commercial sector; the industry …

Exhibit IV—Articulating the Mission

Who are we? Why do we exist?

CRITERIA	ELEMENTS
— incremental	— rationale
— existential	— resources
— economic	— processed
— identity	— products
— action	— markets

We will close this section with an outstanding example of a mission statement that effectively demonstrates the principles that we have developed.

The Preamble to the Constitution of the United States

We the People of the United States, in Order to form a more perfect Union, establish Justice, insure domestic Tranquility, provide for the common defence, promote the general Welfare, and secure the Blessings of Liberty to ourselves and our Posterity, do ordain and establish this Constitution for the United States of America.[15]

BUSINESS STRATEGY IN ACTION

In the case below, Kate Gorham, principal of St. Emily's School, finds herself in a challenging and frustrating situation. St. Emily's is a widely respected Catholic grammar school with a long and honored tradition of serving well the educational and transitional needs of newly arrived immigrant families and other community members. St. Emily's has a clear and compelling mission and a history of strong academic performance. By all accounts, the school's faculty and curriculum continue to serve their students well.

And yet, Kate realizes, the school is on shaky grounds as it looks to its future. The cost of providing quality education is rising, particularly relative to the ability of families in her community to pay, and St. Emily's has been running deficits that have been subsidized by the Archdiocese. Moreover, the continuing support of her parent organization, St. Emily's Parish, and her immediate superior, Father Bennett, is in question as the Parish is experiencing its own difficulties. The School itself is in disrepair and needs to be significantly upgraded. Finally, enrollments have shown a disturbing trend to drop off in the upper grades, and a strong competitor, St. Ingrid's, has been making advances on her southern border.

Despite its proud history, St. Emily's now has to rethink its future and whether major changes are needed in its mission, in its programs, in its role in the community, and/or in its relationship with the Parish. How can Kate interpret St. Emily's enduring mission in the context of the current realities of the parish, the community, and the competitive marketplace?

TEST YOURSELF

Read and analyze the case, St. Emily's School, below. Be prepared to respond to and discuss the following questions:

1. Carefully review St. Emily's mission in light of the criteria and elements described above. How and in what ways does this mission speak to the current situation of the school and the realities of the community?

2. Is the mission still valid? If so, how can Kate use it to create a compelling 3–5 year vision for the school?

3. How can she use the mission and the vision to rally support for St. Emily's School?

ST. EMILY'S SCHOOL[16]

As Kate Gorham inched her way homeward over the normally congested 59th Street Bridge on an overcast Tuesday afternoon in early March, she watched her fellow commuters consider the East River as a preferable substitute to the snarled traffic. Knowing that she was going nowhere fast, she let her mind drift back to a conversation earlier that day with Father Bennett. Kate had been principal of St. Emily's School for the last five years and had been a teacher in the school for seven years before that. Father Art Bennett had been appointed pastor of St. Emily's a little less than two years ago, having previously served as an associate pastor at St. Anastasia's in Orange County for five years and as a rotating counselor in several Diocesan high schools, including Rice and St. Regis before that. St. Emily's was his first pastorate.

"Kate, I can appreciate your desire to have a state-of-the-art computer facility for your children. But let's face it—I cannot go back to my parishioners and ask them to increase their support of the school. It is already a considerable drain on our finances and, with less and less of the children in the school coming from parish families, a number of the members of the Finance Council are having trouble seeing the school as a priority. The suggestion has been made, and I think that it merits consideration, that we take the limited resources at our disposal and focus them on building up the CCD program for parish children, even if this means scaling back parish support for the school.

"With the deficit what it is, we are fortunate that Inter-Parish Financing has been willing to advance us the necessary funds to cover it and also to pick up our insurance costs. I don't want to have to go downtown for more money—especially for something like brand-new computers when we have an adequate lab in place. You're just going to have to do your best with what you have."

Kate appreciated Father Art's concerns. He was new to the parish, which had a largely working class congregation. Sunday collections had been experiencing a slow but steady decline for several years. The weekly bingo game, a parish tradition, the proceeds of which were shared equally by the church and the school, had been dropping off even more rapidly. Moreover, Father Art was now the only priest assigned full-time to a parish that had been served historically by a pastor and two associates.

She had also heard some of the rumblings from the Finance Council and from other voices in the parish that no longer had children in the school. "It's not fair," she thought, "quality education costs money and requires quality facilities, and our children deserve the best programs and resources that we can give them. The computers are only part of our challenge. Our gym, which is one of the few resources that we have that might actually produce some extra money, is in need of a general overhaul, and the roof could go at any time. Our bathrooms are old and in need of repair, and our boiler, which is original, couldn't have more than two or three years left in it. And to top it off, we simply need more space.

"It's ironic; if we would be able to increase enrollment to the point that we would need two classrooms for each grade and the kindergarten, and for the pre-K that we would like to start, we wouldn't have enough space. This school is going to require considerable investment in the next few years, and I'm not sure if the support is there."

Kate remembered wistfully the glowing picture that Monsignor Francis Whelan, the former pastor, had painted for her when he had persuaded her to take the position of principal five years ago. "Kate," he had said, "St. Emily's School has been a polished gem in the Archdiocese's crown since Monsignor Woods opened its doors back in 1938. He saw clearly then that this parish was going to be a crucial gateway—a port of entry—for new immigrants to New York City and to the Church. Nothing has changed to this day to diminish or alter that vision. The neighborhood still attracts a steady influx of immigrants who are at least nominally Catholic, and they still look to our parish, and especially to our school, to help them and their children adjust to their new homeland."

It had all sounded so easy. There was an experienced, committed faculty in place, most of whom Kate had worked with for many years. Seven of the twelve full-time faculty were tenured, including two elderly sisters in habit. St. Emily's had been recognized as a model school by NYC Schools Chancellor Rudy Crew and enjoyed a good reputation in the neighborhood and in the city. With her own children entering their high school years, Kate concluded that this was a good time for her to take on a new challenge and took up her new role with considerable enthusiasm.

In a short time, however, Monsignor Whelan moved on to take the reins of a troubled parish on the West Side. The enrollment decline that had begun in the late '80s continued until leveling off about three years ago at its present 70% of capacity. Financial support from the parish declined while expenses and debts grew, and the 60+ year-old building kept getting older every year. Now, while Father Bennett was willing to continue with the *status quo*, the focus of his attention seemed to be elsewhere, and he was resistant to any attempts to upgrade the school's facilities. Since Father Bennett would likely be at St. Emily's for several more years, the future was cloudy.

ST. EMILY'S SCHOOL—THE HISTORY

St. Emily's School was opened in 1938 to serve the immigrant population that had begun moving into this densely populated, blue-collar section of the city. Monsignor John Woods, the founding pastor, whose portrait still hangs proudly in the entrance hall of the school, had spared no expense to create a real "church" presence for the new parishioners and their children. The school was widely respected as a model of good planning and sound building, both physically and spiritually, for the long run.

The School's mission and values were captured in a letter that Monsignor Whelan had sent to the Cardinal Archbishop in the early '90s in response to questions about which parish schools in the diocese could and should remain open in the face of mounting economic pressures.

Monsignor Whelan wrote:

> St. Emily's is a Catholic school in which gospel truths, values and attitudes are woven into the fabric of education. We view our service of education as contributing to the Church, the world, and, especially, to the local community of New York City.
>
> The Mission of our School is to create and nurture an atmosphere conducive to the development of the spiritual, cognitive, emotional, aesthetic, physical, and social potentials of each child in our care. Respect for one another, in all the diversity of human experience, is a hallmark of our mission, and the School works cooperatively with each family and with our parish and neighborhood communities to foster superior academic achievement and spiritual growth rooted in the teachings of Jesus Christ.
>
> The administration, faculty, students, and families of St. Emily's believe in the dignity of each life and see each child as unique and special.

ST. EMILY'S SCHOOL—THE PRESENT SITUATION

The school building has a rated capacity of 360 spread over 16 classrooms; the school also has a gymnasium, which doubles as a lunchroom, auditorium, and meeting room. Administrative space is crowded but presently adequate, but there is need for a separate computer area. The school presently has no dedicated facilities for art or music programs, and, in fact, dropped these programs, along with the physical education program, several years ago in reaction to the first major budget deficits. Teachers do provide some exposure to art and music as part of their regular lessons, but the details are left up to the individual teacher.

St. Emily's enrollment had held steady at 250–255 students for the past three years. Currently, this includes two kindergartens, two first grades, two second grades, and one section at each of the higher grades. With four presently underused classrooms, there is room for growth or reallocation of space. Possible proposed uses include two pre-Ks, as the baby population in the community is expanding rapidly, and a separate computer lab

The school does have the potential to adapt to emerging technology advances. Thanks in part to the e-rate (which provides a 90% discount worth $45,000), the necessary electrical wiring is in place in all of the classrooms to accommodate modern telecommunications technology, including the Internet. The school's computers, however, are 10-year-old Apple 2Es, and the faculty has little facility, and, in most cases, little interest in the computer as an instructional or administrative resource.

The school population is drawn almost entirely from the immediate local community, with just over 60% of the children coming from parish families. Many of the remaining children and families are also Catholic, at least in name or background, but are not members or contributors to the parish. More than 40% of the families of students presently in the school have immigrated to the US and to the city within the last five years, mostly from South America or Eastern Europe.

The school's academic programs appear to be strong. Students do well on standardized tests, and many have qualified for high school scholarships. Roughly 85% of the school's graduates are placed in the Archdiocese's best high schools.

In economic terms, most families in the school would be considered blue-collar. An analysis of information provided on the applications for financial aid, which over 80% of the families request, reveals an average annual family income of $26,000. A significant proportion of these families fall within what might be considered the "working poor" or the disadvantaged. Although hard to pin down precisely, it appears that over 20 of the children are from single-parent households.

Financially, the school has been running an annual deficit for most of the past four years in the range of $95,000 per year. This has been covered largely by Inter-Parish Financing (IPF), which also has picked up the school's annual insurance costs of $34,500 for the past two years. The school's finances are commingled with those of the parish, and there is no separate reserve fund.

The bulk of the revenues supporting the School come from tuition, which is currently $1,950/child/year, with a 25% "discount" for the second child in the school and a 50% "discount" for the third and each succeeding child. While the school does allow for monthly payments and deferred payments in special cases, it is not able, despite numerous requests, to provide any scholarships.

Additional revenues come from fundraisers, such as three annual candy drives, and from the weekly parish bingo. Together, these provided about $29,000 this past year, but this total has been eroding steadily year by year. The school also derives a modest income from renting out the gym to various local organizations in the evenings and on weekends, but the roof and the bathrooms will need repair for this effort to succeed.

The neighborhood itself is in generally good shape. Comprising mostly modest-sized tenements and subdivided brownstones, it is surrounded by gentrifying neighborhoods and is close to many of New York's cultural attractions. There are some drugs on the streets and occasional incidents of violence involving youth groups, but on the whole, St. Emily's is in a stable area that remains attractive and open to newcomers.

The school does have one major Catholic competitor, St. Ingrid's, in addition to the local public schools, which are considered by many of the parents to be "good but not great." St. Ingrid's parish is located just inside the border of what is usually viewed as the better end of the immediate community. The parish school is in a newer and larger building and tends to cater to a more "upscale"—and upwardly mobile—clientele. Some parishioners from St. Emily's have, in fact, enrolled their children in St. Ingrid's because they perceived it to be in a safer and cleaner neighborhood. Other parish families are also apparently considering making the same move.

The academic programs at the two schools are comparable, as are the tuition charges. St. Ingrid's has been an active and aggressive marketer. They bill themselves as "the safer alternative" and have also promoted the success of their athletic teams and their annual student musicale heavily.

ST. EMILY'S—THE FUTURE

The traffic finally began to clear up a bit on the Bridge, but Kate's challenges remained cloudy. She was keenly aware that she could not allow the situation to drift along on its own momentum for much longer. Some significant decisions and choices had to be made.

She knew that she had a dedicated and experienced faculty, but it was not particularly adventuresome. Only four of the teachers had expressed much interest in modern educational approaches, and the remainder, especially within the tenured group, are fearful of change.

In addition, the financial pressures brought on by the salary agreements in the negotiated teacher's contract continually diverted funds away from building upkeep and co-curricular needs. Kate realized that the school was going to have to find ways to increase or generate new revenues and to sort out competing priorities. She was certain she could not look for much help or guidance from the Parish Finance Council or from Father Bennett.

She thought, "Our parents really like the School and are cooperative and hardworking. They are willing to volunteer to help out at lunchtime and to act as teacher's aides—but then they always seem to want a tuition break in return. They really care that their children get a good education, but few of them have the personal background, abilities, or resources to help in a developmental or advisory capacity.

"The little PTO group is great at organizing a carwash or a craft sale or the like, but they don't have a lot of personal resources. And I'm afraid that they won't be around for a long time. This is still a transient community, especially for those with school-age children, and their commitment to the school lasts only as long as they have a child in the school or until they can move out of the city to a "better" community.

"We have a lot of alumni who say they love us and occasionally come through with a gift. The local merchants and businesses have been helpful from time to time, but they have their own problems."

She reflected that her participation in the Leadership Development Institute (LDI) sponsored by the Archdiocesan Office of Educational Development had probably come along at a good time, although finding time for the workshop sessions had put one more major pressure on her already overcrowded schedule. The requirement to produce a "strategic plan" as part of LDI would, she hoped, help her to bring some of these matters into clearer focus.

The traffic continued to ease up, but the rain, that had been threatening all afternoon, began to come down in force.

KEY POINTS TO REMEMBER

- *The Conceptual level of strategic thinking* is concerned with how we answer the fundamental questions of human organization for our enterprise or unit or activity. These questions are:
  - Who are we? Why do we exist?
  - What do we believe in? What do we hold dear?
  - Where do we want to be? What do we want to look like at a specific future point in time?
- Thus, the Conceptual level focuses on the dynamic relationship and interaction among our purposes, which we refer to as our *mission;* our fundamental beliefs, our *values;* and the degree or extent of achievement of our purpose that we intend to accomplish within a specific period of time, what we call our *vision* or our *strategic intent;*
- Taken together, these three concepts—mission, values, vision—provide or define the context within which we seek to answer the fourth fundamental question:
  - What do we have to do to get there (to our chosen vision)? What is our strategy?
- The essence of *strategic leadership*, the core skill of the *Strategos*, is the ability to articulate, communicate, and demonstrate *mission, vision, and values* clearly;
- "Good" or effective mission statements satisfy several demanding criteria—incremental, existential, economic, identity and action—in providing focus and direction for the organization;
- "Good" or effective vision statements are psychologically and operationally meaningful, they are challenging but attainable, we validate their achievement, and they motivate and attract others to the effort.

CHAPTER 6

Building on the Mission—Identifying Values and Vision

INTRODUCTION

Don Vito Corleone is approached by a major drug trafficker and the other Families to provide the political protection and financing to start the mass importation and distribution of heroin. Despite the potentially huge amount of money to be made, Corleone refuses, saying, among other things, "I don't believe in drugs." Prostitution, bootlegging, extortion, and so on may be fine, but not drugs.[1]

As this vignette regarding Don Corleone's values shows, values are personal and unique to the organization or to the individual. One organization's values may well be anathema to another. Parenthetically, the Don was also not convinced that drugs would be good for the overall success of the family business—another value in action.

We might think of our values as the ultimate criterion for choice and action, as the bases by which we assess and judge the acceptability of options. Our values are our mission taken to the extreme. If we pursue the sources of our aspirations and purposes, if we ask "Why do we aspire to achieve this?" we will find the causes rooted in our core values. We pursue this or that outcome because we believe it to be the expression of something that truly matters—that has value for us. We evaluate possible courses of action on the bases of whether they are consistent and compatible with our core values. We accept or reject a specific act or position in terms of its intrinsic "rightness" and acceptability with regard to those fundamental beliefs on which we base and build our enterprise.

> **WHAT'S AHEAD**
>
> In this chapter, you will learn:
> - How *values* help drive your firm's strategy
> - Examples of effective values and value statements
> - How to transform your mission and values to a compelling *vision* for your organization
> - Key criteria for developing and communicating vision statements
> - How to determine your *strategic cycle* in order to put a definite timeframe around your vision
> - Understand key internal and external factors that may affect your vision (and how to plan for such obstacles)

IN THE REAL WORLD

As the head of a major electric power generating company, you are concerned for the future of your industry. You see operational costs rising rapidly and aging plants becoming more and more expensive to operate as well as undergoing increasing regulatory scrutiny with regard to safety and environmental impact. State regulatory bodies are becoming increasingly resistant to applications for rate increases, and hearings on rate cases are taking longer and longer to resolve, with more and more pressure on the regulators from advocacy groups and more and more public expression of dissatisfaction. Advocates for all of the various alternative forms of energy generation—fossil, nuclear, hydro, solar, wind, and so on—seem firm in their conviction that theirs is the only approach that is safe, clean, cheap, and reliable. They are equally convinced that all other competing forms are dangerous, expensive, and unreliable, and the public is so confused that it distrusts all of the advocates (and your firm) equally and yet it wants access to unlimited power at low cost. And another hot summer of brown-outs or a collapse along the grid seems inevitable.

You have a clear sense of what needs to be done, a vision of the future, if you will, to resolve these issues, but its implementation will take considerable time, perhaps 25 years or more; money, in the billions; and patience, at all levels of society. But the challenges that you face in gaining acceptance of and commitment to your vision seem insurmountable—and not just because of public impatience with the *status quo*, regulatory quagmires, and painful economics.

Your senior management team and your industry colleagues seem to find it easier to focus on operational issues such as temporary arrangements to shuttle power from one part of the grid to another in case of real-time brown-outs or shortages—or on tactical matters such as rate increase cases to shore up cash flows and reserves. You, and most of your senior team, are not that far away from retirement, and you are concerned that your younger managers are getting locked into the same historical habits of thought.

How do you move your vision forward? How can you place it in terms that others can understand and accept intellectually and emotionally? How can you use your vision of a successful, but distant, future to set priorities and sequence actions—to determine what to do first? **The life of a visionary is not an easy one!**

THE KEY CONCEPTS
What is a "Good" Statement of Values?

We will go this far and no farther!
Here is where we draw our line in the sand!

In a sense, the notion of organizational or individual values is a much simpler concept than that of mission. We proposed an extensive set of design criteria to be used in formulating a "good" mission statement—one that performs its decision-making, communications, and motivational functions effectively. The concept of a "good" set of shared values is both much less complex and much more profound. The function of our statement of shared values is to provide the principles by which we intend to guide our behaviors and to judge and assess potential choices. These principles are inherently subjective—they come from the members of the organization, not from analysis. They are, or should be, consensual—they represent the rules or the code by which we have agreed to live and conduct our affairs. They are communal and enduring—they define our culture. They are the expression of what we believe in and hold dear![2]

The challenge with statements of shared values is to ensure that they are more than simply attractive or uplifting abstractions, rolled out periodically for public relations and communications purposes. If meaningful, our values have a prime seat at the table in all of our decision-making and a fundamental question to be asked when considering any course of action would be:

(If we do this) Will we be living our values?

A somewhat ironic, but nevertheless telling, example of the role of values in organizational decision-making comes from the pivotal scene in the classic film, *The Godfather*, described earlier. When Don Corleone says No! to drugs, he is standing on his values even though this may, and does, cost him his preeminent position at the Board table and, ultimately, his life.

We cannot provide you with an explicit list of what would be good values for your organization. We can, however, provide you with some guidance in identifying and formulating your statement of shared values. We find from an examination of the values statements of a number of prominent organizations (a few examples of which will be given below) that there are certain patterns and logic. In general, the elements of such statements tend to fall into five broad classes of values or principles; these are:

- **Professional**: Most organizations have a set of professional values that involve such notions as precision, excellence, zero defects, and intrinsic rightness.
- **Economic**: Most organizations have a set of transactional values that define their exchange relationships with others; examples would include fair return on investment, whatever the market will bear, and to each independent of their ability to pay.
- **Social**: Organizations typically express values regarding their place in the larger society, such as supporting the information needs or facilitating the efficient movement of goods and services.
- **Individual**: Organizations express values that define and shape the organization's relationship with its members/employees. These might include continuous employment, a fair day's pay for a fair day's work, the right of every person to develop his/her potentials fully, and so on.[3]
- **Philosophical**: Most organizations identify higher-level values, often of a metaphysical or even spiritual nature. These might include such things as concepts of integrity, justice, truth, beauty, or freedom.

The challenge, of course, is to create and sustain an understanding and acceptance of our values and to keep these values present and alive in the day-to-day activities of the organization.

Some examples of well-known corporate statements of values would include the following:

IBM®

- Dedication to every client's success.
- Innovation that matters—for our company and for the world.
- Trust and personal responsibility in all relationships.[4]

American Express®
OUR VALUES

Since its founding in 1850, American Express has conducted business according to several guiding principles that over the years have become inextricably linked with the company's brand, products, services, and—perhaps most notably—its people. Generations before the phrase "company values" entered the corporate lexicon, American Express employees across the organization were demonstrating the same core principles upheld by the company today:

> **Customer Commitment**—We develop relationships that make a positive difference in our customers' lives.
>
> **Quality**—We provide outstanding products and unsurpassed service that, together, deliver premium value to our customers.
>
> **Integrity**—We uphold the highest standards of integrity in all of our actions.
>
> **Teamwork**—We work together, across boundaries, to meet the needs of our customers and to help the company win.
>
> **Respect for People**—We value our people, encourage their development, and reward their performance.
>
> **Good Citizenship**—We are good citizens in the communities in which we live and work.

A Will to Win—We exhibit a strong will to win in the marketplace and in every aspect of our business.

Personal Accountability—We are personally accountable for delivering on our commitments.[5]

Wegman's
WHO WE ARE

These five statements explain what we're all about:

1. We care about and listen to our people.
2. High standards are a way of life. We pursue excellence in everything we do.
3. We make a difference in every community we serve.
4. We respect our people.
5. We empower our people to make decisions that improve their work and benefit our customers and our company.[6]

DEFINING THE VISION—WHERE DO WE WANT TO BE AT A SPECIFIC FUTURE POINT IN TIME?

With our mission and values well-defined and providing the foundation for evaluating alternative strategies and resolving conflicts, we are now prepared to return to the third of our original questions regarding our organizational concept: *What constitutes a "good" Vision statement—a description of our desired future that will act as the jumping-off point for our strategic analysis?* How do we translate our sense of purpose and intention into explicit, time-based outcomes to which we are willing to be held accountable? With reference to Exhibit II, how do we define our triangle with sufficient detail and rigor that it can serve as the p latform from which we can launch our detailed analysis and planning effort?

We usually pose this question in an actual situation as follows, "If, at the end of this strategic process, we go away and don't see you again until we reach the target date [t_{p+x}], what should we look for to determine if you have been there and made a difference?" In other words, we need to define our vision or strategic intent as we set out on our journey in terms that will allow us to determine at the appropriate time whether or not we have done what we said we would do.[7] If it was our strategic intent to achieve a certain set of outcomes and conditions by a given date, how did we do and what did we learn in the process that will enable us to continue to extend our vision into the future?

We have found it helpful to assess visions or statements of strategic intent in terms of whether they meet seven basic criteria. These are as follows:

1. **Eyesight**: While it is appealing to dream or fantasize in terms of ultimate visions, BHAGs, and the like, we find that organizations, teams, and individuals function more effectively and are better able to maintain focus when the timeframes chosen for visioning and acting are within "eyesight"—in a range that is psychologically meaningful and that we can "get our arms around."[8]

2. **Concrete**: Visions or strategic intent should be stated in terms that are accessible to the senses, that it, that can be seen, touched, tasted, felt, or smelled in some objective and reprintable way. The judgment of achievement should not be a matter of faith or opinion.

3. **Tangible**: Not only should the outcomes be concrete in the sense that we can perceive them, but they should also be tangible in the sense that they are subject to independent validation by an objective third party.

4. **Challenging**: Our strategic intent, the goals and targets that we set for ourselves, should be demanding and challenging and go beyond that which we could reasonably hope to attain

by continuing to pursue business as usual—by "keeping on keeping on."

5. **Achievable:** Although our visions should stretch and challenge us if they are to be truly motivating, their achievement should still be within the bounds of reason and analysis. Only on the Broadway stage does the continual pursuit of unattainable goals inspire and build character; in reality, it leads to despair.[9]

6. **Assessable**: Not everything is measurable or quantifiable in terms of dollars or units. Nevertheless, we should be able to specify going in—at the beginning—how we intend to assess achievement coming out – at the end [or at the checkpoint].

7. **Communicable**: We should be able to express our vision with sufficient clarity and specificity so that others can say, "We see where you are going!" More importantly, our vision should not only be clear, it should be contagious: "We see where you are going, and we want to come along!"

Note that we have great respect for ultimate or long-term visions, for BHAGs, as ideals to be cherished and sought after and as rallying cries for aligning or binding people together behind a common cause:

"A world safe for democracy"

"A cure for cancer"

"The creation of the perfect, pollution-free internal combustion engine"

These are wonderful and inspiring images. They enflame the imagination and give us the strength to carry on in the face of adversity and temporary setbacks. They are possible but unbounded dreams that we hope to realize someday. As attractive and inspirational as these might be, however, we suspect that they are difficult to manage against. They don't tell us what to do tomorrow, how to set priorities, how to synchronize and coordinate actions.

Our sense of vision, or strategic intent, is not unrelated to these ultimate visions but is, we believe, more pragmatic and operational. We believe that the way to make steady progress toward the achievement of these ultimate visions is to break the effort up into a series of manageable, psychologically meaningful chunks, each of which contains defined targets and measurable outputs, and each of which is informed by the experience of the previous chunk and informs the approach taken to the next chunk.[10]

In terms of the criteria of a good *vision statement* as defined above, a chunk would be that timeframe that is within "eyesight," that is psychologically meaningful to the strategic thinker. If three years out is the extent to which the strategic team can "see" its future in meaningful terms, then that would be the timeframe or chunk for which it would be seeking to define its vision or strategic intent.

Thus, while we remain committed to and motivated by our ultimate vision, our BHAG, our pragmatic question is, "How far along, how far down the road, is it our strategic intent to be in the next chunk of time—the next meaningful period?" This framing of the "vision thing" provides the necessary platform for implementing what we have described as the fundamental mantra of the strategist:

If we want to be .... by ...., then we better be .... by....

"A man on the moon by the end of this decade"

"A 50% reduction in toxic automobile engine emissions within 5 years"

"We will increase customer satisfaction by 10% in the next 12 months"

With such statements of intent, we can fold back from the envisioned future to determine the most likely pathway, the sequence and priority of actions, for getting there—for creating our Zen garden.

Exhibit V—Good Vision Statements

Are definite in terms of timeframe:	By July of 2010 — within two years from today — at the end of the next six months, we will be..., we will have achieved...., we will have the following in place...
Are stated in specific, measurable, observable terms:	Our clients will be of this size and mix...., our new products and programs will include...., our market share will be...., our reputation will be..., our Board will be composed of ... and will be doing...

A summary of the characteristics of "good" vision statements is given in exhibit V. We will conclude this chapter with a discussion of how to determine the right "chunks," the timeframe for our vision, in the next section.

DETERMINING THE STRATEGIC CYCLE—HOW FAR IS FAR? WHAT IS WITHIN EYESIGHT?

"Ok," you might say, "I am convinced. I need to look in my mind's eye some meaningful distance into the future to define my vision. But how do I know how far to look? What is far enough but not too far? How big of a chunk should I consider when determining where I want to be and what I want to look like at a specific point in time?"

We have suggested that a useful timeframe for our strategic vision is one that is within eyesight and that we can feel comfortable with, that our team can "get its arms around," so that we have a sound platform or foundation from which to drive the process. But what is that timeframe?

Conventional approaches often focused on preparing 5- and 10-year strategic plans and one-year operating plans. These choices of timeframe, however, seemed to come more from convenience or habit than from any logic that might suggest that these were the "right" chunks. As one engineer once put it, "Five and ten are nice round numbers. They make for easy analysis and computation and, at least in the p recomputer era, they satisfied the notion of 'slide rule accuracy'!" As a good a rationale as any other—but can we do better?

Using the concept of a "psychologically meaningful" distance into the future as the scope or extent of our vision, we believe that the timeframe for our strategic thought process should be one that makes sense to the strategist and that fits the rhythms of the field or industry in which our industry participates. This suggests that the strategist should consider time or timeframe as a variable and as one of the key choices in the strategic process rather than a constant defined by some "conventional wisdom."

We find it productive at the onset, therefore, to think of timeframe as one of the initial choices made by the strategic team. In general, we would propose that we should extend our vision as far into the future as we can while still feeling that we dealing with a manageable and meaningful "chunk." Thus, while modern technology gives the computational power to develop 25- and 50-year plans and forecasts, we might feel that there are far too many possible intervening events and variables for these to be anything more than academic exercises. Similarly, we might feel that a three- or six-month strategic horizon, while having a great potential to be highly rigorous and controllable, is simply far too short to be meaningful.

Thus, we need to consider what the appropriate timeframe and rhythm is for our particular field or industry, or for our unit or function within the larger organization. We think of this as identifying the effective *strategic cycle* for our endeavor. We may define the strategic cycle in terms of three main criteria:

1. **Intrinsic**: The fundamental nature or natural rhythm of the industry or field in which the organization participates may be defined in terms of the essential or central strategic decision or decisions that define the business. The intrinsic timeframe

or length of the strategic cycle is that period that would be required to make and implement the central strategic decision. As an example:

> In the c hildren's toy business, one could argue that the essential decision is the selection of the line t o be produced for the next holiday season. The overwhelming share of annual business is done at the retail level in the six weeks or so before the winter holidays. This means that toy manufacturers book the bulk of their orders in early summer after the spring trade shows for delivery in late fall. This means that the strategic cycle is defined in terms of the next holiday season and is roughly 12- to 18-months long. By the spring shows, the die for the coming holiday is essentially cast and it is time to start working on the following year. The intrinsic nature of this business, as defined by its core decisions, is quite short and 5- and 10-year strategic plans would be of minimal credibility.[11] A similar case could be made for the intrinsic length of the cycle in the fashion industry.

2. **Regulation**: The intrinsic nature of the strategic cycle for a given industry or field is extended by regulation. This may include any processes or requirements that extend the time of implementation of the core or fundamental strategic decision beyond the execution of the essential technological requirements. Examples would include the issuing of licenses and permits, the review of contracts and agreements, the filing of construction or other plans, inspections, and so on. As an example:

> Recall our example of the head of an electric power generating company. The core strategic decision, we would argue, is whether and when to expand permanent capacity—to build a new power plant.[12] From an engineering and technological point of view, it takes somewhere in the neighborhood of

10 to 15 years to construct the physical plant and have it ready to be brought on line. In practice, however, in the US, the time it actually takes until the plant is up and running, is more like 25 to 35 years. This is because we, for public policy and safety reasons, regulate electric power generation at four independent levels: municipality, county, state, and federal. Each of these has its own methods and criteria and each adds to the actual cycle. Thus, strategists in the electric power business are compelled to think in the 25- to 35-year chunks. This is difficult because this timeframe generally exceeds the strategist's time in office. It is hard to "own" a strategy that began before your time on the job and will not close until after you gone. It stretches the boundaries of "psychologically meaningful." This may explain why so much of the efforts in the electric power business, rate increase cases and sharing extra power on the grid, are of a tactical or operational nature.

3. **Competition**: If regulation has the effect of lengthening the strategic cycle, competition has the effect of shortening it. In effect, the more players there are in a given industry or market, the more likely it is that one of them will make a major strategic move—a technological advance, a new pricing approach, an operational breakthrough—within the normal boundaries of the cycle. Competition adds to the volatility of the industry and effectively makes the industry strategic cycle shorter than that experienced by any single player in the industry. As an example:

> Consider the pharmaceutical industry, specifically the prescription drug component: The fundamental or core strategic activity is the decision whether to invest in basic research aimed at discovering new compounds that will treat disease more effectively than the array of prescription drugs now available. A new drug for treating

cardiovascular disease that provides more positive results with fewer side effects than current products would immediately, once approved and marketed, be worth billions of dollars in revenues to its provider; the research investment decision is quite complex, however, given the realities of the industry. Consider the following attributes:

- On a purely scientific basis, the time from discovery of a new compound on the bench to its being deemed ready for human treatment is in the vicinity of six to seven years.
- Current regulatory procedures typically add anywhere from two to three years or more to this process.
- The degree of competition in the global pharmaceutical industry is such that many firms may be conducting research in the same therapeutic area with each having started at a different time. Thus, the likelihood of a breakthrough or an advance from one of the firms is relatively high, and in fact, such breakthroughs tend to occur every three to four years in the major therapeutic areas.[13]

This means that, if we are to launch a new research effort today, we should be targeting our efforts not at the current state of the therapeutic area but at where it will be 9 to 10 or more years out when, hopefully, our new drug is approved and launched and when the field has already made two or more leaps forward.

Given the high cost of drug development ($600M to $1.2B for a given compound) and the high risk that the effort will not succeed and will not be approved (roughly 1 in 1200 researched compounds are eventually approved), management of the strategic cycle becomes a major task for the pharmaceutical executive. This may help to explain the high rate of mergers and acquisitions we see in the industry—to shorten the scientific process and reduce competition.

Taken together, these three criteria will help the strategic team determine the most productive timeframe and rhythm within which to develop its vision. It can now answer the questions, "How far into the future can we 'see' in a meaningful way? How often should we be checking our actual progress against our initial expectations?"

IN SUMMARY

We have now completed the Conceptual Level of Strategy. We have defined our Mission, our Values, and our Vision. We know who we are, what we believe in, and where we want to be at a specific point in the future. We are ready to use that concept of the future—our Strategic Intent—to guide our strategic analysis and the implementation of our strategic plan. To do so, we turn for direction to the fourth major conceptual question, which we have not discussed in any detail:

What Do We Have to Do to Get There?

We have defined this as our operational definition of strategy. Thus, the question becomes, "What should our strategy be?" We could not answer this in any meaningful way until we determined where "there" was, until we defined our vision. Now, having done so, we find we still cannot respond to this question until we answer one further question:

Where Are We Now Relative To Where We Want to Be?

This is not a conceptual question. It is not a matter of aspiration or opinion. It is a matter of rigorous analysis of objective reality. To answer it, we turn in chapter 7 to the Analytical Level of Strategy.

BUSINESS STRATEGY IN ACTION

To serve as a focus for effective strategic planning, organizational visions need, as noted above, to be specific and comprehensive. Sweeping statements, such as "Our vision is to be recognized as the leader in our field," may work as slogans, but they are inadequate as guides to st rategy formulation and implementation. Good vision statements must touch explicitly on the k ey elements that comprise the organization and its place on the competitive game board.

Thinking back to the St. Emily's case from the last chapter, Kate Gorham realizes that it will not be enough to reaffirm the mission of the s chool and to assert its historical value to the community. The justification for continuing the s chool on mission grounds and the overall vision that you developed previously for St. Emily's are just the first steps. Kate must now craft a substantive vision that lays the basis for implementation for the school if it is to survive. For a school, the key vision elements would include:

- **Performance:** the targeted indicators of achievement against mission
- **Enrollment:** the desired number, mix, and distribution of students
- **Facilities:** the infrastructure needed to deliver the curriculum
- **Curriculum:** the actual program and related School activities
- **Staffing:** the h uman resources needed to deliver the Curriculum
- **Institutional Relations:** the array of other entities with which the School interacts
- **Management & Governance:** how the S chool will o rganize itself
- **Finances:** the economic model of the School; sources and uses of all funds[14]

How would you advise Kate and her colleagues to articulate a vision that will provide the foundation for securing the School's future in service to its mission?

TEST YOURSELF

Please review the St. Emily's case from the prior chapter, and consider the following questions:

1. Develop a comprehensive *three-year* vision for St. Emily's.
2. Identify three to four major strategic initiatives necessary to implement this vision.
3. Determine three to five critical actions to be undertaken in next three to six months.

KEY POINTS TO REMEMBER

- Our *values* are the core, foundational principles to which we turn to guide our behavior and assess and judge potential strategies that we might adopt in pursuit of our mission or purpose. They should be communal, consensual, and enduring and the touchstone against which we evaluate our actions.
- Our *vision* or *strategic intent* is an explicit description of where we seek to move our organization within a given time period. It essentially defines how much of our mission we intend to achieve or how far toward our ultimate objective we intend to progress in that time period.
- Visions are very specific, to the point, and focused. They state what/where we will be—in concrete, assessable terms—by a certain time. They define the outcomes to which we will be held accountable.
- Our *strategic cycle* defines the core rhythm of our enterprise and sets the boundaries for extending our vision. Our cycle is defined by the intrinsic nature of our core "business," the timeframe within which we can make and implement fundamental strategic decisions, and may be modified by external forces such as regulation and competition

# PART III

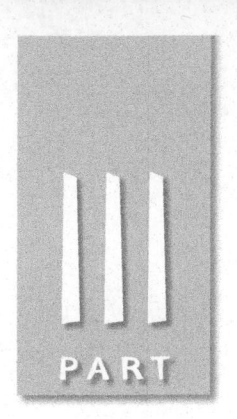

STRATEGY: ANALYTICAL AND OPERATIONAL CONSIDERATIONS

CHAPTER 7

Developing Strategic Perspectives: Macro-Market Analytical Frameworks

INTRODUCTION

> You, who are so blessed with shade as well in light, you, who are gifted with two eyes, endowed with a knowledge of perspective, and charmed with the enjoyment of various colours, you, who can actually see an angle, and contemplate the circumference of a Circle in the happy regions of the Three Dimensions—how shall I make clear to you the extreme difficulty which we in Flatland experience in recognizing one's configuration?[1]

In the last few chapters, we discussed the first of the three key elements of any strategy or strategic analysis: the conceptual foundations of leadership, mission, vision, and values. We also noted that these elements are important to assess both statically (today) and dynamically (over time).

A common error that many business planners and strategists make once they get the "big idea" and vision is that they immediately turn to *implementation* of the idea/vision. It's a good idea, so why not move forward with it? Many strategies and business ideas have died on the vine with their leaders trying to move from vision to implementation (or operations) without first considering what the idea will actually mean in terms of business performance, customer impact, market shift, and competitive positioning. The idea or "what" may be a good one, but it's hard to resist moving directly to the "how" of operations.

But the "why" must be assessed—and carefully measured, forecast, and planned—before a strategic vision can be successfully put into operation. In this chapter, we discuss tools and techniques that comprise the *analytical* component of strategic planning. This oft-forgotten piece is critical to any strategy. Without it, ideas are all too often implemented with no ability to discern what "good" will look like in the market—a market full of competitors, customers, prospects, suppliers, new entrants, and substitutes for everything your business does. As the inhabitants of *Flatland* remind us—having perspective, and being able to see the world from different angles and viewpoints is critical.

WHAT'S AHEAD

In this chapter, you'll learn:

- Why analytical tools aren't only important but are absolutely critical ingredients to a successful strategy/strategic plan
- How to scan a broad business environment and set the context in which to plan (and in which to not plan)
- Key elements of Michael Porter's *Five Forces* model and how they can help you understand a market and its various players and stakeholders
- How to look at—and predict—competitor actions and responses to your strategies

IN THE REAL WORLD

Leaders and strategists are full of great ideas: let's buy that company, sell a piece of our business to this firm, launch this new product, change this existing product, run this advertisement to beat the competition (or to keep from being beaten by them). We read about many of these ideas and transactions in the business pages of our morning papers. We hear how a CEO will buy another company in order to reduce costs, increase profits, create more value for its customers, and build a better working environment for its workers. But have these impacts been measured or forecast, or are they just aAerthoughts (literally) that need to happen now that a merger or new product has been announced?

Middle managers, and many new MBAs, are oAen put in charge of "making it happen" when it comes to some of these strategies. Get the product to market, get the customers back (or just get more customers), get the new firm and its operations and employees integrated into our world. These are the common marching orders that come with the announcement of a new "strategy" or "strategic direction" from management. But instead of jumping right into what we've been trained to do—to "do it"—it oAen makes sense to step back and see what the real value will be of such corporate or strategic decisions. Will this new product actually sell? To whom? And what happens if it doesn't sell? What are our growth targets? Sure, we can make a million of these new products, but what if only a thousand sell? What do we do, then, with our excess capacity? And what about all the people we've hired/acquired to help with this new business idea? What about them?

Sadly, the real world is littered with product and business ideas that sounded great at the time—and perhaps could have been great had a little more analysis and "running of the numbers" taken place. AOL and Time Warner merge, but shareholders have yet to see the gains from that transaction. A drug company in-licenses a promising compound from a biotech firm, and pays dearly for it, but the compound either fails to get past clinical trials or ends up requiring heavy "black box" warnings required by the FDA due to side effects. The Segue, the next step in human transportation, as it was billed, was supposed to be a huge hit ... but then communities outlawed them, and the device went nowhere.

Is this to say that if more analyses of the market, competitive reactions, and so on, had been performed, all would have gone well? Of course not. But if such analyses are not performed, the probability of a business strategy being successful is reduced, and the likelihood of potentially serious financial and operational consequences is increased. Ideas are a good start, and operations are critical to success. But without a clear, quantitative understanding of key market players, forces at work in the market, and potential (financial) risks and rewards to be derived from the new strategy, managers and executives alike jeopardize long-term business success.

THE KEY CONCEPTS

The Big Picture: Scanning the Environment and Setting the Context

When looking at a business, or a product, service, or organization in a marketplace, what do you see? Lots of players and constituents! Competitors, customers, suppliers, and even the press, special-interest groups, and (local) regulators all have some vested interest in the market, product, or service you are evaluating. Some of these players, such as your suppliers and customers, are on your side but others are looking to crush you. Incumbent competitors, new entrants into the market, and dissatisfied customers can all try to slowdown your business and your strategic success.

So how do we look at all of these constituents and make some sense of the landscape in the context of what we're trying to do, strategically? We can make sense of all this, but we need to look at a market and the capabilities our constituents have in terms of the "outside" ones, those that are not part of our firm, and those skills and capabilities that lie "inside" our firm. To do this, we will start with The Big Picture—everything going on—and start to focus in on our business, and our strategy, one step at a time.

We will begin with a broad view of the market and of its key (outside) participants using Porter's Five Forces framework. In short, we want to answer the question:

V. **"Where are we now[relative to where we want to be]?"**[2]:

Where are we now?

a. context	b. capabilities	c. challenges
What's going on out there – outside the walls of our unit – that really matters?	What do we bring to the party?	What are the major gaps between where we are and where we want to be?
• macro? • industry?	• resources? • performance?	• fit? • timing? • capabilities?

Macro-Market Analysis: The Porter "Five Forces" Framework

Michael Porter, a Harvard Business School professor, developed a framework in the late 1970s that still has wide applicability to strategic development, today. His "Five Forces" framework[3] helps us look at a snapshot of a market in terms of how we are positioned relative to the following five market forces/participants:

1. *Competitors*, or firms who directly compete with us
2. *Buyers*, or the people/firms who purchase from us and from our competitors

3. *Suppliers*, or firms who supply our market with products, services, and other "raw materials"

4. *Substitutes*, or other established firms/offerings that compete with us somewhat indirectly. They may not offer exactly what we do, but customers may perceive their offerings as a substitute for ours (and vice-versa)

5. *New Entrants,* or new, emerging firms/products that may disrupt our current market structure—and our competitive positioning—by offering something new/different/better than we do

The chart below shows the interactions of these five forces in a competitive market:

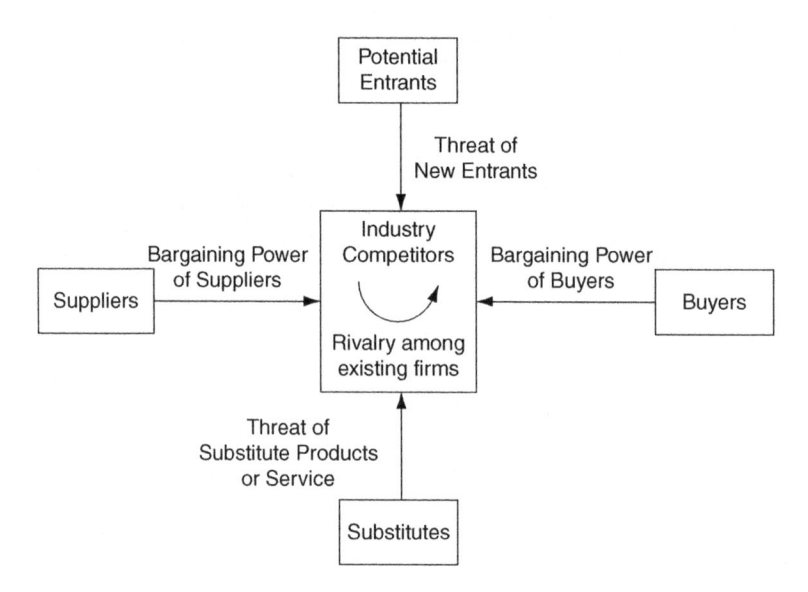

```
                    ┌──────────┐
                    │ Potential│
                    │ Entrants │
                    └─────┬────┘
                       Threat of
                     New Entrants
                          │
                          ▼
                    ┌──────────┐
  Bargaining Power  │ Industry │  Bargaining Power
   of Suppliers     │Competitors│   of Buyers
┌──────────┐───────▶│    ↻     │◀───────┌────────┐
│Suppliers │       │          │        │ Buyers │
└──────────┘        │Rivalry among│     └────────┘
                    │existing firms│
                    └──────▲───────┘
                           │
                       Threat of
                   Substitute Products
                        or Service
                    ┌──────────┐
                    │Substitutes│
                    └──────────┘
```

For example, assume your firm sells consumer electronics like camcorders, televisions, and cellular phones. A firm like Best Buy, for example, competes with many other firms in this market. National chains like Circuit City directly compete with Best Buy™ as do local establishments like Tom's TV and Radio. Other retailers, like Wal-Mart and Target, also compete in the consumer electronics space.

In terms of suppliers, firms like Sony, Sanyo, Motorola, Sharp, LG, and others supply Best Buy (and other retailers) with products to sell. Note that some suppliers may also be competitors. Sony, for example, also sells its products in "SonyStyle" stores and online. Buyers of these products include consumers like you and me, companies (like schools and small businesses that buy laptops at Best Buy), governments, and other institutions.

Substitutes for Best Buy (and other consumer electronics retailers) would include products, services, and/or firms that offer similar results but in different ways. For example, both Best Buy and Circuit City offer installation and set-up services for high-definition televisions and home theater products. However, instead of paying for them to install your products, you could do it yourself, call a friend with installation know-how, and/or contract with a specialized service that only does installations.

Finally, new entrants could come into this market and try to be disruptive. For example, Dell and Amazon.com offer the ability to buy online (with home delivery) many products seen in a Best Buy store. Dell used to sell only computers, but they now sell flat-screen televisions. Amazon.com used to only sell books but now sells (and partners with other sellers) to offer a variety of consumer electronics offerings.

Measuring Relative Strengths of the Five Forces

What is critical to a Five Forces analysis of a marketplace is how these different constituents *interact* and what levels of *power and influence* they have on the market. We will now talk about each force in turn and discuss when each force can be powerful or weak relative to others in the market.

First, let's look at *suppliers*. Suppliers are generally powerful in a market when:

- Market is dominated by a few large suppliers with few substitutes (a so-called oligopoly); e.g., airlines, multicategory producers with patents (Sony)

- Customers are fragmented with little bargaining power; e.g., retail and direct-to-consumer channels
- Switching costs are high (from one supplier to another); e.g., moving from an Intel-based PC to a Mac computer
- "Forward integration" of suppliers: This occurs when a supplier gets more involved in upstream activities in its supply chain. This effect increases the buyer's economy of scale and makes it harder for other buyers to have control over the supply of goods and services. For example, Dell used to just buy computer parts, assemble them, and sell them to consumers. Now, Dell buys—and locks up the supply of—some key raw materials like the flat panels used to make televisions and computer displays

Thus, when supplier power is high, buyers face high pressures on margins and reduced strategic options to combat supplier pressures. Think of airline tickets. With so few suppliers providing flights to/from certain markets, airfares can climb—especially on exclusive routes—and there's not much we as consumers can do about it except pay more for the ticket or connect through another city and increase our travel time.

In terms of *buyers* (or customers), power is high for them when:

- Customers buy in large volumes (and there are buyer concentrations); e.g., bulk purchasing agreements, Costco customers
- Suppliers have large numbers of small operators/stores with high fixed-costs; e.g., retail gas stations
- Products are undifferentiated and can easily be replaced by substitutes; i.e., products are "commoditized" like paperclips, toilet paper, etc.
- Customers have low margins and are price-sensitive; e.g., price-focused shoppers who economize on every dollar they spend

Thus, buyers, whether they be consumers or businesses, are more powerful in a market when they buy commodity-type items in bulk, purchase from a very fragmented supplier base, and focus on getting the best price.

New entrants to a market, whether they be copycats with better prices or new innovators in the market, can also exert power and influence over other market players. New entrants are strong when:

- Barriers to entry are relatively low—low required initial investments, relatively low fixed costs, and easy-to-achieve scale requirements. This is why just about anyone can start a new coffee shop, but very few can start a new airline!
- Current market competitors' experiences aren't fully utilized: If current market players haven't fully utilized their knowledge and insights, a new entrant can come in and be disruptive. The Apple iPod is a good example of this. Portable music devices had been around—like Sony's Walkman—but Sony (and others) hadn't fully developed the idea of stored and portable digital music yet.
- Customers show little/no brand loyalty. If customers (or buyers) aren't particularly brand loyal—e.g., they don't care what kind of bottled water they buy—then a new entrant can possibly steal them from you
- Intellectual property protection is nonexistent. If your product/service isn't protected by patent, new entrants can sometimes easily come in and copy your idea, sell it at a lower cost, and steal your customers
- Qualified expert staff exists in abundance—retail is a good example. There are lots and lots of qualified salespeople, so if you open a new store and offer competitive wages and/or benefits, it may be easy for you to attract talent away from your competitors
- Access to raw materials and distribution channels is open. If the key materials/ingredients you need are easy to obtain, then

anyone else can obtain them! Thus, if someone wishes to copy your business (or strategy), getting supplies from suppliers will be relatively simple

- Switching costs are low. If it doesn't cost much for a buyer to switch from your product/service to another one—think TV stations—then new entrants can steal your customers if they offer something compelling over yours

- Government intervention is rare. If few government regulations/policies apply to your business, then new entrants may have little difficulty competing with you in a market

Thus, new entrants (or *disruptors*) can, if barriers to entry are low, cause damage to your business success. Of course, not every new entrant will be successful, but those with novel approaches to the same business you are in may succeed in taking customers, profits, and strategic success from you.

Next, we examine *substitutes*. Substitute products/services allow buyers to move away from your firm (or your industry) based on a number of strengths these substitutes may have. Note that substitutes' strengths are very similar to those of new entrants. If buyers have low brand loyalty, current competitors offer little in the way of customer service, buyers perceive low switching costs to move to a substitute, and getting the best/lowest price is paramount, then a substitute may prevail in your market. Discount airlines and rail operations are good examples. You can fly from London to another European city on a well-known, "branded" carrier like British Airways. However, if you don't care about frequent flyer points or in-flight snacks, and you are price-conscious, then you can probably get to the same place flying on a much cheaper ticket via RyanAir or easyJet. Alternatively, if you want to save even more money and don't care how long it takes to travel, you may opt for taking a train from London to Paris, for example.

Finally, we look at the intensity of the fifth force, our direct competition. *Competitive rivalry* among firms will be at its most intense when:

- Many competitors of roughly the same size
- Similar strategies in the market; i.e., no differentiation
- Low market growth rates (growth only comes at the expense of a competitor; "zero-sum game" effect); e.g., life insurance sales. Growth in this industry is not that high, and growth is driven largely by brand value, word-of-mouth referrals, broker recommendations, and so on.
- Barriers for exit are high (e.g., expensive, specialized space, equipment, staff). Hospitals in big cities—and their emergency rooms, in particular—are a good example. They're in special spaces with skilled, expensive staff, and since they serve a geographic area, it will be hard for one to "go under."
- Competitive forces affect *all* players, not just us.

Thus, it's important to note that these competitive forces and pressures affect *all market players,* not just us and our firm. Understanding how these forces are interrelated, and often unbalanced, is critical to understanding the power structure of the various players and constituents in a given market. Also note that by no means is a single firm only part of one force. For example, Sony supplies electronic components to other competitors (based on patents), sells directly to consumers, and competes with other manufacturers. Thus, Sony can play multiple roles in a market (as can many firms/concerns).

Limitations of the Five Forces Model

The Porter model is not without its limitations, and several other tools have been developed to make up for some of the Five Forces' shortcomings. At the most basic level, the Five Forces framework is only a snapshot at a point in time. Thus, this model only shows us what a market or competitive space looks like at once. The model doesn't allow for a dynamic, "moving map" view of competitive interactions, responses, mergers, and so on over time.

In addition, (at least) two other key forces are not explicitly labeled. In many situations, the buyer may not be the end *customer* or *consumer* of the product or service. Healthcare is a good example. If your company pays for part of your healthcare, then you aren't necessarily the (entire) buyer of your healthcare services, yet you consume them. When a mother buys her child a toy, Mom is clearly the buyer, but the child is the ultimate consumer. And competitors know this! Competitors will advertise on children's television shows in one way but differently on adult programming—such as ads seen in prime time during the Christmas holidays. Thus, buyers and consumers aren't always the same.

The other force often not explicitly labeled is that of the *government* as a proxy for the effect of regulation and/or legislation. Think of how the government controls certain imports, exports, and prices for certain things. Think of how the government may control healthcare reimbursements (e.g., Medicare in the United States). Thus, the additional two forces of *consumers* and the *government* are important to articulate in industries where they are critical players.

Nonetheless, Porter's Five Forces framework is useful for helping us understand all the players in a market, the dynamics among them, the bases of competition, and the sources and uses of power that each player has. But how does our firm (or our firm's strategy) look in comparison to all these other players? Where are we in this big map, and are we winning, losing, or just treading water? Can we look at ourselves, and at our strategy, in the context of all these other players? In the next chapter, we will focus on how to look at our internal capabilities and limitations and how to map them against other market forces to get a better sense of what we should do to remain competitive.

BUSINESS STRATEGY IN ACTION

Review the MinuteClinic case in the "Test Yourself" section. Note that a new entrant—MinuteClinic—is now part of CVS (the nationwide pharmacy chain) and is encroaching on the markets currently served by several family practice physicians. CVS customers can now go to a MinuteClinic for a certain number of "simple" ailments, like coughs, colds, muscle pain, and be treated by a nurse while in the store (including, at times, prescriptions for basic medicines like antibiotics and pain relievers). While this takes a load off of local family practice physicians, it also means a loss of income from office visits and some follow-up care.

Assuming you are a partner/physician in a local family practice, how do you compete? Should you change the ways in which you compete? What damage can MinuteClinic do, and how can you protect yourself or at least mitigate some of the risks posed by this new entrant? To answer these questions, let's look at the tools from this chapter and see how they might help us devise some strategies before we start reacting and trying to compete.

A Five Forces map will help us see who key players are: MinuteClinic, other pharmacies, insurance companies (who pay for some patients' office visits and care), family practices, and even local/state governments (who pay for Medicare claims and enforce medical care laws). But don't forget the basics from previous chapters. At Family Associates, what do we stand for? What are our values? What is our mission? Does MinuteClinic have the same ones we do? If not, how can we exploit our strengths while minimizing our weaknesses given this new entrant? The tools from previous chapters, and from this chapter, will help us understand our place in this competitive market. But how can we understand how we match up against these market (five) forces? If we look at our firm, what are our strengths and weaknesses? What opportunities can we exploit, but what threats will we need to be prepared for? (More on these in the next chapter.)

To answer these questions, we need to look at our firm and our internal capabilities at a micro-market level to assess our relative position and what we can do to better position ourselves in this marketplace. For that, we will move on to micro-market analyses in the next chapter.

TEST YOURSELF

Read and analyze the case, MinuteClinic, Inc., below. Be prepared to respond to and discuss the following questions:

1. Perform a Five Forces analysis of this market. Who are the customers (vs. buyers)? Does regulation play any role? Are some players in multiple "force" areas?

2. Who has a vested interest in seeing MinuteClinic succeed (beyond MinuteClinic and CVS)? Why? Who would like to see MinuteClinic fail? Why?

MINUTECLINIC, INC.[4]

Welcome to McMedicine. Can I take your order?

"Good morning, Dr. Jones."

"Hello, Mrs. Adams. It's great to see you and Hannah. Look at how big she's getting!"

"We're here for her annual physical."

"It's been a while since I've seen you here. She must have been lucky not to get sick this past year?"

"Well, actually, she had strep throat and then a cough for a while. I just took her to the new MinuteClinic that opened at the CVS in town. It's so convenient—I was there to pick up some things we needed, anyway. And we could get her prescription right there."

"Yes, I've been hearing about MinuteClinic from some of my other patients, too…."

FAMILY ASSOCIATES, INC. LLP

Dr. Henry Jones is the senior partner and founder of Family Associates, Inc., a group practice located in suburban Westchester County. The practice consists of three primary care physicians and a nurse practitioner and maintains an attractive office facility in a residential neighborhood.

The office has five exam rooms, a support staff of eight office assistants and billing staff and maintains regular office hours on weekdays, including two designated "late evenings" each week and Saturday morning hours for emergency visits. Except for Saturdays, the physicians' schedules have always been full, and appointments normally have to be made in advance. In the past, same-day or even next-day appointments have been difficult to obtain, especially for the more popular doctors. On other days, despite the best efforts of the staff, the appointment schedule falls significantly behind schedule and the waiting room is often crowded. The group uses an answering service to take off-hours patient calls and to alert a doctor on-call when the call requires immediate response. The physicians work an average of 50 hours each week.

The group has always prided itself on being available to patients. The group accepts most major insurances in order to maximize the number of patients seen. The practice is committed to the health and well-being of its patients and yet must often make trade-offs between long, attentive appointments for fewer patients and short, efficient appointments for more patients, since overall revenue is dependent on the number of patients seen. The physicians and the staff pay close attention to patient satisfaction and quality of care to encourage long-term relationships and prevent complaints and possible malpractice allegations.

The environment for the practice has been challenging. In recent years, reimbursement rates from insurance plans have not kept pace with the costs of doing business. High fixed-cost expenses for the group include medical malpractice insurance, salaries for the physicians and nurse practitioner, and facility expenses. The cost of vaccine serums is a significant variable expense.

A patient management and billing system maintains the patient demographics, appointment history, and billing history. Patient information and medical history are maintained through paper medical records and charts. The paper-charting system does have some disadvantages. These include manually intensive processes, occasionally chart misfilings, and an inability to take advantage of the speed and convenience of electronic exchange of data with pharmacies and affiliated hospitals. The cost of implementing an electronic medical record system, however, would involve significant financial investment and organizational change.

MINUTECLINIC—THE BIG IDEA

MinuteClinic, then known as QuickMedx, was established in 2000 as a walk-in medical clinic in a Cub Foods grocery store in Minneapolis. In the seven years since its inception, it has served over 700,000 patient visits and introduced a sea change in how medical care is provided and paid for. MinuteClinics are walk-in health centers focusing on diagnosis and treatment of common medical conditions, such as strep throat, mono, flu, female bladder infections, ear infections, sinus infections, and pregnancy testing. Since 2005, MinuteClinic healthcare centers have opened in Wal-Mart, Target, and CVS drug stores in 28 metropolitan centers including Nashville, Indianapolis, Raleigh-Durham, and the Maryland suburbs of Washington, D.C. New centers are now opening in New Jersey, Long Island, Staten Island, and Westchester County. Reuters reported that CVS plans to open 300 new MinuteClinic kiosks in CVS stores in 2007.

In the winter of 1999, Rick Krieger, a strapped-for-time father in Minneapolis, took his son to the city urgent care clinic for a strep throat test and then waited two hours for the simple, five-minute test. Realizing that there had to be a better way to provide simple, yet urgent medical procedures, Krieger developed a new business concept for the healthcare delivery market. Together with two partners, Douglas Smith, MD, and Steve Pontius, Krieger worked on his business plans for the next year and founded QuickMedx healthcare centers in 2000. The centers had four unique and defining characteristics:

1. They were designed to provide walk-in care for very specific and common conditions including: strep throat, mono, flu, female bladder infections, ear infections, sinus infections, and pregnancy testing.

2. They accepted walk-in visits, usually lasting between 10 and 15 minutes in duration.

3. They were planned to provide care under the same roof as another convenient, easily accessible, commonly frequented retail outlet, such as the local Cub Foods Grocery Store.

4. They were designed to serve both the insured and uninsured individuals alike by posting their rates for services and accepting payment only in cash. All services cost a flat $35.

The model offered slim profit margins, though, and there were not enough patient visits to produce the returns the founders had originally projected.

THE EARLY GROWTH

By 2002, MinuteClinic faced a number of problems, the least of which was difficultly raising capital to support its growing operations. As of July 2002, the company had raised about $750,000 in its first round of private venture capital, with the rest of the company's funding coming from internal sources. One difficulty in raising funds early on was that the concept fell in between industry niches where venture capitalists focus. Krieger characterized the nature of the problem, —"Health-care service with a retail flavor is not something that the medical venture capitalists appear to be comfortable with. On the other hand, the retail VCs are not comfortable with the medical attributes."

Ultimately, all three of the original founders left the company during the year, and a new management team took over. A new CEO, Linda Hall Whitman, was brought in to reevaluate the company business plan and scale up the company. With her at the helm, the company changed its model to target insurers and large employers that paid their employees' healthcare costs directly. Under this model, if insured patients preferred not to pay out of pocket, they could use their insurance card and pay a co-payment for services received. For patients who paid out of pocket, the clinics also began accepting checks and credit card payments. The convenience of these centers caught on quickly and their inclusion in a handful of health plan networks by December 2002 continued to fuel their accessibility. Also in 2002, new kiosks were opened in the Baltimore metropolitan area within Target stores. By this time, attendance at clinics had increased 210% from the prior year. And, the infant company took on its new brand identity: MinuteClinic.

MINUTECLINIC GETS LEGS

Late in 2002, the company announced an aggressive growth plan to boost its revenue from $2 million to $100 million in five years, which included plans to expand into two new metropolitan marketplaces in 2003 and four in 2004. At least 10 new walk-in centers or "kiosks" were planned in each marketplace at outlets such as Target Retail Stores and CVS Pharmacies. Along with the growth in the number of outlets came expansion in the types of conditions and age-groups that MinuteClinic was willing and able to treat. The number of afflictions treated by MinuteClinic grew from

11 to over 20, including new additions such as bronchitis, allergies, minor burns, and ringworm. In June of 2004, it also announced that it would begin to provide vaccinations for children and adults, including TDap, Hepatitis A, Hepatitis B, and Meningitis. The new treatment offerings required changes to the original "one size fits all" pricing and the fees for the new services ranged from $25 to upwards of $100.

Other catalysts to the growth of MinuteClinic included large employers such as General Mills and Best Buy, who began to encourage their employees to use MinuteClinics. St. Jude Medical, a St. Paul-based maker of cardiovascular medical devices, reduced employees' co-payments to $10 from $15 or $20 if they used MinuteClinic. The company implemented the lower co-pay in January 2004 for its 1,700 Twin Cities employees and estimated a savings of $20,000 in annual healthcare costs. As a result of these growth drivers, by the close of 2004 the company was treating more than 70,000 patients annually.

The year 2005 produced further significant advancements for MinuteClinic, starting with the announcement of a new CEO, Michael Howe, a native of Minnesota, who had previously served as chief executive of fast-food giant Arby's. Also, in June, MinuteClinic reached an agreement with CVS Corporation to open kiosks in Annapolis, MD, and Minneapolis, MN. In September, MinuteClinic added depth to their Board of Directors by naming two new members, Beth Kaplan of Axcel Partners and Chris Bodine of CVS, who had the expertise needed to propel the fledging company. Ms. Kaplan was the head and co-founder of Axcel Partners, a Baltimore-based venture capital firm. The firm focused specifically on early stage companies, including those in consumer goods and retail. Chris Bodine was the executive vice president of merchandising and marketing at CVS. His responsibilities at CVS included front store and pharmacy merchandising, store replenishment and inventory merchandising, promotional planning, pricing, and marketing.

THE MINUTECLINIC MODEL

The MinuteClinic operating model redefines the 20th century walk-in clinic. The MinuteClinic kiosk staff comprises board-certified nurse practitioners and physician assistants, supported by a Medical Director. Nurse Practitioners have a college degree along with two additional years of graduate-level training in family practice medicine and are licensed to prescribe medicines.

A doctor is on call during all hours of operation. Each new MinuteClinic kiosk requires about $50,000-$60,000 in start-up costs, which cover all the diagnostic equipment. It requires a spatial footprint of only about 75 square feet.

A software program guides diagnosis, treatment, and billing, with up-to-date computerized medical guidelines for diagnoses, best practices for treatment of common ailments, a drug interaction database, and protocols that ensure consistent service. MinuteClinic invested over $1M in the development of this proprietary software, which follows clinical practice guidelines from the American Academies of Family Physicians and Pediatrics. At the end of the visit, the system generates educational material, an invoice, and a prescription, if needed, as well as a diagnostic record that is sent to the patient's primary care provider within 24 hours.

MinuteClinic practitioners maintain a cooperative relationship with hospitals and physicians in its geographic marketplaces by referring patients with illnesses outside the scope of their medical care. Additionally, they will connect patients without primary physicians to one in the area. Dr. Glen Nelson, chairman of MinuteClinic described his staff and services as follows:

> MinuteClinic staff are certified health care professionals who follow strict clinical protocols in triaging, diagnosing and treating simple health conditions. Each MinuteClinic also has a physician available on call at all times of operation. MinuteClinic provides prompt, quality care for a limited set of acute conditions. We consider our services to be a complementary adjunct to the traditional health care system.

VOICES OF DISSENT—AND OTHERS

Throughout this time of growth in patient visits and maturation of the operating model, MinuteClinic has been a target for criticism and skepticism about the quality of the healthcare it provides. Several physician groups voiced concerns including:

- The American Academy of Pediatrics said it "opposes" the clinics because they lead to "fragmentation of care." In particular, the group said children should have a "medical home," a doctor who sees them on a consistent basis.
- A handout titled "Your Primary Care Physician vs. Retail Health Clinics," prepared by the Ohio Chapter of the American Academy of Pediatrics, discouraged patients from making their healthcare choices before consulting their a physician.
- The president of the American Medical Association, as quoted in *The Wall Street Journal*, said, "Serious illness sometimes present with simple symptoms. A cough might be something as simple as a cold, or something as serious as congestive heart failure."
- In a three-minute segment on "Today," with the onscreen subtitle: "Walk-in Health Care: Are Quick Clinics Worth It?", the reporter commented, "Critics are concerned that MinuteClinics are staffed by nurse practitioners who are licensed to treat patients and prescribe medications but have far less training than doctors."

In addition, in late 2005, the company opted to scrap plans to open five kiosks in Rhode Island due to regulatory red tape. The clinic had applied for a license as an organized ambulatory care facility, a category that requires a sink and restroom on site. State health regulators had voiced strong concerns about MinuteClinic's facilities because they did not include such provisions.

New voices also began to add to the chorus in growing numbers—those of satisfied patients. Comments and information about MinuteClinics began popping up on consumer and social networking websites. The following blog was posted on Minneapolis Metblogs in August 2005:

> Today I learned that Minute Clinic is a wonderful thing.
>
> As yesterday afternoon I was hit with one of the common ailments treated at Minute Clinic, I determined that instead of a visit to urgent care, I'd go to Cub Foods. At 9:05, right after opening, I was the first patient. Diagnosis and treatment took about 15 minutes; getting my prescription filled took longer.
>
> Added bonus: treatment is cheap—even cheaper with insurance, as they charge the office visit co-pay, not the urgent care/emergency co-pay.
>
> Plus, you get to watch your tests being performed! Hooray!
>
> P.S. I'm much better, thank you.

MINUTECLINICS FIND A PERMANENT HOME

A press release issued in July of 2006 marked yet another phase of the MinuteClinic evolution. It announced the acquisition of MinuteClinic by CVS Pharmacies, a deal that had been incubating as MinuteClinic grew its CVS-based kiosks to 66 out of 88 total centers in 10 states. By third quarter 2006, the announcements came fast and furious from the now firmly financed organization. In October 16, 2006, MinuteClinic received accreditation for its retail sites from the Joint Commission on Accreditation of Healthcare Organizations (JCAHO). Almost immediately afterward, on October 30, 2006, MinuteClinic issued a press release announcing they had reached and surpassed the 100-clinic milestone across 14 states and that their insurance network was nearing 37 providers across the country, including national plans such as Aetna, Cigna, and UnitedHealthcare.

As of January 2007, MinuteClinic has treated an estimated 700,000 patients since it opened its first kiosk, with half of the total visits having occurred in the past year. It is the first retail healthcare provider to have a national presence, with over 135 kiosk locations. Despite the voices of dissent, not a single medical malpractice suit has been filed.

OPPORTUNITIES OR THREATS?

Shortly after Mrs. Adams and Hannah, Henry Jones stopped to grab a quick cup of coffee with Dr. Bryce Jones, one of his partners.

"You seem preoccupied with something, Hank. What's on your mind?"

"Well, Bryce, it's the new MinuteClinic in town. I'm afraid we'll have to find new ways to keep our patients coming back for our care. I wonder what we can do to stay competitive?"

KEY POINTS TO REMEMBER

- Don't jump from conceptual (mission, vision, and values) to operations. SIZE IT.
- Constituents—who's in the market . . . and who really matters?
- Porter framework—good for snapshot; not good for evolving strategies
- Don't forget multiple roles of some/all players!
- Don't develop analytical components in a vacuum—and they're not a panacea. Be sure to look at analytics in context of mission, vision, and values as well as operations
- When it comes to the analytical component of strategy, avoid analysis paralysis—don't boil the ocean!

CHAPTER 8

Developing Strategic Perspectives: Micro-Market Analytical Frameworks

INTRODUCTION

Analytics themselves don't constitute a strategy, but using them to optimize a [value proposition] certainly constitutes a strategy. Whatever the capabilities emphasized in a strategy, analytics can propel them to a higher level.

Today, for example, some executives still consider it feasible to make major decisions about [corporate strategies] from their gut. However, the best firms are already using detailed analytics to explore such decisions.... In a few years, firms that do not employ extensive analytics in making ... major [strategic changes] will be considered irresponsible.[1]

At the bottom of the Oakland experiment was a willingness to rethink baseball: how it is managed, how it is played, who is best suited to play it, and why. Understanding he would never have a Yankee-sized checkbook, the Oakland A's general manager, Billy Beane, had set about looking for inefficiencies in the game. Looking for, in essence, new baseball knowledge. In what amounted to a systematic scientific investigation of their sport, the Oakland front office had reexamined everything from the market price of foot speed to the inherent difference between the average major league player and the superior Triple-A one[2]

Even a sport, and a huge business like baseball, can benefit from an analytical examination of key "market" factors that affect the business, as Michael Lewis examines in *Moneyball*. We've just talked about how to see the market in terms of its participants, or "teams" in a baseball league context. But now we need to go deeper, beyond our "gut," as Professor Davenport argues, and look more deeply at the team: at the individual players and their strengths and weaknesses in some measurable way.

We will now focus inside our firm/strategy, and we will assess our Strengths, Weaknesses, Opportunities, and Threats using a SWOT analysis framework. Several other frameworks may be useful, too, and we will discuss the highlights of some of them and show how knowing your world better, both outside your firm (or baseball team) and inside, will help you create more competitive advantage vis-à-vis your strategy.

> **WHAT'S AHEAD**
>
> In this chapter, you will learn:
> - How to assess your own firm or department in terms of its strengths, weaknesses, opportunities, and threats (SWOT)
> - Other strategic mapping tools that can help you see how you are similar—and different—from other players in the market
> - The concept of value propositions: what they are, how to frame them, and how to use them to create an advantage for your firm in the marketplace
> - How to start to apply other core MBA courses and skills—like marketing, finance, and organizational behavior—to the development and testing of your strategy/strategic plan

IN THE REAL WORLD

After conducting a Five Forces analysis, in order to get a clearer picture of other market participants and competitors in terms of their potential impacts on your customers, suppliers, new entrants, and substitutes, we now need to find a way to utilize this market intelligence to inform our strategic thinking. If a competitor is about to offer something to a key customer segment of ours, can we catch up? Do we have to catch up? We've known for years that our website technology isn't the best when compared to our peers, so how to we protect this weakness—or strengthen it, if we can afford to—from exploitation by competitors?

Thus, we need to now move from the macro-context—the market and its key constituents and forces—to a context focused on our firm and our strategy. What do we do well or not? What opportunities await us given our strengths and value propositions? What threats will possibly hurt our strategy resulting in customer loss, market share erosion, and so on, and how do we prevent this from happening? To help answer these questions, and to put our strategic thinking through a more detailed test for feasibility, we need to consider our firm's strengths, weaknesses, opportunities, and threats. We also need to see how the bases of competition line up in the market for us (and for our key competitors)? Will our strategy result in something that looks different in the market or more like one of our competitors? How do we really test if our value proposition is *differentiable* in the market?

Let us now begin an examination of our micro-market—of us and of our capabilities vis-à-vis our competition.

THE KEY CONCEPTS

Micro-Market Analysis: The SWOT Framework

To look at our own internal capabilities and then see how they look in the context of the outside market—where our buyers, competitors, suppliers, new entrants, and substitutes lurk—we can assess the following four bases of competition:

- *Strengths*: Our advantages over our competitors, possible new entrants, and substitutes in the context of our customers and suppliers
- *Weaknesses:* Our relative disadvantages—or challenges—relative to other market participants
- *Opportunities:* Areas that we may be able to exploit and to gain competitive advantage (over any other market force) by utilizing our strengths (against our competitors' weaknesses)
- *Threats:* Actions or activities that other market participants may perform to take advantage of our weaknesses (and to thus capitalize on their strengths)

Thus, putting all of these together, we get the *Strengths, Weaknesses, Opportunities, and Threats* or *SWOT* framework. This framework is more micro-focused than Porter's Five forces and allows us to view our (internal) capabilities in the context of the competitive space. A good way to pictorially draw a SWOT analysis is as a 2x2 matrix. On the next page, we show an example SWOT analysis for a large retailer that is considering a move into consumer electronics in order to compete with established competitors (like Best Buy, Circuit City, etc.):

Note a few highlights from this SWOT analysis. First, this retailer has considerable strengths in terms of its pricing philosophy (low prices), leverage with suppliers (since they buy so much), and ability to customize its offerings depending on the types of shoppers it has in a particular area. However, this retailer is weak in terms of providing customer service, a store "experience," supplier rebellion due to continuous price decrease requests, and some recent issues with management and corporate culture.

Strengths:	Weaknesses:
• Unifying principle around low prices that both employees and customers understand and expect from us • Adaptive store operations tailored to local communities and the infrastructure to support it • Size that leads to scale advantage and leverage over suppliers • Efficient operations and dedication to continous improvement • Supplier co-managed inventory and cost sharing • Speed to market of both new categories and business improvements • Breadth of assortment and cross-merchandising potential • Scale and flexibility to drive seasonal opportunities • Culture of humility, respect, focus, and discipline	• Store labor model is not product, sales, or service focused • Brand identity on price – "cheap" stuff • Creating and maintaining an in-store experience (even on a small scale, e.g. projecting HDTV) may threaten their low-cost business model • Vendors are cautious of this firm because of its track record for "beating up" vendors via its demands • Cultural "virtues" in the U.S. market can act as barriers abroad • Saturation of rural markets and risksh of going "urban" may require higher costs, competitive risks and non-market pressures • Rights among leadership, break with founding values • Size ensures that it is always in the media spotlight
Opportunities:	Threats:
• Expand eletronics assortment by a relatively small amount—overlapping with others— to create impression of "same selection and services" with lower prices • Use global sourcing capabilities to create newproducts, and/or lock up supply of overlapping/substitute brands/products • Overlap with specialty retail demographics in key urban locations to create price and "one-stop-shopping" pressures • Provide an effcient, high-volume channel to large vendors of higher end products as underlying economics reinforce attractiveness of scale • Influence industry standards to benefit itself. (e.g. device connectivity) • Leverage online channel more effectively to integrate with stores	• Community opposition to store openings • Legislative changes impacting costs: political opposition • International cultures that may reject our model (e.g. European pricing regulations) • Competition from several angles: on price (Aldi, Costco, Family Ddlar) or differentiation (Fair Care in pharmacy) • Partners difficulties: vendor resistance, or lack of viability • Consumer evolution: access to customers, real-estate limitations; changing buying patterns (e.g., web ordering and home delivery) that lead to disruptive business models • Alienation of most profitable segments: served by competitor's service-oriented labour and store experience. • Fear among communities, media, and regulators about its size and influence

However, this retailer could easily mimic existing competitors in terms of offering similar high-end consumer electronics in order to advertise the "same selection" but with lower prices. This opportunity, as well as the chance to influence standards, give high-end/luxury goods makers the c hance to distribute large volumes through them, and "vertically integrate" by buying upstream products/suppliers and possibly even by creating its own brands/goods, make this r etailer a signifi cant force in the ma rketplace. However, threats to the succes s of this co n-sumer electronics strategy include community disapproval of large stores in their to wns, possible regulatory intervention given this retailer's size and mark et influence, and some emerging new entrants that are advertising low prices but creating more meaningful experiences in their stores and providing value-added services like installation in order to compete.

Thus, a SWOT analysis can be very helpful in terms of mapping a firm's key strengths and weaknesses against the broader market forces that provide opportunities and threats to your success. In fact, if we look at a SWOT matrix in a slightly different way, we can use it to help drive our strategic choices and options:

	Strengths	Weaknesses
Opportunities	S-O strategies	W-O strategies
Threats	S-T strategies	W-T strategies

Here, if we look at the intersections of each of the four pieces of the SWOT matrix, we can develop specific options/alternatives given our capabilities in the current marketplace:

1. *Strengths/Opportunities Strategies (S-O):* Here, the firm's strengths and opportunities are well-aligned. These options should be pursued as they fit well with the firm's strengths in the market, and the firm may have *first-mover advantage* if they can capitalize quickly.

2. *Weaknesses/Opportunities (W-O):* Here, a firm should try to overcome its weaknesses in order to seize the opportunities, if practicable. All too often, firms will attempt almost anything to overcome a weakness in order to take advantage of an opportunity. However, if this requires too much of an investment—in time, money, human capital, etc.—it may not be worth it, and the firm, once able, may not be able to realize a long-gone opportunity.

3. *Strengths/Weaknesses (S-W):* In this quadrant, a firm should try to use its available strengths, again only after assessing the magnitude and potential liability of the weakness, to steel itself

against these challenges/deficiencies. Again, sight is often lost here, when a firm focuses on defending itself too much with its strengths and not utilizing those strengths to garner more opportunities in the marketplace.

4. *Weaknesses/Threats (W-T)*: This requires a defensive positioning from the firm. In this case, the firm should try as best it can to prevent its weaknesses from making it highly susceptible to market threats. Sadly, this quadrant is often written off as "the things we just can't fix," and firms that do this often suffer from sudden market changes and/or ongoing defensive public relations, advertising, and so on. This not only won't help, it will take attention away from strengths and opportunities that would have otherwise been realized.

Thus, a SWOT matrix allows us to see how our capabilities—good and bad—can possibly withstand the market opportunities and threats currently in play. But remember, a SWOT, or a Five Forces model, doesn't provide any concrete *strategies* or *solutions*. These are only tools that can help us analyze a market. Recall that we must also consider the mission, vision, and values (conceptual tools) when developing our strategy as well as operational considerations (the topic of the next chapter). A 2x2 matrix or Five Forces chart does not, in and of itself, constitute a strategy or strategic plan!

Other Strategy Frameworks and "Maps"

The business literature is filled with other great (and terrible) frameworks and tools that can be used to help "map" a firm's competitive position relative to a set of market participants. For example, in a marketing context, *perceptual maps* are good tools for seeing how your firm/strategy may compare to others in the same competitive space. Perceptual maps usually have two axes—representing ranges of effect of different (marketing) elements in terms of how these are perceived by customers/buyers. For example, think of the way your MBA colleagues, dare we say "competitors," fall in a couple of important dimensions when it comes to marketing themselves for jobs:

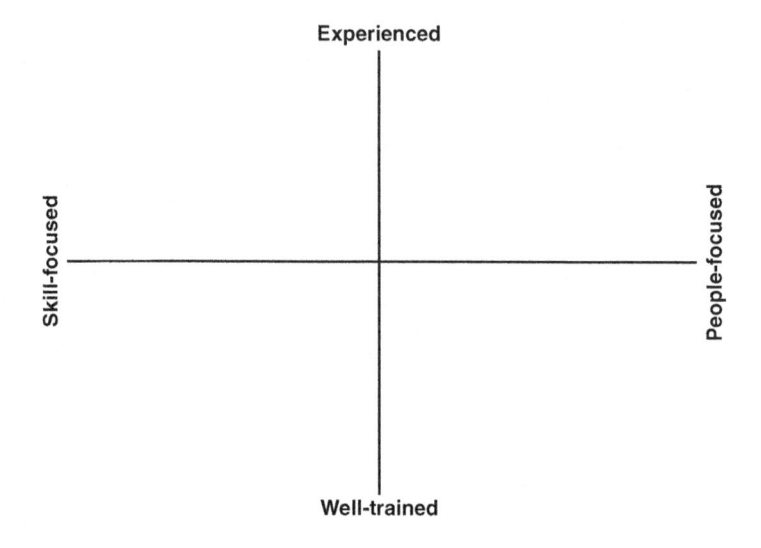

```
                        Experienced
                            |
                            |
                            |
  Skill-focused  _____|_____  People-focused
                            |
                            |
                            |
                        Well-trained
```

Thus, if we believe a firm will interview/hire us based on our relative formal training vs. past experience, we and our colleagues will either have a great deal of experience (with perhaps less formal training) or be well-trained (but lacking "real-world" experience). Thus, the vertical axis, above, allows us to map ourselves, relatively speaking, to our "competition" in this important perception of potential employers. A firm may be more interested in your past experience (in a given industry, sector, market, etc.) than on your formal training. The opposite may be true—a potential employer may prefer your training and credentials (MBA, undergraduate degree, etc.) to your past experiences.

On the horizontal axis, a firm may value technical or industry-specific skills more than relationship (or relationship-building) skills (or just the opposite). For example, an engineering firm may value your past engineering experience while a sales-oriented firm may value your ability to develop relationships with prospects and clients. Thus, knowing how you are perceived in a market, relative to your peers or other "competitors," is very valuable, and perceptual maps help us to see these differences graphically. For example, if you rely on your deep technical skills and experience, then interviewing for a sales or business development position in a non-engineering industry may not be the best fit for you in this "market."

Obviously, other axes/dimensions may be chosen based on what's important in the market, and this framework can apply to many other situations. For example, if we think of retailers as either focused on "price" (selling items based primarily on low prices) or "prestige" (selling branded products at a premium to less price-sensitive shoppers), we can contrast this dimension with, say, the breadth of product selection. The breadth can be either "narrow" (a retailer that sells only a few types of products to a specific audience) or "mass-market" (a retailer that sells lots of different products to many different customer segments).

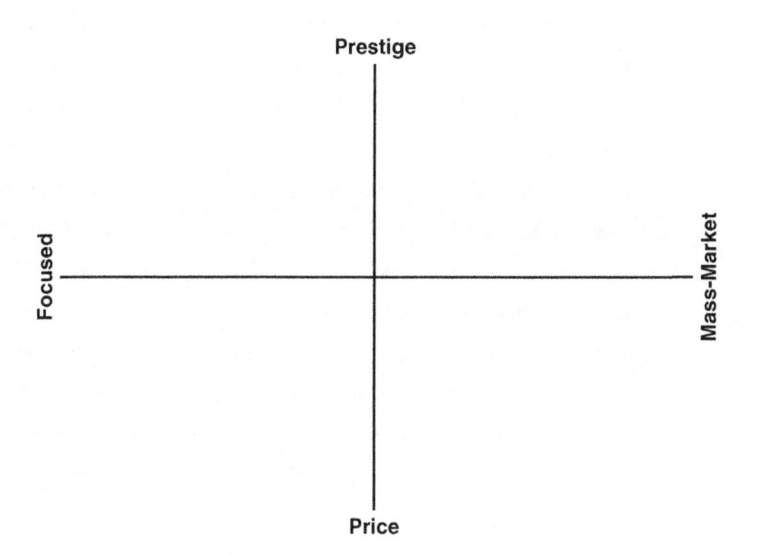

For example, a retailer like Wal-Mart would likely be in the lower-right corner since it focuses on a wide selection of products with low prices. Tiffany and Company, alternatively, would be a focused (jewelry), prestige retailer in the upper leĀ. Other examples can be added, and you can then use this map to see how you are perceived, relative to these two dimensions, versus your competition.

Another framework and tool that we really like is one proffered by Professors W. Chan Kim and Renee Mauborgne of INSEAD. Their framework, called a *strategy canvas,* allows us to show how we differentiate (or not) our offerings compared to our competitors when we look at several bases of competition. At some level, this strategy canvas framework extends the perceptual maps mentioned earlier.

For example, if we own a coffee shop, then we compete on several different bases relative to other players/competitors in the marketplace. For example, we all compete on quality of coffee, variety of different coffees served (both in terms of coffee beans and styles of coffee drinks from drip coffee to espresso beverages), the atmosphere of our shop, whether we sell beans, our wait-times in the shop at peak hours, and the availability of food items in addition to our coffee drinks. Starbucks may sell sandwiches, fruit, and other non-coffee items while Dunkin' Donuts only sells donuts (of various types). Starbucks sells several types of beans by the pound while Dunkin' Donuts sells prepackaged beans and ground coffee (of a small number of types). Starbucks focuses on espresso drinks and thus has somewhat longer lines than Dunkin' Donuts since Dunkin' mostly focuses on coffee with dairy and sweetener additives. If we are to enter this space, we can map out on a canvas how our competition is currently positioned vs. how we would like to position ourselves.

Further, we can see if we're more like our competition than different, and this will help us think about ways to differentiate ourselves. Very oÃen, a firm that thinks it's different from all other competitors may not actually be so different. A strategy canvas will help us see this. Let's take a look at how we might stack up to Starbucks and Dunkin' Donuts with our local coffee shop, M-Beans-A:

Here, the vertical axis, "offerings," measures the extent to which the firm invests in a particular basis of competition. Note, for example, that Dunkin' Donuts invests in their donut foods, but Starbucks seems to invest more in terms of different offerings

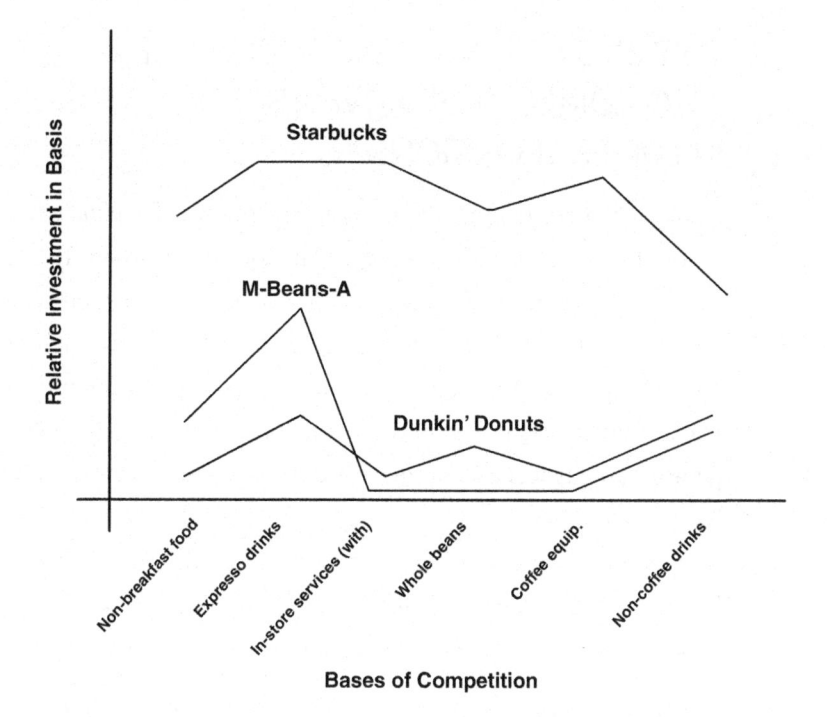

Strategy Canvas: Coffee Shops

Y-axis: Relative Investment in Basis
X-axis (Bases of Competition): Non-breakfast food, Expresso drinks, In-store services (with), Whole beans, Coffee equip., Non-coffee drinks

Lines plotted: Starbucks, M-Beans-A, Dunkin' Donuts

(sandwiches, fruit, canned/bottled drinks, baked goods other than donuts, mints, chocolates, etc.). Our shop offers only a few baked goods, mostly geared toward breakfast, but not as many (or as few) as our competitors. We focus a great deal on espresso drinks, like Starbucks, but we don't sell beans by the pound. While we may wish to be more like a Starbucks than a Dunkin' Donuts, the strategy canvas actually reveals that we're much more like Dunkin' Donuts.

Are there ways we can differentiate? Should we try to be better than Dunkin' Donuts in terms of coffee quality and focus less on espresso beverages? Or should we invest in more (nonbreakfast) food and in-store technology (free wireless Internet access) and attempt to compete with Starbucks on price, our "neighborhood feel," etc.? Thus, a strategy canvas is oAen very helpful in terms of seeing how you and your competitors invest in different areas of competition and which of these bases may be perceived as more or less critical in the eyes of different customers.

TURNING DISTINCTIVE COMPETENCE INTO COMPETITIVE ADVANTAGE: VALUE PROPOSITIONS

Back in the first chapter, we discussed the notion of a *winning value proposition* as a goal of all strategies, missions, and so on. The conceptual level of strategy helps us define the basic innate tools we will use to achieve our goals: mission, vision, and values. The analytical level of strategy—the topic of this chapter—helps us *quantify* and *relate* what we wish to achieve to what others in our market (competitors, suppliers, buyers, new entrants, and substitutes) are doing. All too often, a great vision is proclaimed, and a firm jumps directly to operational considerations without doing the math, first. A few key questions to keep in mind when beginning to examine your mission, vision, and marketplace analyses include:

- Does our idea, product, service, or solution fit, conceptually?
    - Does it support our mission?
    - Does it cause any value conflicts?
    - Is it a key part of our mission—or is it just a nice-to-have?
- Is there a market for it?
    - Is the market made up mostly of our customers or of someone else's?
    - How big is the market (in terms of units, customers, and dollars)?
    - Do we have experience in this market?
- If there is a market, will customers buy it?
    - What unique value proposition will it serve in the market?
    - Will customers identify with this value proposition?
    - What trade-offs will we have to make in order to fulfill this value proposition to our customers?

- How do we best "forge a fit" between the requirements of this value proposition and our current activities?
- Do we have to learn lots of new skills to make it happen, or is it in our "strike zone" in terms of skill sets, etc.

• How many customers will buy it?
- What kinds of customers will buy it?
- Where are they? What other things do these customers buy?
- Will we lose any existing customers when we offer this product?

• If a sufficient number of them will buy it, how much will they pay for it?
- Can we make any money—even if we have a set of willing buyers at a good price?
- Even if we take a loss, is it OK given what our longer-term vision is?
- Will different customers pay different amounts (price discrimination)?

• If they pay for it, will they be satisfied?
- How will we know?
- What if demand exceeds supply?
- Or vice-versa?!
- Will customers make repeat purchases (if applicable) given their satisfaction?

• If they are satisfied, how long will it take our competition to copy or "me, too" us?
- How will competitors (and other Forces) respond when we are successful?
- If someone copies our idea, how will we respond?

• If they are not satisfied, where will they buy it from? What can we do to appease customer service issues?

- What will other market players exploit if our product/concept fails to satisfy customers (or to deliver on its value proposition)?
    - How will we respond?
    - What can we do to help retain customers if something goes wrong?
- Are we developing/selling to be more competitive? If so, what bases of competition are affected favorably by our decisions?
    - How will we look compared to our competitors once we launch the new idea?
    - Will we still look more like some and less like others?
    - Will we truly differentiate ourselves?
    - If we will, what bases of competition will be affected (positively and negatively) by our strategy?

Note that success of a strategy, beyond the conceptual level, hinges on distinctive, competitive, *value propositions.* Why will buyers buy from you? A value proposition that utilizes your strengths and that is perceived as providing more of what the consumer values will be more successful. Further, this will require you and your firm to make trade-offs among activities. Thus, strategy is as much about figuring out what *not* to do or to focus on as it is what to develop and deliver to a market. By forging a fit among your successful (and unique, differentiated) activities in a market in order to develop, and to communicate and to deliver, a compelling value proposition, your firm can best align its offerings with market needs and with your mission, vision, and values.

Note, too, that almost all of the questions above can be answered quantitatively—market share, customer segments, price-points, costs, etc. Such analyses, both qualitative views

CHAPTER 8 • DEVELOPING STRATEGIC PERSPECTIVES

turn distinctive competence

- bases
- sustainability
- transferability
- defensibility

into competitive advantage

of market participants and interactions and quantitative assessments of *what will all this mean*, are critical to success in this phase of strategy development. But don't forget the ties back to mission, vision, and values. And remember, the analytical component is not just a bunch of charts of competitors. Success in this second phase of strategic development depends on sizing, quantifying, and measuring critical customer, cost, price, adoption, retention, and attrition metrics. Otherwise, jumping straight to operations will result in too many unknowns—and a more than likely failed operational strategy from the beginning.

Thus, we have now connected what happens (or doesn't happen) in a market with a set of market players to our overriding mission, vision, and values. Further, we have learned that we need to quantify success in order to operationalize our strategy. A strategy with only an idea and a checklist—with no "sanity check" in the real marketplace environment and context in which you exist—is most likely doomed to fail.

THE ROLES OF FINANCE, ACCOUNTING, AND OTHER MBA CORE COURSES IN STRATEGIC ANALYSIS AND DEVELOPMENT

When many of our MBA students or corporate clients start a strategy course, they ask how this course is connected to other MBA core courses such as finance, accounting, marketing, operations research, and organizational behavior. Sadly, some view a strategy course as a disconnected, "fuzzy" course full of interesting buzzwords that end up getting used by management consultants and managers, alike.

However, business strategy, as a course, is often best taken, and even better understood, after having these other core courses and their tools in one's toolkit. Strategy, and strategic management, should comprise and utilize all of these core skills. Strategy often acts as a glue to help put all of these core pieces together. For example, we cannot effectively assess market potential, for us or for our competitors, if we do not know basic accounting and finance principles. Being able to size a market, understand volumes, costs, and profits, and having the ability to review financial statements (if available) of other competitors are incredibly valuable skills. Also particularly valuable in the analytical component of strategy is knowledge of marketing—both the three "C's" of company, customer, and competitor, and the four "P's" of products, price, promotion, and placement. Knowing how competitors price their offerings, position them in the marketplace, and affect our own company and customers is paramount to effective analysis of a potential market or opportunity. Finally, organizational behavior, and assessments of leadership styles, management philosophies, networks of market participants, etc., are critical to understanding and to developing effective visions and missions (and then being able to analyze them astutely in a marketplace).

Thus, as you conduct analyses of possible strategies, alternatives, and/or pathways from the present state to the desired future state (or vision), don't forget all those important skills learned in other core courses. The more managers and leaders use them in the context of strategy development and management, the more effective these strategies will be. Otherwise, a strategy will be disconnected from core business principles. And it will likely fail.

BUSINESS STRATEGY IN ACTION

Let's return to the MinuteClinic case in the last chapter, but this time, let's focus on Family Associates' strengths, weaknesses, opportunities, and threats given MinuteClinic's entrance into its market. A SWOT analysis will help us see how our practice stacks up against the competition in this market by assessing our strengths, weaknesses, opportunities, and threats. We can use the intersections of these—strengths/opportunities, for example—to develop some options to consider moving forward.

A strategy canvas can also help us see how we compete, and are perceived by patients, with this new entrant in the market. Can we afford to give up these basic items to MinuteClinic? If not, how can we make up for these lost visits? Since reimbursements are maintained by the insurance companies, and we cannot always set our prices, how can we negotiate to get more favorable rates?

Even if we believe we have some options to help us minimize our weaknesses and protect us from threats, how do we put these options into part of our day-to-day operations? That is, how do we take the insights we gain from our SWOT and strategy canvas and turn them into actionable tasks/initiatives with appropriate tracking of key metrics to ensure success? For that, we will move on to operational considerations, including how to measure what "good" looks like and how to plan tasks that achieve desired outcomes, in the next chapter.

TEST YOURSELF

Review the MinuteClinic, Inc. case from the last chapter, and, using the tools of this chapter, answer the following questions:

1. Assume you are a partner with Family Associates. What strengths, weaknesses, opportunities, and threats do you see in your market given the entrance of a MinuteClinic? What specific strategies, offensive and defensive, might you posit to counter these "new entrant" effects?
2. How does Family Associates compete in the marketplace? What are the key bases of competition for any player in this evolving "retail healthcare" space? Use a strategy canvas to show Family Associates and MinuteClinic in these terms.

KEY POINTS TO REMEMBER

- SWOT—good for internal planning, but just like a Five Forces analysis, a SWOT doesn't tell us specifically *what to do*
- Use strengths to exploit opportunities and to defend against threats.
- Improve weak areas, if possible, to avoid future risks.
- Even a defensive approach, in areas of weaknesses that are also vulnerable to outside threats, should focus on damage control. Don't try to fix everything!
- Other tools, like strategy canvases, can also aid in determining key SWOT areas and give us insights into how different and/or similar we are to our key competitors
- Any strategic analysis should incorporate key learnings and frameworks from other MBA core courses. Strategic thinking and analysis should *never* be divorced from these other areas!

CHAPTER 9

Developing Strategic Perspectives: Operational Considerations

INTRODUCTION

Your boss has asked you to drive from Chicago to Oskaloosa, Iowa, a journey of 317 miles. He's prepared a budget for you with clear metrics. You can spend no more than $16 on gas, you must arrive in 5 hours and 37 minutes, and you can't drive over 60 miles per hour. But no one has a map with a route to Oskaloosa, and you don't know whether you'll run into a snowstorm on the way.

Ludicrous? No more so than the way many companies translate their strategic plans into operations.[1]

If it can be measured, it can be improved.[2]

Now that we have discussed how to think conceptually (mission, vision, values) and analytically (macro-market, micro-market, and SWOT), we have to tie our market-validated, rationalized plan to the way we do business every day: our operations. A conceptually "good" strategy that has been vetted against external and internal strengths and weaknesses now must be put into operation if our vision and mission are to be realized.

However, this is a critical connection point that is often assumed to be easy. Remember, a firm has employees, shareholders (internal and external), customers, and other stakeholders. All of these constituents want to see a strategy succeed, but often for different reasons. Shareholders want returns on invested capital. Customers want new, better, and/or more innovative products. Employees want a sense of purpose and to be compensated for their value-added. Thus, putting a strategy into operations is much more than just "doing it." We have to think carefully about key *stakeholders*, and we have to be able to objectively *measure* our success (or lack thereof). All too often, metrics and measurements of success are only measured financially. However, we must also measure how our customers react, how ready/stable our own internal business processes and operations are, and how we are learning and growing as an organization as part of our strategy.

Thus, we come to the concept of *management dashboards,* which help us watch a few—emphasis on *few*—key measures in a number of categories to help us see how things are proceeding as we operationalize our strategy. However, having a dashboard isn't enough. Just as with a car, it may have a dashboard, but you have to know where you are going (vision) and know if you are getting there well or not. "Success" won't be measured only in terms of speed on the speedometer (or distance traveled on the odometer) but also on being on time for a meeting (your watch), being prepared for the discussion (agenda), having enough fuel (fuel gauge), and possessing enough cash to pay for your share of the meal (cash in your wallet or available credit on your credit card). A number of financial, internal operations, customer, and learning/

growth measures can be measured. And, as Edwin Booz said, *"If it can be measured, it can be improved."*

But what if something goes wrong? What about that snowstorm on the way to the meeting? What about cost overruns? Employee attrition (or new hiring)? What if competitors don't act as you thought they would? All too often, even the best of strategists, using the best of action plans to put their strategies into operations, fail to anticipate, plan for, or even consider what might happen if all the planning goes wrong. We all try to keep enough fuel in our cars so that we never run out of gas. But sometimes it happens. And sometimes a flat tire messes up our entire daily schedule, no matter how much cash you have or how well your agenda is prepared for the meeting you will now be either late to or not able to attend.

Therefore, near the end of this chapter, after we have discussed how to measure success—what "good" looks like—and how to create effective action plans to turn your vision into discrete, measureable actions, we will consider what happens on those strategic "rainy days." How do we expect the unexpected, plan for it, be ready for it, and able to handle any other contingencies that come our way in the course of executing our strategy? As a senior executive at a retail consumer electronics firm said to his team once:

> When something happens, a store catches fire, a competitor tries to engage us in a price war, a new entrant tries to take away our customers, whatever, I don't want us to be surprised. Instead of having to scramble to respond, I simply want to be able to pull the answer out of my file drawer . . .because we had already thought about the situation months ago, and we have a script for how to handle it now.[3]

WHAT'S AHEAD

In this chapter, you'll learn:

- A useful tool for measuring success in putting your strategy into operations: *The Balanced Scorecard*
- How to measure customer effectiveness and satisfaction
- Ways to measure the effectiveness of your own internal business processes and operations—the things you and your firm do every day
- Methods to measure financial success of your strategy (using basic accounting measures)
- How to measure your growth and innovation—personally and as a firm—as you put your strategy in operations; that is, how well is your strategy paying you and your firm/people back in terms of their learning and growth?
- Ways to develop *action plans* that you can explicitly tie to your balanced scorecard
- How to handle those times when your action plan doesn't work (those "hurdles" or "roadblocks" we've been talking about as part of achieving our ultimate vision)

IN THE REAL WORLD

The business literature and daily newspapers are filled with countless stories about great ideas (and visions) that seemed to have credible value propositions that could just never get off the ground. Continental Lite, a discount version of Continental Airlines, never really made it. Neither did Song as part of Delta Airlines. But Ted, part of United Airlines, seems to be flying with few issues.

Krispy Kreme donuts were the rage, and they started selling coffee in their stores (to compete with local Starbucks, etc.). But customers started trying to get healthy. Krispy Kreme tried to offer lower-fat options, but it didn't "stick." Wal-Mart tries to sell appliances—refrigerators, freezers, etc.—but ends up getting out of the business. All of these firms have bright management teams, loyal customers, and lots of internal and outside "strategists." So what happened? These ideas tested well in the marketplace but ultimately couldn't be effectively put into operations. Did management not measure the right things? Were action plans not specific enough? Were contingency plans never developed, or if so, were they executed too late?

Many great ideas, from the Sony Betamax (eventually beaten by the VHS standard for videotaping) to Sony's Blu-Ray high-definition DVD technology (which eventually emerged victorious over the competing HD-DVD standard), have sometimes blossomed but sometimes bottomed out. What makes them different? Is it how well finances for these projects are measured? How well internal operations (marketing, sales, product development, etc.) are working? Whether the firm and its people are learning and growing along the way? Or is it just that customers didn't like it (or liked it and didn't buy it)? The answer to all of these questions is YES; a number of customer, financial, innovation and growth, and internal process issues cause some strategies to succeed…and others to fail. So how can we measure our success (or can we even know what success looks like early on)? These questions get us to the core of operations—and of putting a strategy into operations.

THE KEY CONCEPTS

Metrics and Measurement: The Need for Assessable Strategies

Ideas and visions are terrific, and if they can be analytically validated and substantiated, all the better. However, having a conceptual and analytical basis for a vision doesn't help us much with putting it into operations. Granted, we could create task plans, project plans, Gantt charts, and other popular outputs, but how will we know if we're making progress? If we're meeting our vision? If our prior analyses were correct?

Too often, managers try to project-plan their way through a strategy without ever stepping back and asking, "What does 'good' look like?" Even strategists who don't skip the analytical components often immediately jump to work- and task-planning with only one or two metrics used to define success: time and budget. If we can implement our vision within x months at a cost of no more than y dollars, we will be "successful." But do our customers like what we did? Did we grow and learn as a company? Did our internal business processes need to be improved/changed in order to be effective? Did we implement our ideas on budget but at too much of an (opportunity) cost for it to be worthwhile? Managing the implementation of a vision by only considering time frames and budget requirements is simply insufficient.

Recall our framework from earlier discussions:

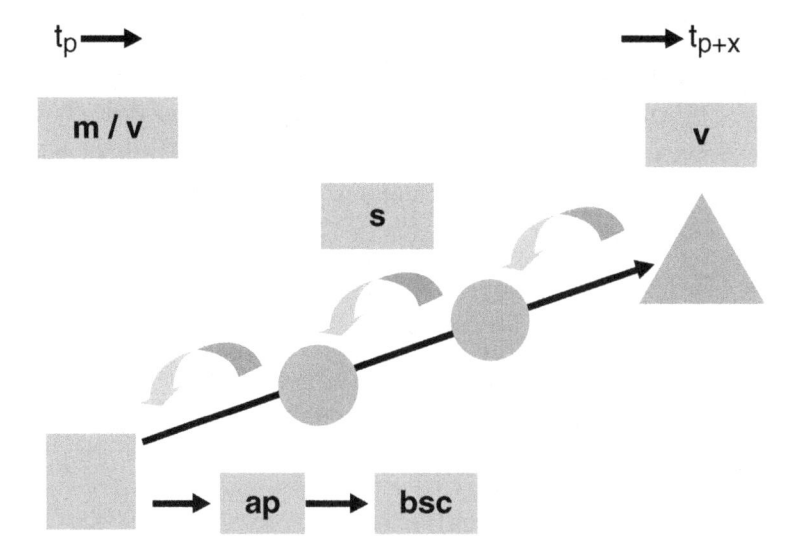

$t_p \rightarrow$ $\rightarrow t_{p+x}$

m / v

v

s

ap → bsc

Here, we focus on defining our vision (v), using our mission and values (m / v) to help define our strategy (s) that will take us from the present time (t_p) to a definite point in the future /EQ/ (t_{p+x}). We use the process of "folding back" to understand what we must accomplish in terms of milestones and the hurdles we must overcome.

Now we add two new items to our framework. At the present time, we now must develop *action plans* (ap) to put our strategy into operations, and we need to create a *balanced scorecard* (bsc) to measure our progress against targets that define our success (or what "good" looks like). In this chapter, the key pieces we will focus on will be connecting our vision (v) to our actions (ap) and measuring our success using a scorecard framework (bsc). Thus, *operations* in a strategic context means *putting our vision in place through measurable, objective, deliberate actions,* as shown in the chart, below:

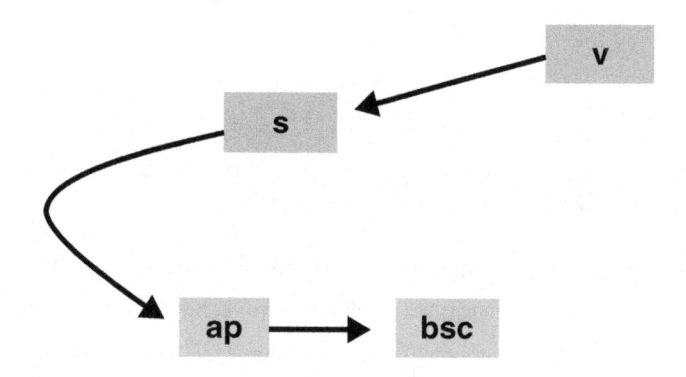

The Balanced Scorecard: A Simple Operational "Dashboard"

In order to measure the effectiveness of putting our strategy into operations, we propose a framework developed by Professor Robert Kaplan, of the Harvard Business School, and David Norton, a management consultant in the 1990s. Kaplan and Norton's approach is in widespread use today, and it continues to be the basis for a great deal of management reporting and operations management around the world in both for-profit and not-for-profit entities.

As the chart below depicts, our vision and strategy (v / s) and our action plans (ap) drive us to measure the effectiveness of these using a four-part framework called the *balanced scorecard*. The balanced scorecard is so named because it effectively *balances* our strategic intent with our actions while allowing us to measure or *scorecard* our efforts along the way:

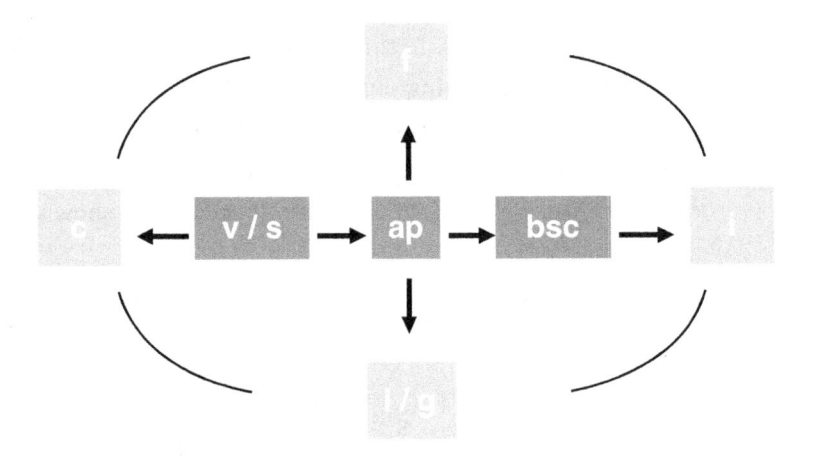

The four parts of the scorecard are:

1. *Financial* metrics (f): These measurements allow us to assess the financial position and achievements of our actions. Standard accounting and industry-specific measures are often used here; e.g., return on invested capital (ROIC), payback, return on equity, and others. Industry-specific measures will vary, but for example, a retailer may track sales per square foot and inventory turns. A healthcare insurer may track medical loss ratio, and a restaurant may track average order price (per person or per table).

2. *Internal business process* metrics (i): These metrics, which are often confused with financial indicators, measure the

effectiveness and efficiency of our day-to-day business processes. For example, a manufacturer may track defects per thousand or total assembly time. A credit card company will keep notice of delinquencies and of new cards issued. A retailer may look at coupon redemption rates and effectiveness of its advertising campaigns (in terms of foot traffic in the store, etc.)

3. *Learning and growth* metrics (l / g): These measurements allow us to see how our organization, our people, processes, and technologies, learn and grow by virtue of our strategy. Are we learning about new markets, products, and/or services that we are offering to new customers? Do our people get enough training and growth opportunities as part of our strategy?

4. *Customer* metrics (c): These indicators give us the opportunity to see how our customers view, react to, and identify with our strategy. Are our customers satisfied? Do we retain many of them or is there too much attrition? How are we at acquiring customers in the first place? What segments of customers do we serve/not serve, and how are they responding to our actions in the marketplace? Again, different industries may have different measures; e.g., retailers track repeat customer visits while a consulting or law firm may focus on new customer acquisition, in terms of sales/proposal effectiveness, and then how long they are able to retain them).

It is critical that any measure used in the scorecard be *objective, measurable, and reportable.* If all parties (inside and outside the firm) cannot agree on objective definitions for each measure, then the scorecard will be worthless. Similarly, if the metrics cannot be measured and reported periodically without requiring massive amounts of database redesign or calculation, then the s corecard won't be an effective management tool at all. All too often, managers use scorecards with vague metrics like "increased employee morale," and "more satisfied customers," without really thinking about what it will take to define it, measure it, and report it.

But beware: a common tendency that we see when managers create and use scorecards is that they become too cumbersome and include, as we have seen, literally hundreds of metrics and measurements. This is simply not strategic! Recall that you can drive your car to get from Point A to Point B by only really paying attention to two or three key metrics: speed, fuel level, and perhaps any "error alarms" that may arise such as low tire pressure, high engine heat, or high transmission speed (the red zone on your tachometer).

Thus, when executing a strategy, keep it simple, keep it focused, and keep it clear. While there is no magic number of metrics that will create optimal success, the fewer metrics you use, the better. This will make your scorecard easier to manage, easier to communicate, and easier to track against. We have seen large firms with large departments dedicated to nothing but scorecarding. While in some cases, precision manufacturing, for example, this may make some sense, in general, strategies that are well conceived in mission and vision, well analyzed in a market context, and well planned in terms of action tend to require simple, compact, and easy-to-update scorecards (and supporting resources to manage them).

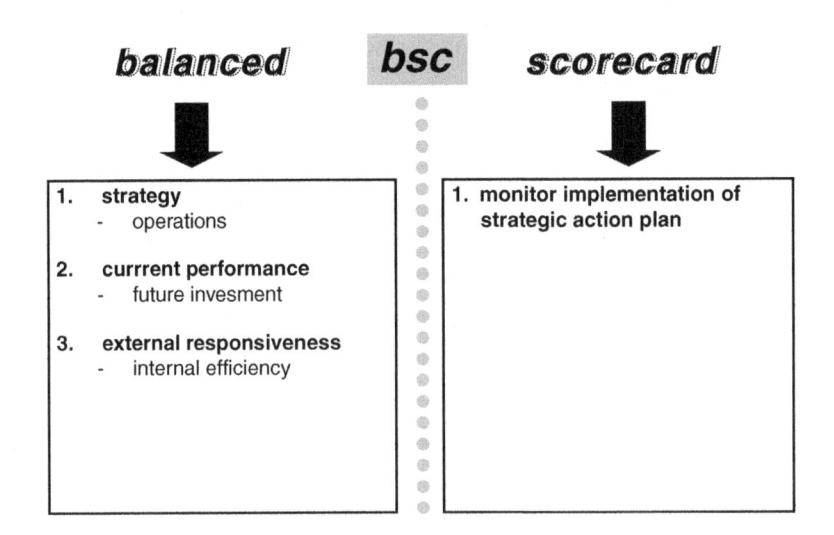

balanced   **bsc**   **scorecard**

⬇   ⬇

1. **strategy**
   - operations
 	
2. **currrent performance**
   - future invesment
 	
3. **external responsiveness**
   - internal efficiency
	1. **monitor implementation of strategic action plan**

To put this in context, consider the two terms, *balanced* and *scorecard*. As we can see, the balanced scorecard effectively *balances* our strategy, current performance and operations, and the demands placed on us from external (market) forces with need to change/affect all of these in order to be successful with our new strategy.

Thus, as many have put it, implementing a strategy is akin to changing the tires on a racecar as it continues to speed around the racetrack. Now we will discuss metrics in each of the four parts of the balanced scorecard.

Customer Metrics: What Do Our Buyers Want?

Customer metrics should help us evaluate and report on customer perceptions, attitudes, and actions with respect to our strategy (which, again, links our actions to our vision). Common metrics include satisfaction, acquisition rate (how many/often do we get new ones), retention rate (how long do we keep customers or how many stay with us over time), attrition (how many leave), etc.

Depending on the industry/market in which your strategy is being executed, other customer metrics may make sense. Repeat visits to stores, how much they spend, results of product/service surveys, and many others are possible. The key, though, is to not necessarily measure what you think your customers think is important. You must find out from *them* what's important, using surveys, focus groups, salespeople, etc., and then devise simple measures and tools to track effectiveness. Common areas of focus for customer metrics often include:

- Satisfaction
- Churn: acquisition, retention, attrition
- Lifetime value: how much we can expect to make in revenues or profits from our customers (often used as a financial measure, also)

- Market share: how much of the market we own vs. competitors (both in terms of units and dollars, if applicable)
- Households: In some contexts, a firm may want to know how many households it serves (as a multiple of the number of customers it has)
- Segment-specific metrics: If a firm segments its customers in some way(s), by geography, psychography, profitability, tenure, etc., some segment specific metrics may make sense. For example, a credit card company may monitor certain delinquency states (not paid in 30 days vs. not paid in 60 days) for some cardholders (high-risk defaulters, for example) compared to others for whom they may measure, say, credit limits more closely

Thus, with a clear understanding of customer needs—which should be tightly aligned with your value propositions developed earlier—the general manager (and *Strategos*) should be able to build a scorecard for customer success.

Financial Metrics: Getting It Done on Time and on Budget

When it comes to financial metrics, many of us think of "income statement" quantities or ratios like return on investment, profits, inventory levels, etc. Depending on the focal points of your strategy, you may choose to use some of these or other financial measures important to your industry or specific actions. Average basket or "ticket" is used to see if a retail sales force is successful at creating more sales per customer. If you are revamping a compensation and incentive scheme for your employees (or business partners), you may wish to track average bonus and/or average merit increase payouts.

In most firms, the financial metrics are well-established, understood, and distributed. However, in many cases, these are the *only* metrics used to gauge success (especially for earnings-per-share-focused public companies). Again, these financial metrics must be balanced with those in the other three areas in order to have a higher probability of operational (and thus strategic) success.

Internal Business Process Metrics: Excellence in Internal Operations

Like financial measures, many firms have a good sense of what internal process metrics drive their businesses. Manufacturers know how to manage cycle times, defect rates, inventory stock-outs or surpluses, and labor utilization (overtime, etc.). Professional services firms know very well how to control and report utilization of their staff (how "busy" they are in terms of billable time) and realization of their staff's billings (the percentage of optimum billable dollars per employee that is collected from clients). For example, if an attorney is fully utilized (busy eight hours a day) but only 50% realized, then we should find out what the 50% of non-revenue-producing activities are. These may be acceptable, or we may need to task this attorney on other "realizable" tasks.

Pharmaceutical firms know how to manage drug development pipelines, drug manufacturing, distribution, and pricing. The list goes on and on. Oddly, however, these internal business process metrics are often either confused with financial ones or managed separately from other scorecard areas/measurements. For example, the quality control group may know how many defects per thousand a plant creates, but the good folks in finance may not know (or track) the relative financial impact of these defects. (And neither one of these groups may know the true customer impact since that often falls in the marketing area!)

Of particular note in the internal process area is the management of multiple business partners that may have come into play due to partnerships, alliances, joint ventures, or outright mergers or acquisitions. *Horizontal integration* occurs when a firm buys a competitor in order to increase market share, spread costs out over a larger pool of assets, etc. For example, when American Airlines bought TWA, it was able to get TWA's fleet of aircraft, its St. Louis, Missouri, hub, and profitable routes/customers that it couldn't have easily tapped before. When a company buys a competitor, or horizontally integrates, a special emphasis is placed on the merging/consolidation of internal business processes (such as ticketing systems, aircraft maintenance, baggage handling, advertising and marketing, and customer service in the airline example, above).

Vertical integration, on the other hand, occurs when a firm decides to move either "upstream" or "downstream" in its range of activities to try to control more of the processes (and assets, management, etc.) of the functions that its industry performs. For example, Dell Inc. used to just be an Internet-based seller and builder of computers. Dell would buy components from manufacturers, assemble computers based on customer specifications/orders, and then ship them directly to paying customers. In recent years, however, Dell has vertically integrated by moving "upstream" in its supply chain. It buys more raw materials, now, like chips, flat-panel displays, etc., in order to keep component prices under control and to effectively lock-up supply of key components from its competitors. (This type of vertical integration is often called *forward integration* in the sense that Dell moved upstream from buying just assembled components to the more "raw materials" of computers, televisions, and cameras.)

Another example is wine sellers. Some simply buy wine from wineries and resell it in retail channels (playing the effective role of wholesalers). However, some wineries sell directly to consumers. A third option is when a wine seller, such as a local store or importer, buys vineyards and production facilities in order to make the product that it ultimately sells. Finally, when Sony bought Columbia Records, Sony did so to become an "entertainment company" and in order to control the production and distribution, literally, the pressing of albums and CDs, for its artists. Prior to the acquisition of Columbia Records, Sony simply bought CDs from pressing plants/manufacturers and resold their artists' work to retailers. Sony could also move the other way in its efforts by buying a retailer, or by setting up its own as it has with its SonyStyle stores, to control its music business from artist recording all the way through retail distribution.

Thus, when companies horizontally or vertically integrate, a particular emphasis is placed on the monitoring and management of internal business processes (which have become more complex due to another firm's processes coming into the mix). Common internal business process metrics, which are often very industry/market-specific, include:

- *Acquisition* metrics: raw material quality, consistency, purity (could also be applied to customer metrics in terms of target-market effectiveness of advertising, etc.)
- *Manufacturing* metrics: cycle times, defects, shipping commitment accuracy
- *Selling* metrics: sales lead-times, "penetration" effectiveness or "conversion" rate (that is, how many prospects are converted to customers)
- *Service* metrics: service quality, "attachment" rate (that is, how many products or dollars of add-on sales and service our service employees create for us with customers)
- *Operational* metrics: first-pass rate (percentage of claims that are adjudicated correctly, for example, by an insurer), call-center hold or wait times (how long you wait to speak to a customer service agent, for example), "six-sigma" manufacturing controls
- *Collaboration* metrics: how many drug compounds are approved based on collaborative efforts, how many joint sales have we achieved, how many cross-sells have we made (for example,

when a bank sells a credit card customer a mortgage or home equity loan)

Again, many internal business process metrics are just that: internal. While some useful classifications are above, these depend largely on what a firm does in its day-to-day operations and business. Many are dictated by the industry a firm is in (or even by regulations the firm must meet) but depending on your strategy and action steps, you may need to create additional ones to suit your specific needs/situation.

Growth and Learning Metrics: Assessing What We Do in the Context of Doing It Better

Finally, we look at the *learning and growth* component of the balanced scorecard. This is perhaps the most neglected—or unrealized—component of performance management. Financial, business process, and customer targets can be achieved, but what if we burn out our employees to hit them? What if our employees don't learn anything new (or better) as part of this new strategy? Mergers and acquisitions often fail specifically for these reasons and little (mutual) learning takes place, at a staff or management level, to reinforce and to embrace differences in operations, financial management, and/or views of the customers.

Thus, learning and growth metrics are often good proxies for effective communication and change management within (and outside) an organization. Common metrics include:

- Training effectiveness
- Employee retention
- Employee growth (both in terms of numbers and promotions/advancement)
- Inter- and intra-firm communications (for example, how many joint conferences, meetings, planning sessions, etc. do we hold, and are the results what we expect?)

CHAPTER 9 • DEVELOPING STRATEGIC PERSPECTIVES 201

Don't forget these when developing a scorecard for strategy effectiveness. Remember, you may know what your strategy is, but if others don't share the same sense of mission, vision, and analysis of the market, your strategy will only remain yours. These types of metrics in the learning and growth area help us understand how well we manage the rollout of a strategy, or of any communication or initiative, as well as how our most critical asset, our people, view the job we're doing.

An easy way to think about how our balanced scorecard is tied to the pieces/elements of our vision is as follows:

vision / strategic intent

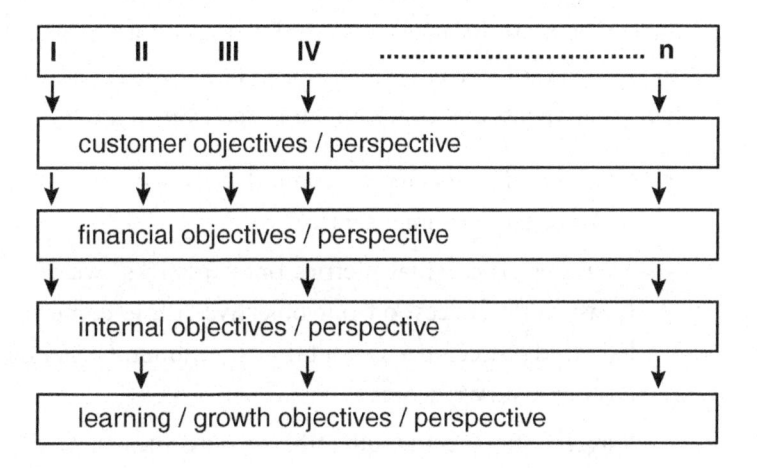

I	II	III	IV	....	n
↓			↓		↓
customer objectives / perspective					
↓	↓	↓	↓		↓
financial objectives / perspective					
↓		↓			↓
internal objectives / perspective					
	↓	↓			↓
learning / growth objectives / perspective					

If our vision or strategic intent comprise a number (n) of milestones and/or components (i.e., the arrows we get when we "fold back" from our vision to the present state), we should be able to match each piece of our vision to a specific metric in our balanced scorecard. For example, parts I, IV, and n tie to our customer objectives, above. All pieces of our vision tie to financial measures. Parts II, IV, and n apply to our learning and growth as an organization and as a market player. It's important to note that if some parts of your vision don't tie to specific metrics, you should revisit your scorecard. Conversely, if you have metrics that you collect, track, and report, but they aren't tied to your vision, then why are you collecting and reporting them?!

Action Planning: Concrete Task Planning and Management for Your Vision and Strategic Intent

Now that we understand four critical dimensions to measure the success of our operations, how do we now "do it?" Recall that the operational component of strategy, at its most basic level, is achieving our vision through (measurable) action. Thus, we need a framework to help us plan tasks (with targets, objectives, etc.) for each of the indicators in our balanced scorecard. For each metric (in each balanced scorecard area or *perspective*), we need to articulate clearly the four components that comprise our *action plan* for strategy success:

- *Objective:* The specific outcome that we wish to achieve; e.g., improve our customer service
- *Measures:* The actual metrics or "yardsticks" we will use to measure the success of our objective. These come from our balanced scorecard; e.g., wait time for inbound callers, average customer survey scores
- *Targets:* The specific, quantifiable outcomes that will define success, in terms of your measures, in meeting your objective; e.g., decrease wait time for inbound customer calls by 10%, improve our overall average customer satisfaction from our surveys by 5%
- *Initiatives:* Tasks, and those who are accountable for them, that will enable you to hit your targets for your measures, which will then lead to success of your objectives

The chart on the next page illustrates how to build a solid action plan using the balanced scorecard "customer" component.

Note that objectives can have multiple measurements, but measurements can only have one target. Several initiatives, however, can relate to several targets (and vice versa):

balanced scorecard (customer perspective, only)

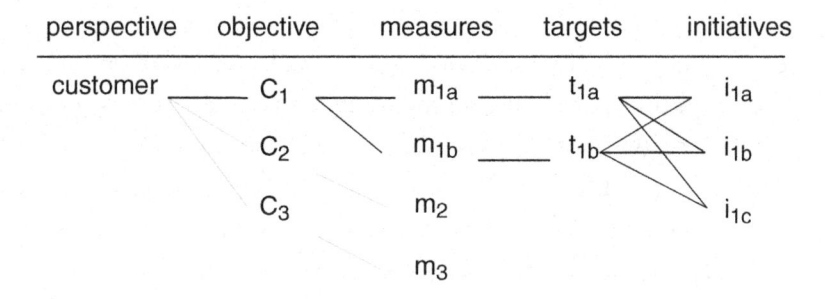

perspective	objective	measures	targets	initiatives
customer	C_1	m_{1a}	t_{1a}	i_{1a}
	C_2	m_{1b}	t_{1b}	i_{1b}
	C_3	m_2		i_{1c}
		m_3		

We cannot emphasize enough the need to make the action plan simple, focused, and with commonly understood language. Objectives should be clear, and measures (including their calculations) should be spelled out so there are no issues wi th interpretation. Targets should be reasonable and based on either past performance or improvement efforts, or on industry norms. Initiatives should be straightforward, and each one should have a clear manager and/or point of accountability. In fact, in our experience, the more the initiative managers are involved in helping define the action plan (and scorecard), the more successful the operations will be.

Benchmarking: Tying Operations Back to Conceptual and Analytical Frameworks (For You and Your Competition)

Once we have a clearer sense of market players and their impacts (the macro-market results) and a sense of our firm's capabilities in the context of our market (the micro-market analysis), we can begin to put our strategies into action and develop operational plans as long as we have a clear sense of metrics (from our balanced scorecard) and a task-level plan to execute (our action plan). However, a very useful process to go through at this point, either inside your firm or with the aid of external consultants, is to *benchmark* some (if not all) of your key metrics and see how you currently stack up compared to your competitors.

For example, if you are trying to improve your customer service experience, you may want to see how some of the metrics of your competitors perform against your metrics. What is the average time on hold for our top competitors? Are we not doing as well? If so, why not? If we are doing as well, does it make sense to then focus on this area? The answer may be "yes" if we believe improvements in this area will lead to significant competitive advantage. However, if efforts may not, then we may be better off working on other ways to improve our customer satisfaction; for example, by decreasing total call time, and decreasing the number of transfers/handoffs needed to resolve issues.

Imagine creating your balanced scorecard for all of your key competitors. If you can, you will be able to see how they exceed or lag your own operational performance. However, getting access to these kinds of measurements is very difficult if not impossible at times. Thus, the use of an outside research firm or consultancy may be beneficial. Often, outside researchers and consultants conduct studies in various areas and collect statistics for a wide range of companies (often in specific industries). Further, an outside firm will bring some objectivity to your scorecard metrics and provide some views that you may find helpful outside of your own offices.

One caution, however: beware of the "myth of best practices." Many times, consultants and researchers will elaborate on "best practices" in an industry or for a certain set of operational procedures. Many of these are common across the usual business disciplines such as best practices in direct marketing, manufacturing controls, procurement, information technology management, management reporting, and so on. However, one interesting paradox often occurs when a firm embarks on a "best practices" implementation or wishes to be "best in class": the firm ends up spending a great deal of money on some improvements that, while best in class, don't necessarily lead to improved business results (or even customer awareness). Further, if all firms in your industry are chasing after the same "best in class" practices, then by definition, there will be little differentiation among your and your competitors' capabilities!

This is not to say the pursuit of "best" capabilities is unwarranted entirely. However, often, "good enough" is just that—good enough in terms of what your internal operations and external customer expectations want. And in fact, if surveyed, many customers would *not* necessarily be willing to pay more for their products and services just to improve some capabilities (like wait times) on the margin. Therefore, we caution you to beware of the "best practices" paradox. Many of the things you do can be improved, surely, but this doesn't mean they necessarily have to be the best to be competitive (or differentiable) in the market. Further, if you and all of your competitors chase the same goals of "best in class," then by definition, nothing will distinguish you (or them)—other than perhaps how fast you can achieve these practices.

Scenario Analysis and Contingency Planning: Strategic "Rainy Days"

But what if something goes wrong? What if your action plans aren't achieved in the time frames you planned? What if targets are not met? Objectives not fully achieved? Does this mean your strategy was worthless? Of course not. In fact, all too often we have noticed clients who will develop strategies; prepare conceptual, analytical, and operational analyses; devise solid action plans and scorecards; and then put it on a bookshelf for months or even years (with no reviewing of these important strategic components over time).

Instead, the firm (or leader) will just start managing various tasks in the hope that some improvement across all dimensions will be sufficient. Sadly, this is often not the case. And in fact, when difficulties arise, or competitors, suppliers, new entrants, substitutes, and/or regulators perform unexpected actions, the firm and its leaders are often caught completely off-guard, and as a result, the *entire* strategy and action plan gets scuttled (or at least severely decreased in scale and in scope). As such, we believe that of equal importance to your action plan and scorecards are the *contingency plans* around all of them. What will we do if we cannot get the new system implemented by year-end? What if our customer service is perceived as worse instead of better when we implement some key initiatives? What if a competitor "scoops" us in the market; i.e., develops and releases a product just like the one we are developing but six months ahead of our target launch?

The key to better preparing your strategy, your plans, and your metrics for these "rainy days" is to have a good and always-updated knowledge of:

- Key *end-states* that may occur in your market, e.g., a competitor goes out of business or is acquired by another competitor, a competing product comes out before yours, customers rebel against your new offering (or you need to recall it due to technical defects), etc. Note that some end-states could be very positive for you as well based on strategic success.
- Possible *scenarios* that may lead to these various end-states. That is, what key events, actions, responses, and inputs must happen in order for the end-state to come true? What do you have to do (or not do) to allow them to occur?

The chart on the next page depicts how to think about various scenarios, fueled by various *enablers* often tied to your scorecard metrics and suspected forces and actions in your market, and what will have to be true in these scenarios to see the end-state that you envision. Note that the way to develop these scenarios is to work from right to left; that is, start with the possible end-state and then work "backwards" in terms of what will have to be true for that end-state to exist. Eventually, you will get to key enablers (or disablers) that will likely fuel these various pathways. The goal of your strategy is to disrupt competitive scenarios, if possible, while giving ones in which you prevail the best possible chance of success:

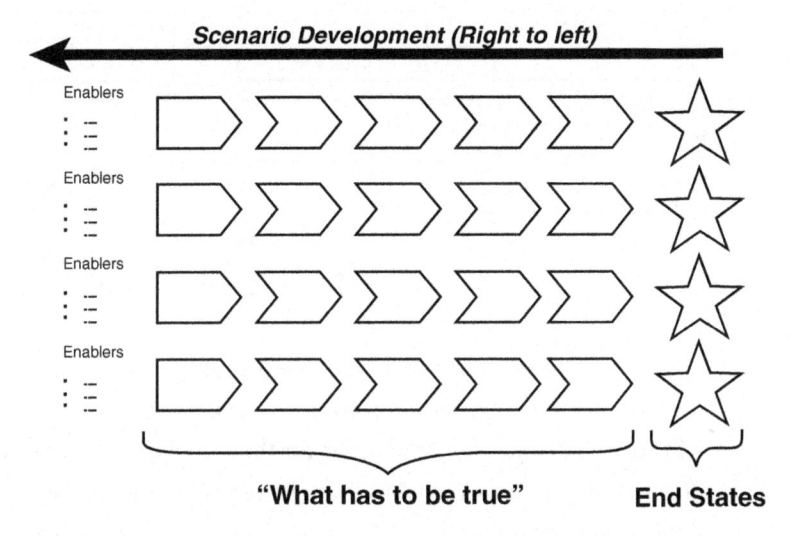

Scenario Development (Right to left)

"What has to be true"   End States

As an example, consider the ABC Toy Company, a retailer of toys for children. At the core of ABC's strategy is the focus of becoming the best store/toy *experience* for its customers (children) and buyers (parents, etc.). Thus, ABC wishes to differentiate itself by delivering on the value proposition of providing unparalleled experiences with toys instead of just being a "retailer" of them. ABC will allow, for example, children to play with toys in the store, and salespeople will be on hand to help answer questions that purchasers/parents may have about various toys including safety, accessories, age-appropriateness, and so on.

Assuming ABC wishes to achieve this outcome or end-state, what would have to be true in order for them to win? An example of the key steps needed (not necessarily in serial fashion) is shown below:

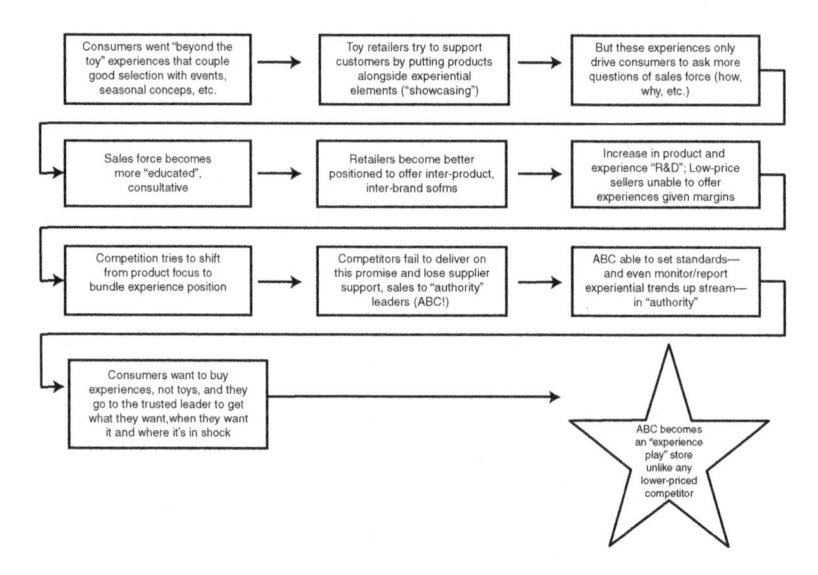

```
[Consumers went "beyond the toy" experiences that couple good selection with events, seasonal concepts, etc.] → [Toy retailers try to support customers by putting products alongside experiential elements ("showcasing")] → [But these experiences only drive consumers to ask more questions of sales force (how, why, etc.)]

[Sales force becomes more "educated", consultative] → [Retailers become better positioned to offer inter-product, inter-brand sofms] → [Increase in product and experience "R&D"; Low-price sellers unable to offer experiences given margins]

[Competition tries to shift from product focus to bundle experience position] → [Competitors fail to deliver on this promise and lose supplier support, sales to "authority" leaders (ABC!)] → [ABC able to set standards—and even monitor/report experiential trends up stream—in "authority"]

[Consumers want to buy experiences, not toys, and they go to the trusted leader to get what they want, when they want it and where it's in shock] → ★ [ABC becomes an "experience play" store unlike any lower-priced competitor]
```

Here, note that each rectangle is a presumption about what either ABC or its competitors, customers, suppliers, and other "Forces" will have to do or become in order for them to win. Note that some boxes imply actions that ABC will have to take with customers. Others include internal processes and operations (like sales force training). Each of these boxes could lead to initiatives, for example, for consideration in action plans (and subsequent measurement by scorecard metrics). By mapping out these possible scenarios, including ones in which ABC is prevented from achieving its goals/outcomes based on market reactions/responses, the strategist can more clearly see what has to be done, and done well, in order to properly put a coherent, measurable strategy into operations.

BUSINESS STRATEGY IN ACTION

To see how the balanced scorecard can help us monitor and measure our strategic efforts, let's consider the situation of Astral Pharmaceuticals in the case below (in the Test Yourself section).

Astral has six possible alliances/partnerships/joint ventures it can consider. Let's assume for the time being that all potential business partners line up well with our mission, vision, and values, and that from an analytical perspective, each potential suitor has merit in terms of a market potential, etc. (These assumptions are likely not true, but we will leave the detailed conceptual and analytical evaluations to the reader in the next section.)

Now, let's think about what kind of balanced scorecard will help us measure business partnership success (in whatever form the business partnership ultimately takes). Looking at the four components of the scorecard, we could propose the following initial entries:

- Financial: generate enough profits to accelerate Astral's research agenda
- Internal processes: fully utilize the expertise of the sales force (and keep them busy full-time)
- Learning and growth: develop knowledge and intellectual capital in key therapeutic areas
- Customer: maximize the value of our long-term customer relationships and prevent attrition at (almost) all costs

This is just a start, but we can now look at how the six possible alliances/partnerships satisfy (or not) each of these metrics. Most if not all of these potential partners will positively impact the first three metrics, above. But the fourth one, maintaining and maximizing our long-term customer relationships, is hard to achieve with any of the business partner candidates. In fact, with some partners, we may see exactly the opposite effect: attrition of some of our key customers/accounts.

Thus, we see that a viable strategy depends on finding the right mix of alliances, not just one single path. We cannot assess single partnerships in and of themselves, and we must look at potential opportunities in a broader (market) context.

TEST YOURSELF

Read and analyze the case, Astral Pharmaceuticals, below. Be prepared to respond to and discuss the following questions:

1. Which two (or three) of the six overtures do you think make the most sense for Astral (and in what order)? Consider these not only in the context of fit with your mission, vision, and values, but also consider whether the various potential partners make sense from an analytical perspective (customer/market dynamics, etc.).

2. Now that you've examined the conceptual and analytical phases of strategy with these various potential suitors, which two (or three) do you think make the most sense operationally for Astral? Are these the same two (or three) you identified before? If so, why? If not, why not? What single best overture should Astral then consider if they could only ally with one?

3. Assuming Astral's board approves your (two or three) recommendations above, what scorecard would you use to manage the integration of the new partner firms (Astral and its intended business partners)? Be sure to develop a few—and only a few—customer, internal process, innovation/growth, and financial metrics that would apply. (We've given you a bit of a head start in the previous section.)

4. Using the balanced scorecard you just developed, what key elements of an integration action plan would you propose if you were put in charge of making these new relationships work? For each balanced scorecard perspective, map out what specific objectives, measures, targets, and initiatives you would plan to make this new business relationship work. Remember, each initiative has to have an objective target, align with your objectives in your scorecard, and be measurable/reportable in some quantifiable way

5. Finally, what happens if one of the nonchosen suitors comes along and offers a more compelling deal (financially, etc.)? Or what if two of the suitors who you considered but didn't work with choose to ally to compete against you? Articulate what impacts these types of market disruptions would have on your scorecard and action plans. What contingencies might you plan for in order to ensure higher chances of success?

ASTRAL PHARMACEUTICALS, INC.[4]

Astral Pharmaceuticals is a US-based firm engaged primarily in the discovery, manufacture, and distribution of ethical [physician's prescription required] drugs for the treatment of human illness. Astral presently markets its products in over 100 countries around the world although the bulk of its sales (70%) are in the US.

Astral was founded in 1920 by two University-based medical researchers. The company's first major product, an anti-depressant, was launched successfully in 1929. This established Astral as a leading player in therapeutic compounds for diseases of the central nervous system [CNS], a position that it still holds today.

Over the years, Astral has developed and marketed compounds in several other therapeutic areas. Presently, it participates in eight major areas, making its product line one of the broadest or most diversified in the industry. It plays a significant role in anti-infectives, an area in which most of the major firms have supported products; respiratory, where it shares the bulk of the market with Glaxo and Rhone Poulenc; and Women's Health Care, where it has held a dominant position in oral contraceptives. Astral's major competitors in the CNS area are Glaxo and Pfizer.

Historically, Astral has been a solid performer. Current year revenues reached a record high of $5.2B, of which $4.3B came from ethical pharmaceuticals, and the remainder from infant formula

($0.7B) and animal health ($0.2B). The company also realized revenues of $0.15B from its agricultural products group (not included in the $5.2B).

Over the past decade, the firm has maintained an average net profit margin of roughly 17%. This has been down slightly in the past few years, ranging between 12% and 14%, as government and market pressures have challenged industry margins and forced prices down. The rapid growth of generics has also depressed industry margins. These factors, along with the continued growth of managed care companies, are to continue for the foreseeable future. Thus, Astral, which experienced a compounded annual growth-rate (CAGR) of 18% in revenues and 24% in earnings from operations (EFO) over the past five years, is facing a forecasted CAGR of only 6% in revenue and 10% in EFO for the next five years for its current businesses.

Astral's current performance makes the Company the world's tenth largest pharmaceutical company. There are, however, several problematic aspects to this rosy picture. In the last fiscal year, 48% of Astral's sales, and a greater proportion of profits, came from four compounds. Of these, one (Astral's family of oral contraceptives) is already off patent but has been sustained so far by a strong detailing effort and customer loyalty. The largest product in the line, a Central Nervous System (CNS) compound, will be facing major direct competition for the first time as a large European firm had just had a lower-cost compound with comparable results approved for sale in the US. Astral's remaining two high volume compounds will come off patent in 1997 and 1998.

Astral's R&D efforts have been only limited success recently, and the Astral pipeline of potential new products is thin. The company expects to gain FDA approval for from 3–5 new products in the next five years, but none of these is expected to be a "blockbuster" (annual sales greater than $1.0B).

The company does have a strong, experienced sales force, which is generally assumed to be the largest in the industry. It also has solid manufacturing capability and the capacity to absorb significant growth. R&D expenditures lag behind the industry leaders. Astral currently devotes about 7.5% of sales to R&D while Merck and Pfizer, for example, both presently spend in excess of 11% of sales on R&D.

Astral has made three minor acquisitions in the past several years, each time of a small single product firm with the express intention of filling out the product line. If measured separately, these three acquisitions would have accounted in total for less than 15% of sales in the past year. The company is presently engaged with Lilly in a joint marketing effort for a gastrointestinal compound. This compound was developed by Astral but fit well with Lilly's line and experience in detailing GI drugs.

The Astral Group also includes a relatively small but sound over-the-counter (OTC) division with annual revenues of $0.8B (not included in the $5.2B for the Pharma division). The OTC division has had little success in transferring Astral compounds over to OTC status and derives 3/4 of its revenues from a line of personal care products that were acquired in the `60s.

Astral is also presently a minority investor in two biotech startup situations; Astral was recruited for these projects by a venture capital packager and the firm's direct involvement has been limited.

Astral's involvement in the global marketplace began in the late 40's through a joint venture with the Zambon Group (Italy). This effort is no longer active, and Astral presently drives its worldwide activities internally.

Given the high level of merger and acquisition and joint venture activity in the pharmaceutical industry, it is not surprising that Astral has been sought out frequently by a variety of firms and brokers. At the moment, the company is considering roughly six overtures of various sorts. Management realizes that it cannot pursue all of these simultaneously, even should they all prove to be attractive, and still direct current operations effectively. It is looking, therefore, for a strategic logic for setting priorities and allocating its efforts.

AGRINETICS

Agrinetics, the agricultural products division of Chemtronics, a major British chemical company, has expressed an interest in acquiring Astral's agricultural product group. Agrinetics is presently the fourth largest provider of agricultural products (fertilizers and crop protection compounds) and is looking to grow aggressively. The acquisition of the Astral Agritech line would move it immediately to a strong #2 position (Astral Agritech is presently 7th in global market share).

Agritech was the first non-ethical drug unit added to the Company and was started originally to market several fungicides that had been developed in Astral's labs. The group has experienced steady growth and strong performance over the years, providing the firm with an average EFO of 22% over the past four years.

Chemtronics has indicated that it would be willing to pay a reasonable multiple of current sales for the unit. These funds could be used to accelerate the Company's lagging R&D effort or to pursue high potential acquisitions in the emerging biotech arena.

Chemtronics is a broad range producer of commodity and specialty chemicals. It does not have an ethical pharmaceutical unit but has contracted several of its European facilities out to generic pharmaceutical producers.

HUMANIA

Humania is a pharmaceutical firm based in Sweden. It has specialized in anti-inflammatory products and is a world leader within this therapeutic area. It has had little involvement in any other areas, preferring to license any compounds that it might identify in other treatment areas to other firms for development. Humania has not established a US operation, again preferring to license its compounds to local firms. Presently, both Bristol Myers Squibb and Upjohn are marketing ethical products under license from

Humania. SmithKline Beecham represents several Humania OTC products.

Humania has approached Astral with an offer to license its newest product, an anti-inflammatory that has proven particularly effective in the treatment of viral infections of the joints. The drug is presently #1 in the European market but has not been submitted to the US Food and Drug Administration (FDA) for approval.

Under Humania license proposal, Astral would assume responsibility for the admission of the drug to the US market. It would provide Humania with an upfront fee for access to the technology and would absorb any costs attendant to gaining FDA approval. Once approved, Astral would market the drug under a "Humania Astral" label and would provide Humania with an ongoing licensing fee.

Astral presently has only a limited presence in the anti-inflammatory area (two minor compounds for treating muscle stress) and no promising compounds in its pipeline.

BIONAMICS

Bionamics is a California-based biotech start-up launched four years ago by three former Genentech scientists who have been doing promising work on an Alzheimer's prevention product utilizing a novel but as yet unproved gene-splicing approach.

Bionamics received investigational new drug (IND) approval two years ago but have now hit a financial "wall." The necessary research protocols to proceed through Phases I and II will require a major investment (estimated to be in the range of $215M). If successful, it is anticipated that the product would be a major blockbuster, easily achieving annual sales well in excess of $2.0B.

The owners of Bionamics have been working with a venture capital packager who has approached Astral. The initial proposal is for an alliance in which Bionamics would bring the product and the researchers and Astral would provide the necessary risk financing as well as manufacturing and marketing resources. The president of Bionamics would head up the effort with an advisory committee made up of equal numbers of representatives from both parties. Bionamics and Astral would each own 50% of the finished product.

Astral is headquartered in New Jersey and maintains a sales office in Los Angeles.

TSUJITA PHARMACEUTICALS

Tsujita is the third largest firm in Japan. Until this time, it has had little exposure or experience outside of the Pacific Rim. There have been indications recently, however, that its president, who was educated in the United States, aspires to having Tsujita be the first Japanese pharmaceutical to have a major presence in this country.

Tsujita has approached Astral with a proposal that the two firms enter into a joint venture to co-develop a promising new compound for the control of cardiovascular disease due to hypertension. The initial work on the compound has been done in Tsujita's labs, and preliminary results suggest that the compound may reduce significantly the potential for cardiac trauma for patients with diagnosed hypertension.

There are indications that the compound is potentially unstable and that the formulation process is likely to be difficult and expensive. This will undoubtedly result in a high cost per dose for the drug if and when it is approved. Thus, Tsujita, which is confident with regard to its R&D capabilities, is looking to Astral to provide manufacturing and marketing expertise.

Both the Japanese and US markets are likely to continue to evidence strong demand for cardiovascular (CV) products, and the proposed compound has breakthrough possibilities. In the US, the CV market has been shifting strongly to generics, which now account for about 56% of total sales. Astral presently has a limited involvement in the CV area with three well-established but relatively low volume compounds available. All three have several years remaining on patent.

UNIVERSITY MEDICAL CENTER

A distinguished team of academic researchers at a major University Medical Center in the Midwest have recently presented a series of papers at medical conferences describing breakthrough experimental work in the treatment of small cell cancer. Their proposed treatment protocol involves a balanced combination of chemotherapy utilizing new formulations with a revolutionary biotech product that would be administered orally.

The research has been funded to date by a series of government grants, mainly from the US National Institutes of Health (NIH), and two sizable grants from the Robert Wood Johnson Foundation. As the project moves to the preparation of an Investigational New Drug Application (IND) for submission to the FDA and to the launching of an extensive clinical trial process, considerable funding from new sources will be required. Also, the university, a private institution, has most of the financial problems confronting such institutions. It sees this compound as providing it with an entree into a new, long run revenue stream but lacks the expertise to undertake a full commercialization effort. Thus, the university is looking for a partner.

Through alumni contacts, the University has approached Astral with a proposal to establish a partnership for completing the project. The university would provide the concept and the lead researchers and Astral would provide the expertise needed to move the compound through the regulatory and product launch phases. The partners would share equally in any commercial success.

MICROPHARMA

Micropharma is a small firm located in the Boston area. It has just received FDA approval for its first product, a new non-insulin compound for the control of childhood diabetes. The compound has considerable market potential; it has also opened up a promising new area for further research. Micropharma sees itself primarily as a research shop and intends to concentrate its efforts on pursuing further research on derivatives and extensions of its initial studies.

Micropharma has already made arrangements to outsource the manufacture of the compound and is now looking for a marketing partner. It has indicated an interest in exploring a sales and marketing contract with Astral. Under the proposed arrangement, Astral would be the sole US representative for the product and would be compensated on an agreed-upon percentage of sales basis. Micropharma would not engage in any direct sales or marketing efforts but would work through Astral.

Astral does not presently have any products for the treatment of diabetes in either children or adults.

KEY POINTS TO REMEMBER

- The third piece of strategic thinking comprises *operations*, or the key levers that help us translate our vision into action. However, creating a list of actions is easy. The key is to create an action plan that can be *measured* with a sense of what *targets* make sense.
- A *balanced scorecard*, which balances our measurable actions and effects on our *customers, internal processes, financials,* and our own firm's/people's *innovation and growth* can help us monitor and measure our effectiveness at taking our vision into action.
  - *Customer* metrics should focus on customer impact: satisfaction, repeat customer visits/sales, customer attrition, and customer feedback on our operations/interactions with them.
  - *Financial* metrics should help us understand how well our strategy is being put into operations from a "dollars and sense" perspective. Are we giving our shareholders a fair return? Even if we're taking a loss, are we managing it? Are we decreasing inventories, cutting costs, raising margins, etc.?
  - But remember, financial measures aren't necessarily just those you see on an income statement. Industry-specific ones, like medical loss ratios for insurance companies or gross margin return on inventory (GMROI) for retailers, can also be useful financial measures.
  - *Internal process* metrics, which are often confused with financial ones, should measure how well we do our "day jobs" in terms of our normal operating procedures. For example, in retail, "shrinkage" is a measure of how much inventory is lost (or potentially stolen) as a percentage of total inventory (either in units or dollar

terms). While this may appear to be a financial metric, it actually points to internal loss prevention processes and controls (critical for retailers), and if shrinkage is too high, store security operations may need to be enhanced. For manufacturers, assembly-line metrics like cycle times, down times, defects per thousand, etc. are useful process metrics

  ○ *Innovation and growth* metrics should focus on how we, both the firm and people, learn and grow as a result of our strategy. Are our employees leaving, or do we challenge them (and compensate them) enough to stay with us? Do we offer training to help our employees learn new skills, or do we just expect them to do the same tasks for years? If we develop products, are we just refining the same basic concepts, or are we truly creating new, innovative products?

- *Action plans* should be created for each balanced scorecard component, and each plan should comprise key objectives, measures, targets, and initiatives for each scorecard measure. In this way, specific tasks/initiatives are planned (or stopped) in support of our key metrics and measurements.

- Don't make the mistake of creating thousands of metrics …and thousands of initiatives! Over-tasking is a common effect of putting a scorecard in place. Make sure your scorecard is simple, not too expansive, and focuses on a few key observable measurements. This will make action plans easier to create and initiatives easier to delegate and to achieve.

- Finally, be sure to consider what might happen if things go *wrong.* Develop action plans and *contingency plans.* Have an idea how you may react, change internal operations, etc. *before* hurdles get in the way of our strategic milestones.

PART IV

PUTTING IT ALL TOGETHER: IMPLEMENTING A STRATEGY

CHAPTER 10

Completing the Process— Developing the Strategy

INTRODUCTION

And the next day, Moses sat to judge the people who stood by Moses from morning until night. And when his kinsman Jethro had seen all things that Moses did among the people, Jethro said:

> What is it that thou doest among the people? Why sittest thou alone, and all the people wait from morning till night.

And Moses answered him:

> The people come to me to seek the judgment of God. And when any great controversy falleth out among them, they come to me to judge between them, and to show the precepts of God, and His laws.

But Jethro said:

> What thou doest is not good. Thou are spent with foolish labor, both thou and this people that is with thee: the business is above thy strength. Thou alone canst not bear it. But hear my words and counsels, and God shall be with thee.
>
> Be thou to the people in those things that pertain to God, to bring their words to him, and to show the people the ceremonies and the manner of worshiping, and the way wherein they ought to walk, and the work they ought to do.

> And provide out of all the people able persons, such as fear God, in whom there is truth, and that hate avarice, and appoint of them rulers of thousands, and of hundreds, and of fifties, and of tens, who may judge the people at all times.
>
> And when any great matter soever shall fall out, let them refer it to thee, and let them judge the lesser matters only: that so it may be lighter for thee, the burden thus being shared out unto others. If thou doest this, thou shalt fulfill the commandment of God, and shalt be able to bear his precepts: and all this people shall return to their places with peace.

And when Moses heard this, he did all things that Jethro had suggested to him.[1]

This familiar passage from the Book of Exodus is often cited as providing the rationale for the delegation of authority, for span of control, for distributed leadership, for training and development, and for all the other elements of formal organization. Moses may well be a great leader, but his strengths clearly lay in articulating and celebrating mission, values, and vision, and not in developing effective strategies to transform these into reality. After all, he and "these people that are with thee" had been, and would continue, wandering in the desert for many years.

Jethro's (who is undoubtedly the world's first management consultant) message to Moses is clear. It is not enough to be a visionary—and you certainly cannot do it all yourself! And if you try, by sitting all day while everyone waits for you to make every decision and resolve every issue, everything will come to a grinding halt in the desert, and your vision will never be achieved!

Jethro then goes on to advise Moses as to what he should be doing as the leader: analyze and assess the challenges in the external environment; assemble and organize your capabilities and resources, especially your human capital; use your vision to identify and order the major projects and milestones; anticipate the problems that may occur along the way; and prepare and implement your strategic action plans. In other words, become a *Strategos*—a strategic thinker!

"Ok," you say. "This sounds good, but advice is cheap. How do you do it? I've got all the pieces: conceptual, analytical, operational. How do I put it together in a Strategy? What should my strategy look like, what should it contain?"

WHAT'S AHEAD

In this chapter, you will learn:
- The basic principles, the three fundamental questions, of *folding back* to determine the timing and sequencing of the key *milestones* in achieving your vision
- The Third KEY to Strategic Thinking—the complete FOLDING BACK mindmap
- How to create your *strategy on a page* as the Fourth KEY to Strategic Thinking

and as the basis for communicating and monitoring the implementation of your strategy
- The requirements of a comprehensive *strategic action plan*
- A final summary of the overall *Strategic Thought Process*

IN THE REAL WORLD

Your Division of a major educational and consulting services organization includes 11 distinct "products," ranging from extensive executive development programs for senior executives to customized strategy formulation consultations for individual firms to general managerial training for middle managers to state-of-the-art update conferences in specialized functional and technical subjects. Each of these intellectual products has its own distinct markets, customer sets, technologies, and methodologies. This has led you to organize your division by product-market category (for example, Finance for Nonfinancial Managers; Strategic Leadership for Not-for-Profit Executives; Public Sector Management Systems; and so on) with a key manager heading up each of these areas.

You expect each of your 11 unit managers to develop and execute effectively a winning strategy in his/her particular market area or line of business and to do so in such a way as to remain the market leader in both quality and innovation in each market sector. You also expect each unit to meet its economic goals, and you have agreed to overall economic targets with your senior management.

At the same time, you realize that the dividing lines across product-market sectors are vague and that there is much potential overlap in terms of potential external customers (a not-for-profit executive may choose to attend a private sector general management program to obtain a broader perspective) and of internal competencies and expertise (your financial consulting staff may be equally comfortable with public and private sector finance issues or with cost accounting and capital budgeting techniques).

Thus, you need both a strong integrated Divisional strategy and a series of strong individual unit strategies as well as the means to monitor and coordinate the entire array so as to maximize synergy and avoid conflict and wasteful redundancy.[2] How can you achieve consistency and comparability across line-of-business strategies while allowing for local flexibility and creativity within individual unit strategies? How can you get your unit managers to function as a strategic team while aggressively pursuing opportunities in their separate lines of business? **Sounds like a job for the true *Strategos*!**

THE KEY CONCEPTS

Let's review what we have done up to now. We have fully developed our concept of our organization, its mission, values, and vision, in terms of its past, its present, and its desired future. We have defined our aspirations and described, in vivid terms, what the fulfillment of those aspirations would look like.

Next, we asked "What's going on?" both in the external environment (the world outside our organization) and in our internal environment (our capabilities and resources, our structures and processes) that might materially affect our ability to reach our targets. We tested the feasibility of our vision and used our analysis to identify the gaps, both in the market and in our organization, that we would have to focus our strategy on closing.

Finally, we focused on our operating processes and procedures in order to build the delivery system, the "factory," needed to produce the outputs (the results) called for by our vision and to monitor our performance so that we might continue to adapt our efforts in real time in response to experience.

We have, in fact, set the stage for creating our strategy and moving to implementation—to action. We are now ready to use our vision, our chosen future, in the context of our analysis and our operational systems and structures to choose our strategy—to answer the final question we posed back in chapter 5: **What do we have to do to get there?**

Folding Back—The Fundamental Questions

When we introduced the key concept of *Folding Back* in chapter 2, we argued that our image of the desired or chosen future, our vision, provided the best vantage point or perspective, given current information, from which to chart the path connecting the present to the future (see exhibit I). Before we could do so, however, we had to gather and synthesize that current information—the best intelligence that we could assemble about the feasibility of our vision in the context of external and internal realities. With that effort now behind us, let's turn to the fundamental questions of *Folding Back*.

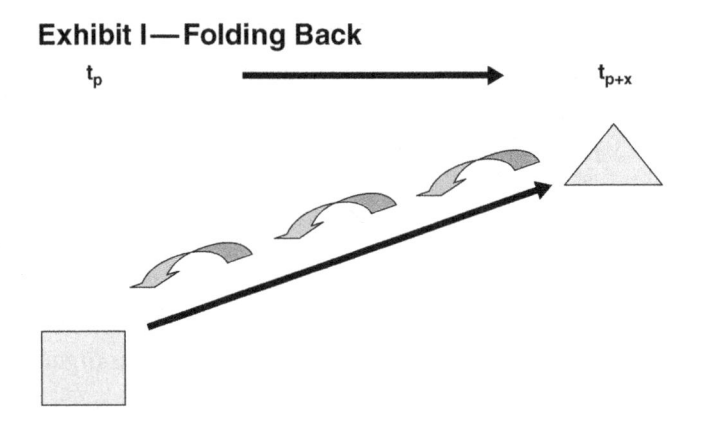

Exhibit I—Folding Back

t_p → t_{p+x}

VI. What are the major stages/phases that we will have to accomplish along the way?[3]

Perhaps the most difficult aspect of moving from vision to strategy is to resist the temptation to try to do everything at once—to seek to implement or achieve the entire vision immediately. True visions as we have seen are complex and can involve many components both in marketplace performance and in internal organization and operation. It would be foolish to presume that we could put all these elements in place simultaneously. Moreover, there is likely to be an interdependency among components such that it is necessary to have one in place before moving to another or that getting one stage of a process done first will facilitate the implementation of the next phase.

Just as strategic thinking is a process, strategy implementation is a process and the challenge is to find the sequencing or staging that best uses resources and provides the momentum needed to complete the entire process. This does not mean that we should always order the components in terms of importance or difficulty. The issue is to do "first things first." Using the platform of the future, our vision, we can see clearly what is foundational, what the "first things" are that will lay the necessary bases for later accomplishing the important and the difficult. Even better, we can see where completion of one phase sets up the leverage and synergy necessary for the next stage. Finally, each of these stages or phases, which we have termed *milestones*, serves as valuable checkpoints for evaluating and, if appropriate, modifying and adjusting our strategy.[4]

VII. What obstacles are likely to get in our way?

We have noted earlier that our sense of vision involves the pursuit of achievements that would not come in the normal course of events if we were simply content to pursue business as usual or to "roll with the flow." We would expect that progress along our charted strategy would not be a simple, orderly progression from here to there. In fact, we would expect, and we should anticipate, that we are likely to encounter any number of obstacles (roadblocks, detours, potholes, distractions, and a universe of other man-made and natural disasters) at every step of the way.

Thus, rather than waiting for such events to occur and then hoping to be able to respond and not lose confidence or momentum, we aggressively seek to identify and prepare for them. In fact, these obstacles are the very challenges that we identified in the Analytical phase and are the *gaps* between our current state and our desired future state that our strategy must speak to and close.

The example that we gave in chapter 2 of getting the renovations of newly rented space done in time to secure a Certificate of Occupancy in time to open the new facility on the targeted date demonstrates the relationship between milestones and obstacles. The C of O is an essential milestone in this strategic project, and we all know that public agencies move at their own speed, so this is an obstacle or potential delay that we must anticipate and plan for in our strategy.

Other examples of such obstacles that occur in the normal course of implementing typical strategies might include:

- **Lack of capacity**: creating the need to construct a new facility in order to have adequate capacity and to employ state-of-the-art technology in producing a breakthrough product;
- **Absence of demand**: requiring that we create public awareness of, and demand for, environmentally safe materials before launching a new product line;
- **Resource scarcity**: recognizing the necessity of establishing alliances with suppliers and distributors in order to ensure a steady flow and availability of product;
- **Lack of credibility**: the need to understand the issues that the public cares about and to gain credibility and visibility on those issues before running against an incumbent for public office;

In each of these examples, the obstacles or barriers are those things that either must be removed or overcome, or put in place or done, to reach the next milestone.

Note here that we have focused on knowable or anticipatable obstacles that would predictably occur in the staging or phasing out of a complex strategy. Experience tells us that obstacles and potholes are likely to occur for which we can neither control nor predict the timing, severity, or nature of their impact. In fact, the critics of rational planning disciplines point to the potential of such events (natural disasters, scientific breakthroughs, political unrest, and so on) to dismantle the best of plans.

We acknowledge that even the best strategic thought process, the most thorough analytical effort, cannot identify or predict the timing and occurrence of all likely disruptive events. It is our position, however, that the fact that the probability or the timing of such events may be uncontrollable and not perfectly knowable does not remove them from the purview of the strategist. We believe that there are two broad classes of such events:

- **Those events that are knowable (can be expected) but not predictable (schedulable)**: For example, we know that hurricanes and tornadoes will occur, and we can even narrow down the range of dates within which each is most likely as well as hypothesize about likely location, but we cannot, with current knowledge, predict the exact date, intensity, duration, and path of a given storm. Similarly, we know that the economy (national or global) will be cyclical in nature, as will the stock markets, but we cannot predict with certainty the timing or the amplitude of the swings—nor always anticipate the events that will trigger the emotional and analytical responses that launch the next swing.[5]

These unknowable aspects do not prevent us from knowing that such events will occur nor do they prevent us from developing and holding in readiness *contingency plans* to be enacted *when* such events do occur—and they will.[6]

- **Those events whose occurrence is neither expected nor predicted**: Here we get to the truly unknowable. We cannot define in advance the event so we cannot predict its occurrence. We can, however, say that such events will occur. Our sense, also, is that the number and likelihood of such events is small or can be reduced to a limited, although unknowable, set by rigorous application of the analytical tools outlined in chapter 7. What would be left would be the truly unknowable, and even here we can anticipate that such will occur and will exist.

What does this mean for our strategy? It means, first, that it should be *robust*, that is, grounded in a strong consensus on mission, values, and vision, and buttressed by rigorous, ongoing analysis, and an alert, flexible operating system so that it can withstand major shocks. It means, second, that it should be *resilient*, that is, it should have the flexibility and adaptability to be able to question current arrangements and to move quickly in response to changing conditions without losing sight of either the mission and core values or the vision.[7]

VIII. What are we going to do to overcome these obstacles?

Here we come, at last, to what might properly be called *strategic planning*. We have used our chosen future (our Vision) to identify and order the critical milestones along a timeline—to define our Strategy. We have found the potential obstacles and events that might prevent us from reaching each milestone and have determined the gaps that have to be bridged. We now need to move to implementation. We need a *strategic action plan*.[8]

Our strategic action plan provides the guidance and direction for implementing our chosen strategy. It specifies, step by step, who has to do what when in order to move along the timeline—along the intended strategy.

Note that, while our overall strategic thought process has encompassed the entire timeframe of our vision, and all of the milestones and obstacles along the way, our strategic action plan can and should focus on defining the actions and decisions that need to be undertaken to achieve the first milestone—to overcome the initial obstacles.

The first milestone becomes the initial checkpoint from which we can assess our progress and make whatever adaptations and changes in our strategy that our experience to date suggests are appropriate. Each milestone provides the opportunity to restart or recycle our strategic thought process and to develop the action plan for the next phase.

Taken together, these three questions constitute the process of *Folding Back*, of moving from our vision of a desired future to the specification of the steps that have to be taken in the present to achieve that future. Thus, *Folding Back* is the Third KEY to Strategic Thinking. The process is shown in Exhibit II. Note that this is not a snapshot at a point in time nor is it a moving picture. It is in effect the mindmap of the *Strategos*—holding the actual present and the desired future simultaneously in mind.

Exhibit II—The Third KEY—The Complete Mindmap FOLDING BACK charts the vision

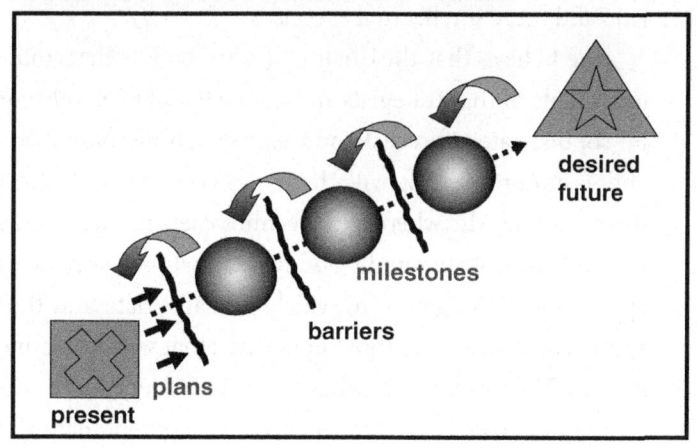

In the next two sections, we will provide detailed guidance on the critical elements of a comprehensive Strategy and on the requirements of an effective action plan. These two components will complete our development of the strategic thought process.

Developing the Strategy—"Strategy on a Page"

We turn now to the actual articulation of the strategy that we have been laying the groundwork for throughout the entire strategic thought process. To be effective and meaningful, a sound strategy must be both comprehensive, covering all of the aspects of our organization and of the marketplace that have to come together for us to succeed, and readily understandable, so that it gives clear guidance to all members of our organization so they can play their parts effectively without limiting their flexibility and creativity.

To be credible and practical, strategic action plans, much like the overall strategic thought process, have to be prepared largely by the leaders and managers who will be responsible for implementing, monitoring, and adapting them. Such plans should be brief in order to be accepted and acted upon rather than set aside as unrealistic and mere intellectual exercises.

We believe that the quality of a strategy is determined by the judgments of the strategists and not by the illusion of rigor fostered by sophisticated forecasts and extrapolations based on numbers and assumptions that will change as soon as we begin to act on them. In a world where new technologies, models, and analytical methods propagate rapidly and disseminate at warp speed, it is the application of judgment to widely available data and the ability to secure commitment to those judgments that will determine strategic success. Thus, in the end, while we believe deeply in the importance of rigorous analysis, it is leadership and judgment that will make the difference (see Exhibit III).

Exhibit III—On Strategic Analysis

- **All players have comparable access to the same macro data – the same conceptual and analytical frameworks.**
- **Therefore, they have access to the "conventional wisdom" of the feild.**
- **The challenge is what to do with the information.**
- **How does it yield a winning strategy for the individual organization?**

The level of detail and specificity in an effective strategy lies somewhere between the graphic timeline shown on our mindmap and the exhaustive strategic planning reports full of endless task lists and multiyear quantitative projections traditionally prepared by strategic planning departments and external consultants.[9] The latter, given their volume and the time that it takes to prepare them, are often out of date by the time they are promulgated and end up as doorstops.

We prefer an approach that we have dubbed "Strategy on a Page." This is the Fourth KEY to Strategic Thinking—the ability to capture the essence of your strategy, with all its critical elements on a single page. We believe that this approach facilitates communication in and across units within an organization as well as between the organization and its publics or stakeholders. We also believe that it facilitates ongoing monitoring and assessment and the flexibility needed to make changes in real time on the basis of evolving experience. Our approach is summarized in exhibit IV and its key elements discussed briefly below.

Exhibit IV—Strategy on a Page
what are we going to do to get where we want to be?

- **strategic intent**
- **elements**
  - Program/activity/product mix
  - Marketing (context, competitive dynamics, clients/customers)
  - Facilities
  - Organizational renewal/R&D
  - Financial
  - Human resources
  - Management/organization/governance
- **critical success factors**

As we can see, the purpose of any strategy is to answer the question:

What Are We Going to Do to Get Where We Want to Be?

The response to this question may be divided into three main components; these are:

1. *Strategic Intent*: What do we intend to do, to accomplish within the current *strategic cycle*[10]; in this sense, strategic intent refers to that portion of the vision that we are committing to achieve in the next cycle or to the progress toward the ultimate vision or BHAG that we are proposing to make in the

next cycle. Our strategic intent provides the baseline against which to assess actual performance and is the basis for exercising accountability;

2. **Elements**: the strategist has essentially seven major *elements* or components of the organization which are under his/her control or influence and which can be manipulated and acted upon in formulating the overall strategy; these are:

    - *Program/Activity/Product Mix*: What are the things that we actually intend to do or to provide to the market in the next cycle or plan period? What is our intended portfolio of offerings to potential customers? This should include consideration of our current mix as well as offerings to be added and to be dropped.

    - *Marketing (context, competitive dynamics, client/customers)*: Our strategy must incorporate a clear and accurate sense of how our relevant marketplace is structured and how it operates and behaves—and how our strategy both accommodates and exploits this.

        Thus, we need to understand the evolution of our field or industry. Is it growing, stagnating, shrinking—domestically or globally? Is it becoming more or less regulated? Is it driven primarily by technology and innovation, by pricing, by customer service?

        What is the nature and intensity of competition within our field or industry? How do we define or identify potential "customers?"[11] How do those customers make their decisions? What constitutes a winning *value proposition* from the customer's perspective?

    - *Facilities*: What will be needed by way of capacity, equipment, space, and so on to support our strategy? What are our technology needs? What are our overall infrastructure needs?

    - *Organizational Renewal/R&D*: In addition to competing effectively in real time, our strategy must include maintaining

and growing our readiness to compete in the future.[12] Thus, we need to ask what we are doing to maintain the vitality, commitment, and effectiveness of our members and what we are going to stay at or ahead of the curve in product/process innovation and quality.
- *Financial*: We need to understand fully the economic model of our firm and our industry. We need to translate our strategy into economic or financial terms in order to determine whether it is within our means and to resource it properly. Finally, we need to express our strategy in terms of the expected flows of revenues and costs so that we can make judgments about whether to pursue the strategy and can then monitor its performance in operation.[13]
- *Human Resources*: Our strategy should include a careful delineation of the human resources needed in terms of competences, availability, capacity, numbers, and so on. It should assess where our current human resource complement is either fully utilized by current commitments or not fully prepared in terms of new or enhanced competences and skills required by the strategy. It should also include the necessary recruitment, training, and performance management programs.[14]
- *Management, Organization, Governance*: Finally, our strategy needs to be clear on how we are going to organize ourselves to operate—what roles, functions, positions will be needed and what the structure or table of organization will look like. We need to define our operating procedures—will we be organized and operate as teams, as functions, as territories, etc.? How will we communicate and interact? How will decisions be made and by whom?

3. **Critical Success Factors:** the final component of our "strategy on a page" is the identification of the *critical success factors (CSFs)*, those things that we absolutely must get right, that must occur, that must be put in place if our strategy is

to succeed. These could range from something as simple as getting a license to do business in a particular jurisdiction to avoiding injuries to key players throughout the season to establishing a clear differentiation on the customers' mind of the additional value of our product on service grounds when our competitors have identical technical characteristics. We would argue that this set of CSFs should be small but powerful; perhaps no more than three to five for a given strategy. If the strategy is well-designed both internally and in terms of its appropriateness for the marketplace, its requirements for success should be expressible in a limited but highly leveraged number of central points. Again, doing so makes both monitoring and adjustment easier and establishes a clear foundation for accountability.

So how does this work in practice? Remember our Director of executive development programs for a major educational and consulting organization at the beginning of this chapter? His response to the challenge that we laid out for him, *How can you get your unit managers to function as a strategic team while aggressively pursuing opportunities in their separate lines of business?* was as follows:

> Once a year or so, I would take my entire management team off for a two to three day retreat away from the office—very much in the tradition of strategic retreats. We would use some of that time to review our performance, collectively and by unit for the past year, but we did most of this by prior circulation of reports—and, of course, I had individual performance reviews with each of my unit managers separately from the retreat. We spent most of our time sharing our impressions of our shared marketplace and how it was changing and in exploring the unique aspects of each of the unit's markets. We would end by setting a collective vision and broad goals for the Division for the coming year, including

defining such policies, practices, and objectives that every one of the units would have to achieve.

As a last step, I would then require each of the unit managers, with their teams, to prepare and submit to me within a week his/her "strategy on a page" for the unit, including specific performance targets, timetables, budgets, and so on. We would then take another day, back at the office, to combine and integrate these, to identify and resolve conflicts, to look for synergies, and so on. These then became our operating unit strategies for the coming year.

The message to all of my managers was as follows:

> You should treat your "strategy on a page" as a living document and as the basis for conversation during the year. I expect to be able to call you into my office on short notice with your strategy for a real-time update, to be able to ask, "How are you doing against your projected timeline? What's working and what's not working? What can I do to help?"

Notice two things: first, I am not trying to play "gotcha" or to micromanage; I just want to make certain that we are always acting from a strategic perspective and that we maintain the focus and the flexibility to make course corrections in real time. Second, this is the basis for a dialogue, for identifying issues, opportunities, and special circumstances, and not for exerting control. I have to be willing to listen to the insights of my managers and to make adjustments on the basis of their inputs, even if it means waiving or relaxing some of the conditions that we had agreed earlier every unit had to satisfy.

Preparing the Strategic Action Plan

With our Strategy on a Page in hand, the last step that remains is to translate it into the specific step-by-step *action plan* that we will follow; the components of an effective action plan are shown in exhibit V.

Exhibit V—The Action Plan

Who is going to do what? When? How are we going to know how we are doing?

- For each "stage" or "phase" or "milestone," develop a plan that will overcome or minimize the identified obstacles to achievement.
- The plans answer the question: *How will we achieve, in the chosen time frame, the Central Success Factors (CSF) needed to ensure our success?*

Good action plans include the following:

- **Objectives:** What, in measurable terms, do we want to achieve?
- **Challenges:** What are the significant challenges we face, internally and externally, to achieving these objectives?
- **Resources:** What resources will be required to implement our plan? What do we have on hand? What do we need to acquire? And how will we acquire them?
- **Participants:** Who will have a role to play and what are these roles? How will we recruit, prepare, or free people up to participate?
- **Plans:** What are the steps? What's the timing? Who will do what? When? What will motivate the participants? How will we monitor and assess progress and make adjustments? How will we assess achievement?

BUSINESS STRATEGY IN ACTION

In the case below, David Stanley, the newly appointed director of marketing for Graham, Smith & Bendel, a high-level management consulting firm, has been charged by his boss, Aaron Nettles, with implementing a new strategic approach for the firm. Stanley, who recently succeeded William Graham, the founder of the firm, as its CEO, had, as one of his first acts, instituted a far-reaching reorganization in order to respond to what he saw as major changes in the nature of the consulting business, particularly in the way that firms sought to develop new business. Nettles perceived a need for the firm to become more proactive in marketing its services and felt there was a need for someone to "shake things up," especially with the senior consultants whom he saw as comfortable and set in their ways. Nettles selected Stanley, a newcomer to the firm, to drive this process and to chair the new business committee, which was supposed to generate new strategies, encourage cross-selling, and so on.

Although undertaking the task with high hopes and considerable energy, Stanley has found the going slow and possibly treacherous. His senior colleagues, whose representatives sit on the committee, have been modest in their support and their representatives have been notable for their spotty attendance at meetings and passive engagement when they do attend. Stanley knows that Nettles has great expectations for the committee and is likely to expect visible results in the near future.

How would you advise Stanley to proceed? How, if at all, should he modify the approach that he has taken to date? Can you help him develop his Strategy on a Page and implement an effective strategic action plan?

TEST YOURSELF

Read and analyze the case, Graham, Smith & Bendel LLP., below. Be prepared to respond to and discuss the following question:

1. Develop your Strategy on a Page for implementing the cross-selling concept. Prepare a strategic action plan for putting your strategy into effect; be specific about such thinks as:

    - Specific actions and the time frame for each
    - How and why change will occur
    - What your role will be

- Who will participate in the planning and implementation
- How will you overcome resistance

GRAHAM, SMITH & BENDEL LLP[15]

Graham, Smith & Bendel is a highly respected management consulting firm. GSB has an impressive list of past and present clients, and for more than 30 years, under the direction of William Graham, has been a profitable but conservative consulting firm. Headquartered in London, GSB had established fully staffed branch offices in New York, Paris, and Tokyo during the 90s in order to serve the growing global needs of its long-standing clients.

> Our fees are higher than our competitors' (Graham said), but our clients know we will not take on an assignment unless we have the expertise to do it right. We are cautious adding staff. We bring them along slowly until we are confident that they have proved themselves ready.

While competitors expanded rapidly during the late 1990s, GSB refused to add inexperienced staff. They frequently turned down assignments rather than add "unproven" staff. As a result, the mid-2000s found GSB with solid profits but slow growth and a declining market share.

At the time of his retirement two years ago, 11 functions reported directly to Graham. Basic consulting services were grouped in five departments. Each was headed by a senior consultant, who reported to Graham. In addition, six service departments also reported to the president. Before his retirement, Graham named Aaron Nettles as his replacement. Nettles, 59, had been with the firm for 27 years and was Director of consulting projects, dealing with marketing.

AARON NETTLES, PRESIDENT

Nettles described his feelings on succeeding William Graham as President and commented on his style as compared to that of his predecessor and mentor:

> Sir William [Graham had been designated a Knight of the British Empire by HRH Queen Elizabeth II in 1990] was a consultant's consultant. He continued to head up a number of our key account projects even while running the business. His secret was his ability to find good people, groom them slowly, and then give them almost complete freedom to do their job. Once he felt you were ready, he told you explicitly what objectives he wanted met, listened, altered them if you made a good case, and then gave you autonomy. With his highly decentralized style and his many talents, he probably could have had 50 people reporting to him.

Nettles went on to explain that, though he respected Graham, he was neither comfortable with Graham's style nor content with slow growth. Within six months, he acquired two smaller consulting firms. One, Executive Recruiting and Placement (ERP), was well regarded as a management search firm, operating on a regional basis from Los Angeles. The second, Arista, Inc., specialized in sophisticated research and engineering studies. With its headquarters in Frankfort, Germany, Arista had a growing reputation in high technology and in the power and transportation industries. As Nettles noted with regard to these acquisition:

> ERP and Arista were firsts for us. While we have offices and do business around the world, our growth and expansion until now has been internally generated and grounded in our roots in the UK. This was our first major effort to integrate established non-British firms into our culture.

Heartened by what he saw to be the initial success of these two acquisitions, Nettles next acquired Filer Associates, a Paris-based market research firm about three months later. Filer, highly regarded for the quality and integrity of their work, had become overextended and resisted laying off personnel during recent slow periods. As a result, they were close to bankruptcy when they agreed to join GSB.

Although all three acquisitions were made by exchange of stock, Nettles felt that the firm would have to accelerate its growth and generate more volume and profits. As he stated,

> We have an excellent reputation and great opportunities to grow. Mr. Graham built an outstanding group of people but never really tried to capitalize it; his view was that our sales efforts should be as 'professional' as an MD. I believe we must seek to make fuller use of the talents of our three new divisions, and we have to get more synergy out of our existing groups.

REORGANIZATION

After the Filer acquisition three months ago, Nettles announced a major reorganization. Three long-service GSB consultants, Michael Shamtun, George Reldan, and Patricia Leon, were named vice presidents and put in charge of groups that had hitherto reported directly to the president. In addition, several service activities were divided into smaller departments.

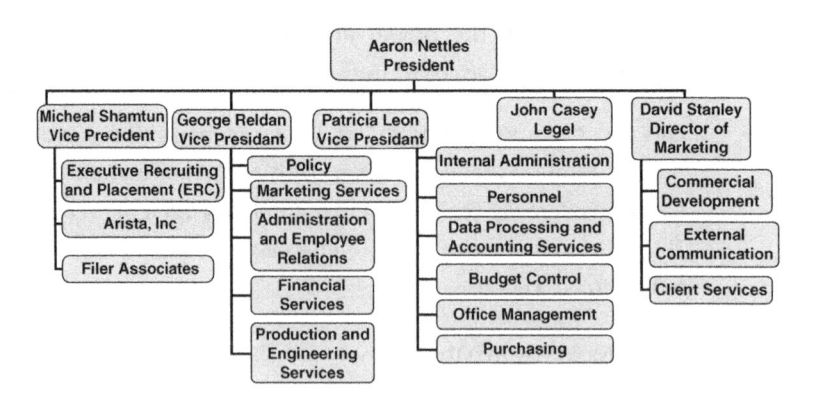

```
                          Aaron Nettles
                            President
   ┌──────────┬──────────────┬──────────────┬──────────────┬──────────────┐
Micheal     George        Patricia        John Casey    David Stanley
Shamtun     Reldan         Leon            Legel        Director of
Vice        Vice           Vice                         Marketing
Precident   Presidant    Presidant
   │           │             │               │               │
Executive   Policy      Internal        Commercial
Recruiting  Marketing   Administration  Development
and         Services
Placement               Personnel       External
(ERC)       Administration              Communication
            and Employee
Arista, Inc Relations   Data Processing Client Services
                        and Accounting
Filer       Financial   Services
Associates  Services
                        Budget Control
            Production
            and         Office Management
            Engineering
            Services    Purchasing
```

Nettles explained his reasoning for the reorganization:

> I want to maintain our decentralized structure, but I also want more coordination among key departments and more time to devote personally to key accounts. When we get a project it usually falls within the scope of one of our five consulting departments (policy, marketing, administration, finance, or production and engineering). It is assigned to a senior consultant from that area and he or she builds a project team. They may draw on people from other areas by checking with their department heads. This works pretty well but with Reldan, who has worked previously in our financial services and policy practices, heading up all five groups—he can save me a lot of time overseeing the makeup of key project teams and balancing workloads.
>
> I also expect Reldan to get more business from our current customers. Frequently, for example, while working on a financial project with a client, the potential for a marketing or personnel project will emerge. In the past, our people were virtually conditioned not to seek such a project for another group within our firm. Mr. Graham felt this was "solicitation" and not ethical. "If the client needs more work and feels we can handle it," he used to say, "then they will invite us to make a proposal." We have missed too many opportunities this way.
>
> Also, bringing in these new units gives us a perfect opportunity to shake things up a bit. We have been rather set in our ways in our principal practice areas for a long time, and this should enable us to breathe some new life into the firm without directly criticizing anyone.

THE MARKETING FUNCTION

To assist Reldan and Shamtun in marketing GSB services, Nettles named David Stanley to the new position of director of marketing. Stanley was a relative newcomer at GSB, having been brought in less than two years ago by Nettles. Stanley, at 37, had been a director of marketing for a small consulting firm before accepting Nettles's offer to join GSB.

Since joining GSB, Stanley has butted heads with some of the firm's veteran consultants. A few have complained to Nettles that Stanley doesn't really understand GSB's business or clients and that he is trying to drive change without taking the time to understand what does and doesn't work at GSB. George Reldan has been a particularly tough critic, saying that Stanley is arrogant and doesn't belong in the job. Nettles regards these complaints as proof of the need to reconsider some of GSB's habits and traditions; he remarked:

> I am convinced that Stanley, and the skills and perspectives that he brings, has the potential to make a real contribution to the Firm. And, realistically, the firm needs someone to "shake things up." Stanley is an outsider—that's good. But this firm has always been slow to accept newcomers in all of our practice areas. Many of the practice heads see their areas as independent business, almost fiefdoms, and seem to resist "selling" on moral grounds. I am pleased that the folks from ERP recently sought Stanley's help in their effort to expand their practice to Chicago and New York.

At the same time, Nettles indicated that he couldn't afford to create a wedge between himself and the firm's veteran consultants, including Reldan, because the firm needs their technical expertise and values the close relationships they have built with clients.

Stanley has two staffers working for him who carry out commercial development activities. While they do some limited marketing to prospects, mainly responding to RFPs (requests for proposals) from potential new clients, their main function is to work with consultants across the firm to develop proposals for existing clients. Stanley also has small client services and external communications departments under him. But he considers his most important responsibility to be his post as chairman of the New Business Committee, which was created by Nettles at the time of the reorganization.

NEW BUSINESS COMMITTEE

As part of the reorganization, Aaron Nettles formed a company-wide New Business Committee to foster greater interchange of ideas within the Firm and to promote new business. The Committee was composed of the head of each of the five consulting groups under George Reldan. In addition, Shamtun designated one representative from each of Shamtun's three divisions. Nettles asked David Stanley to chair this committee.

Although GSB's headquarters are in London, the Filer representative has been the only one of Shamtun's people to attend the Committee's monthly meetings. The Arista representative has missed several meetings and the ERP representative has had problems making the trip from Los Angeles on a regular basis. These representatives are kept informed of committee work and are expected to attend three major meetings held in March, September, and December. Patricia Leon, Vice President of Internal Administration, is also a member of this 10-person committee. Leon has an extremely tight relationship with Nettles and had been his "second-in-command" for many years. The rest of the Committee saw Trish as Nettles's representative and believed that she served as his "eyes and ears."

As soon as Nettles announced the creation of the Committee, Stanley moved quickly to get the effort up and running. He described his approach:

> I wrote a memo to each member as soon as the committee was announced three months ago. In it I laid out two basic objectives and suggested some procedural guides. But I left things open until we met and sorted things out face to face.

The two basic objectives stated in the memo were:

1. To facilitate communication among organizational units with an eye to sharing successful techniques and helpful data.
2. To implement an integrated action plan for the business that will foster greater growth than the sum of what is possible in individual units.

While Stanley believed in the value of collaboration, he questioned whether the Committee was a viable approach, at least with its current composition; he remarked:

> So far, I am getting nowhere. Over the last three months, 11 meetings have been scheduled, but three were canceled because key people were out of town on client business. Of the eight we held, only our last one included all 10 members, and that was the biggest fiasco of all. I prepared a detailed agenda and asked each representative to make a one-hour report on his/her department's plans and opportunities for synergy. They had all agreed to do their homework, and I blocked out two days to allow ample time to critique each unit's inputs.
>
> I was optimistic that they would really develop the basis for a more integrated marketing approach because our earlier two meetings generated a lot of good discussion. These meetings dealt strictly with exchange of techniques, and everyone said they got a lot out of them. As soon as we shifted from sharing information to implementing changes, however, they clammed up.
>
> I'll bet that half of the people from Reldan's group hadn't spent more than 10 minutes preparing their presentations. It was particularly embarrassing because it was the first meeting that both the Arista and ERP representatives attended; and they had both put a lot of time into their presentations, even if they were more descriptive than prescriptive.
>
> I specifically asked Reldan to assign the heads of each of his five groups to this Committee to get their commitment, and he went along. Perhaps they are just too busy, and I ought to get them either

to name an alternate or send their junior people to the monthly meetings.

Then the top people would need to come only to the three meetings attended by Arista and ERP. Perhaps I could get more debate and honest exchange of ideas from their subordinates. Reldan's department heads virtually refuse to dig in and criticize one another's operations. Nettles is looking to me to generate new business from existing clients, and I know I can do it if these people would take off their department hats and try to think in terms of the whole Firm. He promised to help when he gave me this job and I certainly need it. It's just that I'm not sure what to ask for. He is very busy and has a lot of confidence in me. I would hate to let him down.

PERSONAL BACKGROUND ON DAVID STANLEY

David Stanley, 37, is married with two preschool-age children. He had taken the job at GSB, hoping that, while it involved more responsibility, it might involve less travel, enabling Stanley to spend more time with the family.

Before joining GSB, Stanley was the Director of Marketing for Deveraux, a small, but highly successful, consulting firm. Prior to being promoted into that role, Stanley was one of the firm's most productive consultants, starting his career in the Firm's Houston office. He routinely out-stripped all of his performance metrics and, after tours of duty in Vancouver, Atlanta, and Philadelphia, was put in the marketing role and moved to the Firm's headquarters in Toronto. As the Director of Marketing, Stanley personally was involved in the pursuit of nearly every one of the firm's largest new business opportunities:

> I love selling [Stanley said]. I enjoy getting in there and winning the client's trust. I like the competitive challenge of figuring out how to shut out the competition.

In the Deveraux culture, the people who brought in the business, the "rainmakers," reigned supreme. Consultants who could sell earned the biggest bonuses, got promoted, and won the attention of the Firm's senior management. The Firm also recognized the need to have consultants with technical expertise, but these individuals were not held in particularly high esteem if they did not also sell. As Stanley described the environment at Deveraux:

> A lot of the technical people weren't very client-focused. They often couldn't take the shortcuts you need to make to meet the client's needs because they were so caught up in doing everything in a completely perfect way from a methodological standpoint. I often had to act as the client's advocate and be very directive with the team, telling them when they were getting too "Ivory Tower" for the client. While I respected that these guys usually had a lot more technical know-how than I did, it was ultimately my job to decide what was in the client's best interests.

Deveraux's consulting culture was sink or swim. The Firm often would hire a pool of new associates with the tacit understanding that only a very few would succeed. More seasoned consultants would size up the new hires and quickly shun anyone who did not appear to have "the right stuff." Once a new consultant brought notable value to an engagement, he/she would get additional mentoring from the senior team. Without creating this initial success for oneself and "earning" the right to be developed, a new consultant would find him/herself shut out of project work and unable to achieve his/her billing targets. People at Deveraux would talk quite openly about who was succeeding and who was "dead weight."

> I hated the culture when I joined Deveraux [Stanley said]. It was harsh, but ultimately it works. Darwin knew what he was talking about with survival of the fittest.

When Nettles recruited Stanley for the position at GSB, he jumped at the opportunity. While he was attracted by the generous compensation package, the main appeal for Stanley was having the chance to move to a larger firm with more responsibility and more opportunity to have a major impact. As he remarked, "We knew that the move to London would be disruptive, especially for two Midwesterners, but the opportunity was just too good to pass up."

DAVID STANLEY AT GSB

Stanley has been frustrated in his nearly two years at GSB, questioning whether he made the right decision in joining the Firm:

> Everything here is done at a snail's pace. No one seems to be willing to go out and push clients for more business. I don't see how the Firm can possibly survive if it doesn't get a lot more aggressive. The risks are enormous.

Stanley recognized that he hasn't made a lot of friends at GSB:

> People here don't want to accept the reality of what I'm telling them. It's a little bit of the "shoot-the-messenger" syndrome, in my opinion. Part of the reality is that the people who can't change won't survive. No one wants to hear that.

Stanley is excited about chairing the New Business Development Committee. He viewed it as his "golden opportunity" to get noticed and have a meaningful impact on the Firm's direction:

> There are huge untapped opportunities here, but everyone is so complacent. Clients don't just drop work in your lap anymore. You have to hustle. You always have to be looking ahead. No one here seems to be doing that. No one has a clue how to think like a client. I'm not sure any of them have ever sold anything. Frankly, I'd like to cut my losses and replace them with people who know what they are doing.

His frustrations were reflected by his direct reports' disappointment with their experiences in working for Stanley. As one marketing staffer remarked:

> We were excited when David first joined us. We thought we'd finally have an opportunity to learn from a real professional marketer. The

reality hasn't measured up. Mostly he just wants us to do exactly what he tells us to do, and he never offers any explanation or rationale for anything. He doesn't take the time to solicit any of our ideas, and he seems to have no interest whatsoever in our development. We're certainly cranking out more proposals than ever, but I sure don't feel any excitement about what we're doing. I don't even care whether our proposal gets a favorable response anymore.

Stanley's frustration with his staff is magnified by what he views as Reldan's lack of commitment to business development:

I know Nettles has told him it is the firm's top priority, but I don't think Reldan is really on board. I know he doesn't much like me or my way of thinking. He's very old school; he loved the gentleman's way Graham did business. But he needs to recognize that even Graham must have known the Firm couldn't keep doing business the same way. Otherwise Graham wouldn't have named Nettles as his successor.

[With respect to the new business committee] Reldan is just going through the motions. He sends his people to the meetings, but I don't think he's really conveyed to them that what we're doing is mission critical. During the meetings, his team members seem to shut down when we start to talk about what isn't working and what needs to change in concrete terms. I think they are afraid of saying something that will get back to Reldan and tick him off. At least the people from Arista and ERP seem to be making a good faith effort, but that won't last if Reldan's team doesn't get engaged. I already feel like I'm starting to lose their focus.

I don't want to drag Nettles into this if I don't have to, and I imagine Patricia Leon's been keeping him informed anyway. I'm not sure he's entirely objective where Reldan is concerned—they have a long history. I also don't want him to think I can't get things done on my own.

CHAPTER 10 · COMPLETING THE PROCESS

KEY POINTS TO REMEMBER

- *Strategic Thinking* is a continuous, dynamic process linking purpose and aspiration to performance and achievement with Four KEYS:
  - *If we want to be by ... then we better be by ...*
  - *Diagnostics*
  - *Folding Back*
  - *Strategy on a Page*
- There are three levels or phases of *Strategic Thinking*:
  - *The Conceptual Level*: where we define our *mission and values*, our core purposes and reason for existence, and our *vision*;
  - *The Analytical Level*: where we assess the feasibility of our *vision* and to identify the gaps that must be closed by our *strategy*;
  - *The Operational Level*: where we create and operate the organizational systems and processes needed to implement and monitor our *strategy*
- The Strategic Thought Process involves 8 fundamental diagnostic questions:
  - *Who are we? Why do we exist?*
  - *What do we believe in? What do we hold dear?*
  - *Where do we want to be? What do we want to look like at a specific future point in time?*
  - *What do we have to do to get there?*
  - *Where are we now?*
  - *What are the major stages/phases that we will have to accomplish along the way?*

> - *What obstacles are likely to get in our way?*
> - *What are we going to do to overcome these obstacles?*
> - The final output of the *Strategic Thought Process* is a comprehensive *strategy* supported by a detailed, explicit *strategic action plan.*

Acknowledgments

We have both been blessed with challenging students, demanding clients, and a vast network of professional colleagues and mentors at Columbia and elsewhere who have encouraged us to put our *Strategic Management* course on paper. First, we thank our department chair, Sherry Glied, of the Department of Health Policy and Management, Mailman School of Public Health. Sherry has provided support for our course developments over the years, and, at times, has been known to threaten bodily harm if we *did not* write this book! Susan Cohen, our departmental coordinator, has been extremely helpful in terms of supporting our research, providing expert counsel on how to frame our concepts, and being our head cheerleader during this process.

We are particularly indebted to our long-time friend and collaborator, Ian Wilcox, vice president and pharmaceutical practice head at the Hay Group, with whom we have joined on so many projects over so many years. Ian provided the opportunity for and collaborated in the development of many of the cases that we have included, and we are grateful for his support and for allowing us to use some cases developed in conjunction with Hay.

We also are indebted to Alison Boyle, a former Mailman student, for her terrific MinuteClinic case. Gajendra Gharia, our superb teaching assistant during our first offering of *Comparative Strategic Analysis* was very helpful as a sounding board as we developed some of our frameworks.

Also, we cannot express our gratitude enough to our editorial team at Kaplan Publishing. Shannon Berning, our acquisitions editor, kept us on pace and encouraged us when we were too tired or too busy (or both) to write. Joshua Martino was extremely helpful as our development editor. He patiently read all of our babble and made sure it made sense to a broader audience. Fred Urfer, our production editor, provided great guidance, as usual, during the copyediting, proofing, and production processes.

Finally, our families deserve a huge amount of credit for putting up with us, individually and collectively, during the writing of this text. We weren't always as available, as spouses, fathers, and friends, while we were on the phones late at night, and we have our families to thank to for their tremendous help and support. Without them, our text in strategic thinking, and in fact, our own life strategies, would not be complete.

Columbia University
New York, New York
June 30, 2008

This book has been a long time in coming. That it is here at all is due primarily to two people. The first is Ellie, my wife, partner, and principal editor, who has been known over 44 years to ask occasionally, "So, when are you going to write your book?" The second is Paul, my co-author, friend, and protégé, who called one day last summer and said, "I have a contract for us to do *the book!*"

Without their su pport and encouragement—and gentle nudging—I would still be giving the same answer that I had used for years when students asked, "Professor, where have you written this so we can get a copy?" My response has always been, "I'm too busy teaching—advising, whatever—to find the time to write. Maybe when I get older." So here it is—I guess that I've gotten older!

The philosophical roots of the ideas, concepts, and approaches that run through the b ook go much deeper. As Paul and I have said throughout, *strategy* starts with the subjective and the emotional—with human purpose and beliefs, with dreams of what can be, with the conviction that we can choose and achieve the future. We hold these values in trust to our families—to those who showed us the way and shaped us. My parents, Tom and Mary Agnes Ference, blessed me with their unwavering faith in me, with a love for learning, with a commitment to community service, and with a dedication to making sure a thing was done right—no matter how hard. My aunt, Kathryn Benn, gave me a love for reading and a fascination with ideas and words. My grandmother, Mary Benn, taught me what to hold dear—to believe in. I think that they would be pleased.

I was started on the path leading to this book by two wonderful teachers, Bertha Raynovich and Helen Morgan, who taught me Latin and Literature, and who gave me my first teaching experience, *Macbeth*, as a high school senior. Thanks to them, I found, and have never lost, my fascination with the learning process.

I learned my trade at the feet of masters, especially Herbert A. Simon, my mentor and advisor and inspiration. My appreciation also to Richard M. Cyert, Victor H. Vroom, James G. March, Harold J. Leavitt, and H. Igor Ansoff—my Carnegie Tech GSIA faculty. There were truly giants in those days!

At Columbia, I have been privileged to work with and learn from a most generous group of colleagues and friends. Boris Yavitz, a master of imagery and articulation, started me on the path to the open-systems perspective that informs our strategic thinking framework by making the connections between my engineering experience (yes, I was a rocket scientist of sorts!) and the key role of vision and imagination. Kirby Warren and John Hutchinson taught me to teach by coaching and by example and then gave me the opportunity to test myself with the most challenging audience—experienced corporate executives. Finally, my first two bosses, Deans Courtney Brown and Hoke Simpson, challenged me to make the transition from theory to practice by making me a profit-center manager!

Fred Putney and Norman Toy, my consulting partners at the Riverside Group for over 40 years, have been a constant source of friendship and challenge, always reminding me of the importance of the underlying economic and financial realities of any enterprise, and working together to build the bridges between for-profit and not-for-profit management—a theme that runs throughout this book.

I am grateful to the friends and colleagues who have read, commented on, and greatly improved the earlier versions of the text, especially my long-term collaborator, Ian Wilcox. Others who contributed greatly to the review process include Joann Baney, Ralph Sabatino, Brooke Williams, and John Winkleman. A special "thank you" also to Lynn Russell, whose coaching and guidance has greatly improved all of our exhibits.

Perhaps the best part of "doing the book" has been my deepening friendship with my partner and co-author, Paul Thurman. We met years ago as teacher and student and are now truly friends, colleagues, collaborators in every sense. I can frankly say that without his commitment and enthusiasm, this book would never have happened. Thank you, Paul.

Now it is done. My sons and their wives, Tom and Jill, Michael and Noelle, will finally be able to answer TJ, Sydney, Colin, and Casey, and Brooke and Jerry will be able to answer Morgan, Griffin and Justin, when they ask, "What does Grandpa do?"

And to Ellie, I can say, "None of this would have ever happened without you. You are my wisest reader, my best editor, my safe harbor, the center of my life." Now, should you ask, "So, when are you going to write your book?" I can answer, "Thanks to you, it's done."

Thomas P. Ference, PhD

Sir Isaac Newton was right; I have only accomplished my goals thanks to the tall shoulders of so many other giants. Tom Ference, my co-author, uber-mentor, and good friend, was the first person to ever teach me "strategy" at the Columbia Business School (even though I had been "doing it" as a consultant for years before his course). Tom's mentorship and friendship have paid immeasurable dividends, and I am honored to have my name next to his on the cover of *his* book. He and Ellie continue to be good friends, and I apply his support and wise counsel on a daily basis. (Tom's grandchildren and my children have also become good friends. While we're not making any matrimonial wagers, we're optimistic!) Thanks, Tom, for everything. And even that greatly underestimates your contributions.

Gil Irwin, my mentor and former boss at Booz & Company, (formerly Booz Allen Hamilton) deserves huge credit for this book, as well. He taught me the craft of consulting and, unbeknownst to me, how to think strategically. (I just didn't realize it until I took Tom's course!) Doug Figg and Doug Price, deserve special credit as terrific clients and even more as supportive friends and professional colleagues. The Dougs were instrumental in helping me develop and to refine a course for National Cancer Institute postdoctoral fellows and Oxford-Cambridge (and National Institutes of Health) scholars that focuses on leadership and strategic thinking in laboratory science.

Rob Min, deserves much credit for helping me with the analytical tools component of this text (especially with some statistical methods including the "kurtotic" method of management). Thanks, too, to Jeff Levin-Scherz, a former student, colleague, and member of the Harvard School of Public Health faculty, for his assistance and help with my strategy course at Columbia. Connie Tchang was very helpful in terms cleaning up and improving many of our charts and exhibits, and Lydia Chan, in addition to taking care of my two young children and getting all "As" in her night college courses, was extremely helpful in terms of preparing our final manuscript. Teddy Zmrhal, my entrepreneurship advisor, deserves a great deal of credit for reviewing some of the case solutions and course materials developed over the years.

But the overwelming majority of the credit goes to my beloved wife, Andrea, for her continued support, patience, and "shoulders."

Writing three books in one year was a tall order, and I simply could not have completed it without her. Thanks so much, Andrea; your love and devotion to our family—and to my professional aspirations—have been irreplaceable. And you did it all while working two full-time jobs—your professional career as a marketer and your personal one as CEO of our household. Our two angels, Vanessa and Lisa, aged a year while writing this book. Vanessa, our two-year-old, started to talk while Tom and I prepared this manuscript, and one of her first words was "book," which she would say to me as she pointed to my laptop on so many nights before bedtime. Lisa, our six-year-old, learned how to play softball and soccer in the past year, and she even convinced me to coach her kindergarten and first-grade teams. (Apparently, she thought I had too much free time!) She also started reading while we wrote the text, and once in awhile, she would read some of what we wrote and would comment on our "cool charts." (Tom is convinced she will soon become our literary agent.)

Finally, I acknowledge the love of my father, Clovis Claude Thurman. In his 79 years, he was a tough dad—the kind who loved you when you followed the rules but who also reminded you, in a rather "focused" way, when you didn't. He was the first *Strategos* in my life. And although he had only a sixth-grade education and spent his life as an automotive and Diesel mechanic, he understood the importance of values, the need for a mission, the non-negotiable requirement for a sound plan of action, and the inherent desire to measure—and to decisively implement and to improve—one's performance. Some in my family believe he obtained these skills as a Corporal in the United States Army during World War II. Or as a poor farmer growing up in rural Oklahoma. Or as a mechanic where it either "worked" or "didn't work, yet." But regardless of the root cause, his mission, vision, and values were clear. And they are as much a part of me as my breath and heartbeat have been to this day.

Paul W. Thurman, MBA

ACKNOWLEDGMENTS

Update 2016:

Much has happened since we first published this book with Kaplan in 2009. Paul remarried and now has four daughters, with his wife, Crissa, in their blended family. Lisa, now 14, and Vanessa, now 10, still call Paul, "Dad," while Stella, 13, and Tahlia, 9, are now proud--we hope!--to call Paul their stepfather.

Tom celebrated 50 years on the faculty of Columbia University back in June of this year--a truly remarkable accomplishment. Tom and Ellie still enjoy their garden and their grandchildren, including their latest, Nicki, all of whom they get to spend a bit more time with now that Tom is teaching a bit less and enjoying his "free time" a bit more.

We have both been incredibly blessed by the support, helpful commentary, corrections, and improvement suggestions by the countless friends, clients, staff, faculty colleagues, teaching assistants, and students with whom we have shared this text over the past several years. Once our book went out of print in late 2015, we received many letters of encouragement--demands, actually--that we self-publish our text so others could have access to it.

This happy event caused us to review our manuscript, make a few edits, but to largely keep it as it was in 2009. As our wives have insisted, "Why mess with perfection?!" While we won't claim to be that good, we do believe our frameworks and ideas have stood the test of time. We may add further chapters on digital and social strategies, "big data," and strategic thinking for the new (Millennial) generation. We may also add a case library/companion text at some point. Please stay tuned!

Regardless of what we do next, we thank you for your continued good feedback and successful implementations of the thoughts we've put forward, here.

Tom and Paul
Columbia University
New York, New York
December 20, 2016

Test Yourself "Answers"

In the following sections, we will provide a brief discussion for the cases found in the "Test Yourself" section at the end of each chapter. We should note that these are not "answers" or "solutions" in the traditional sense of problems but rather are a discussion of the issues and factors that you should take into account as you review and analyze the complex situation laid out in the case. We will point out and provide examples of where the concepts and tools presented in the text are relevant in formulating your response to the questions raised for each case. We will point you toward what we would think of as a broad "solution channel"—which may include many specific "paths" or strategies that might be considered in pursuing a defined vision.

Our Cases are drawn from actual organizational settings and are inherently complex. Each case will typically involve both qualitative and quantitative information and will require both rigorous analysis and the exercise of informed personal judgment. Each Case will also either suggest or yield a number of strategic options, alternative specific solutions or strategies within a broad solution channel, each of which might be appropriate or effective for a particular understanding of the organization's purposes and strategic intent/vision. The analyses of each Case will necessarily involve predictions about future courses of events, including the responses and independent actions of other organizations and individuals that cannot be known and that will be influenced at least in part by the actions that you recommend and take. Thus, the effectiveness of any proposed strategy is both probabilistic and contingent on the behaviors of others, individually and collectively, and on events not fully predictable or under our control. Success is also dependent on how effectively we implement or execute it—and even this is relative to how well the other players on the Gameboard execute their strategies! As in most truly competitive situations, in sports or in business, it is not enough to be "right," conceptually and analytically, we must also play well—and the other guy may still play better! As one wit once put it:

> Strategy is like shooting through a moving forest at a moving target from a moving platform!

"If this is so," you might ask, "why bother? Why not just go out and play it by ear?" The answer is in the nature of the *Strategic Thought Process* itself. As we have presented it throughout the book, this process involves:

- Being clear and articulate, developing a consensus (regarding your mission, values, and vision), and resolving any difficulties or ambiguities here before moving forward;
- Folding back from your vision, your strategic intent, to identify potential solution paths or strategies, within a broad channel, that might move you from your present situation to your desired end state and defining the major milestones or checkpoints along those paths from which you can assess and modify your efforts;
- Using your strategic intent, your vision, and your understanding of the major elements of the solution path to guide a comprehensive analysis of the critical factors, internally and externally, including the likely behaviors of colleagues, competitors, and customers;
- Identifying the barriers and obstacles that will have to be overcome and the initiatives that will have to be undertaken to

progress along the chosen path, or from path to path, milestone by milestone;

- Developing detailed strategic action plans that can be implemented and assessed, particularly at each checkpoint, to move dynamically and flexibly along the solution channel;
- Identifying and undertaking the leadership and managerial actions and behaviors needed to secure, motivate, and sustain the commitment of the organization and its members to the strategy in pursuit of the vision.

We would suggest that this is the thought process that you should follow when reviewing the cases. The key issue is not in finding the "right" or "school" solution, as there is not likely to be a single "right answer," even ours, but in developing a proposed strategy that "hangs together"—and that is internally coherent:

- Are the mission and vision clear?
- Does the analysis support the feasibility of the vision?
- Do the strategic plans provide the best chance of achieving the vision?
- Do you or the key characters know what to do to lead the effort?

For a general format, please see the outline in the box below:

CASE ANALYSIS

Prepare a concise analysis of the Case that is responsive to the following points:

- What are the issues (strategic, tactical, and/or operational) that are presently confronting the organization or institution, or the key decision-maker, described in the Case?
- What are the conceptual factors (mission, values, vision) that are relevant to these issues?

- What are the external/environmental factors that are relevant to these issues?
- What are the internal factors (structure, processes, people) that are relevant to these issues?
- What is the strategic intent of the institution—or of the key decision-maker?
- What alternative strategies would you consider and which would you recommend to the institution? To the key decision-maker? Why?
- What are the three to four most significant/first priority actions that would have to be taken to implement your recommended strategy effectively?

Chapter 1 Burton, Wells & Co.
OVERVIEW

The case sets up four dynamic tensions:

1. <u>Strategy vs. Expedience</u>: Farber's basic argument boils down to "let's not leave money on the table because of cumbersome bureaucratic procedures—let's do the deal and worry about the details later." The counterposition is that "we have carefully designed review processes in order to keep our focus on our strategic purposes and avoid rushing willy-nilly after every (dangerous?) opportunity that presents itself. After all, a poorly-conceived deal can go bad." Remember also that Sales gets paid on commission based on revenues generated, the top line; the role of Administration is to ensure that revenues translate to profits, the bottom line. Further, in the leasing business, the actual bottom line may not be realized for some time, even years, after the business is originally booked.

2. <u>Professional vs. Managerial vs. Leadership</u>: Putnam's first concern is to determine whether this is a sound business deal—packaged by Farber and reviewed against the proper metrics. Second he must deal with an implied challenge to the formal organizational system and processes—Farber is pressuring a subordinate of Putnam's (Troy) to set aside or alter review procedures established by a cross-functional task force at the corporate level. Finally, he has to resolve the preceding issues in such a way as to maintain the willingness of all involved to continue to work together and to avoid increasing tensions and interdepartmental conflict. Thus, Putnam must seek a resolution that is *professionally* sound and that preserves the existing *managerial* system and is within the limits of his authority. In doing so, he must provide the *leadership* needed to retain the commitment of all involved to the firm's strategic

purpose. Thus, it is important not only *what* he does, but also *how* he does it;

3. <u>Expedite v. Exception</u>: Farber is asking for an exception, to skip steps or waive tests or lower criteria, in order to meet a deadline. Under what conditions would it be appropriate or defensible to grant such an exception to established policy and would this situation meet any of these? If an exception is not appropriate, would it be possible and appropriate to expedite (speed up) the complete review process by deploying additional resources, working longer hours, etc? Under what conditions would this be acceptable and how would you account for the diversion of critical resources from other projects and deals to this "special" case?

4. <u>Person vs. Process</u>: Farber's main argument for an exception, or for expediting, seems to be his personal credibility: "Trust me, and I'll back you up if anyone complains." Burton, Wells has, however, gone, for strategic reasons—the changing nature of its book of business—to a carefully designed formal process in order to have a consistent approach to focusing effort, allocating resources, and assessing performance in order to compete on an increasingly complex and risky Gameboard (see exhibit I). How can BW effectuate this change without losing the ingenuity and enthusiasm of key individuals such as Farber? And should there be special cases—separate rules for special people?

ANALYSIS

Reviewing the facts presented in the case in the light of the above issues, we can reasonably draw the following conclusions:

- The ball is clearly in Putnam's lap. It is the role of his unit, and, therefore, his responsibility or job as the head of the unit, to deal with the challenge that Farber has raised—both to the role of the review procedures and to the authority of the Administration unit. If he would, instead, try to pass the problem on to David Wells, he would be failing in the responsibilities entrusted to him, he would not be doing his job, and he would be bringing the need for his unit into question;

- The strategic mission and values of the Firm are stated clearly in the comment from Joseph Burton on p. 16 and seem to call for a complete and thorough review of the proposed deal in service to both the Firm and the customer;
- Putnam's authority extends to conducting the review and to approving (signing off on) the deal or not; it does not extend to making "arbitrary or capricious" changes in the process without a collective corporate decision—even if it would make Art happy and reduce short-term conflict;
- Therefore, given the process, the impending, deadline, and Troy's "red flags," the proposed deal must be reviewed under the existing process and a determination made in keeping with the existing criteria.

This is the straightforward part of Putnam's decision process—to make a professionally sound decision within the current managerial system and the governing mission and strategy. What remains is the leadership challenge of deciding just how to go about doing this so as to "keep the peace" and avoid elevating the level of the tensions noted above. We suggest that you consider the following in deciding how Putnam should proceed:

- There are no good grounds for granting an exception. A rushed, big-ticket, high-risk project for a new customer with high potential for future business would seem to be the worst, rather than the best, case for suspending the rules. And "trust me" is not enough, even if we have the greatest respect for

Art, because, if we would do so and the deal would go bad in some way, the blame would fall not on Art but on Administration whose job it is to provide a check-and-balance on Sales' enthusiasm;

- This situation is not taking place in a vacuum. There are, undoubtedly, multiple deals in various stages of development and review being presented by other Vice Presidents and Sales reps and how this event is handled will be visible and set precedent for others to follow;

- Given Art's stature, the potential value of the deal, and the tight deadline, there may well be a good argument for expediting the process by 'throwing' additional resources (analysts, etc.) at it—but these resources will entail costs and will disrupt other work in progress;

- Once this situation is resolved, it would seem appropriate and timely to review the process, after all, it is new as the business it is designed to review, to see if it is working as intended and how and where improvements might be made, and to determine whether the organizational and management systems (teams and work groups, compensation and incentive processes, and so on) are fully aligned behind the new business strategy.

Whatever specific path Putnam chooses to follow will have to balance the above considerations.

Chapter 2 Ivtak Americas Group: The HR Challenge

OVERVIEW

The case contains many issues, ranging from the strategic to the purely operational and from the conceptually profound to the mundane. The heart of the case is that Cat is being asked to, in effect, create a new role at the Group level for HR managers. She is told by her functional boss, Pierre Balmains, and her new line exec, Roberto Cuevas, that they are looking for her to become a "true business partner" with the various country and business unit heads. This concept would seem to suggest that Ivtak is looking for HR managers who can take on and perform effectively as executives, as strategic business leaders, as general managers, or as part of a general managerial team as opposed to the more traditional HR roles of functional specialist or technician, internal consultant, or staff administrator.

To do this, Cat will have to "step back" and reflect on the broader conceptual challenges of the case rather than simply diving in and providing a series of solutions or answers to the more specific or obvious questions raised by different speakers (Who to appoint to Argentina; whether to outsource the personnel date base). In that regard, Cuevas' comment on page 42 is a "trap:"

> Let's sit down and discuss your <u>solutions</u> [emphasis added] as soon as you get back.

If Cat were to do so, she would be tacitly accepting the role of tactical problem-solver for such tasks as assigned to her by her boss. Neither of these has any particular urgency as presented and, in fact, should not be dealt with until she has had the opportunity to formulate the broader strategy she wishes to pursue in responding to the mandate to become a true "business partner."

Both of these are tactical decisions; they represent potential "means" for implementing a particular strategic perspective. For example, until she knows how she wants to approach this partnering challenge both with her line colleagues, including Roberto, and her functional community, including Pierre, she really cannot know what sort of team she wants to build and what sort of individual, or bucket of skills, she wants and needs in Argentina.

ANALYSIS

There are at least four major conceptual dimensions that Cat must take into account in formulating her strategy for approaching her new position:

- **Strategic:** What is the meaning of *"business partner?"* Pierre clearly wants her to secure a "place at the table" for HR in the strategic decision-making process; Roberto is looking for a real-time, action-oriented member of his operating team. To define this role personally, Cat will have to deal with the following:
  - The evolving nature and changing needs of the global electronics industry.
    - Issues would include new concepts of talent and career, building sustaining common cultures across diverse sites, supporting the performance of culturally diverse distance teams, etc.
  - Ivtak has a particular culture with a strong emphasis on the scientific mentality, "a collection of researchers and academics," with an emphasis on intrinsic product attributes and little patience or interest in details or in the softer side of the business—including operations and marketing!
    - Ivtak has a history of being effectively "siloed" and functional in its orientation—and what we now call HR has been largely traditional personnel. How does HR move from specific tactical or operational concerns (which would keep HR pigeon-holed) to a focus on emerging issues inside and outside the firm.
  - The potentially competing viewpoints and "true" intentions of her two key bosses.
    - She is receiving mixed messages from Pierre and Roberto. How can she clarify and with whom is she expected to partner—Roberto, other key group executives, other HR Heads, etc.?

- She clearly needs to fight off pressures to make decisions or provide solutions to current issues, such as outsourcing, until the new HR concept can be developed and implemented.

- **Behavioral:** Having defined the strategic issues, Cat will also need a clear strategy for dealing "on the ground" with the people involved. Issues include:
  - Informational needs: On the overall corporate business situation, on the Americas Group specifically, on the personal strategies and situations of Pierre and Roberto, on her predecessors, on the proposed candidates for the Argentina post, on the outsourcing proposal, and so on.
    - She needs an explicit timetable and process for acquiring information including who to speak with, individually and/or in a group, about what.
  - Dealing with her two key bosses and their differing expectations.
    - One can argue that it would be premature to move on the Argentina appointment or to make a decision on the ISP outsourcing proposal and yet Roberto wants "solutions" immediately. She must establish herself as an independent player and not simply as a subordinate or team member in order to gain control of her agenda.

- **Organizational:** Cat next needs to consider the form that she wishes the unit to take in terms of relations with the other business functions at the group and country levels and the nature and composition of the new HR "Team." Issues to consider include structure and reporting lines within the HR community (e.g., functional teams that coordinate across countries vs. multifunctional country teams), necessary skill mixes at the country and group HQ levels, a prioritized agenda of strategic issues, and a work process for managing the overall effort (regular meetings, information systems, etc.). The push from Roberto to appoint a new country manager for Argentina from a list of prescreened candidates is a good example of the need to put tactical issues in a strategic context.

- HR Manager – Argentina: Roberto is pressing Cat to appoint a new HR Manager for Argentina (her former position). She knows all three of the proposed candidates, although none well, and is not convinced that any of them are an ideal choice, either in the old HR environment or in the new "business partner" context that she now trying to formulate in her mind.

    While it is clearly important to fill the Argentina position, it is less than clear how the appointment of any of these will advance the HR agenda, as opposed to using HR posts for individual career-development experiences.

    This appointment is a key step in Cat securing effective control of her own strategy, the shape of her organization, and the composition of her team. The choices made by Roberto as finalists reflects a more operational or functional view of HR than that implied by the "business partner" concept. The inclusion of DeJesus particularly suggests he is more concerned with advancing other agendas than in strengthening HR—further evidence that the candidate will have to educate and manage upward.

- **Operational:** The final dimension that Cat should consider would be the making of specific operational decisions in a partnership context. The proposed outsourcing project would benefit ISP and may well be a sound approach to the more conventional technical personnel functions of HR. It is unclear how it would affect evolving global HR strategy. Also, the issues and tensions that would be involved with a major systems conversion driven by outside technical folk might put unnecessary stress on the unit and be premature in the context of the evolving strategy. Critical issues would include:

- The readiness of the HR organization to undergo major system changes while in the processing of developing a new strategy and absorbing key senior level transfers and appointments
- The wisdom of making decisions about which policies, procedures, files, etc. to standardize and transfer to an outside vendor when the role of HR systems in the firm is being reconceived and redesigned
- The value of allowing a newly established HR team to create its own concept of how best to organize and perform its multiple functions

In summary, Cat must decide how to deal with these four sets of considerations in taking up her new position. How she does this, and particularly how she approaches her first few days, will determine whether she will be able to fulfill the strategic challenge that she has been given. Her entry strategy, her initial actions, will be crucial to and must be consistent with her strategic vision. Thus, her first concerns must be to:

- Provide an explicit definition or understanding of what it would mean for HR to function as a full "business partner" within the firm
- Develop a personal, detailed strategy for positioning herself as a strategic business leader or a general manager, and not as a functional manager, technical specialist, or consultant
- Articulate a comprehensive strategy in terms of goals, priorities, and actions for establishing the HR function at the group level as a full partner and for avoiding being locked into tactical issues and assigned tasks

Chapters 3 and 4 Fidelity Corporation
OVERVIEW

Fidelity may well represent the classic example of an organization that is successful despite itself. It continues to persist in its traditional approach to business—it's hard to call this a "strategy"—despite overwhelming evidence of a dramatically changing marketplace and despite growing polite but intense disagreement among various "camps" within the firm. Reputation, momentum, and the (shrinking number of) loyal clients of the cadre of (aging) senior partners, along with a good market, are carrying the firm for the moment, but dark clouds are clearly gathering on the horizon. And the hiring of a group of "old pros" who have been let go by their firms as part of rebuilding efforts and who are also steeped in the old ways may well be clogging the arteries at Fidelity.

We note several aspects of the marketplace and of the firm itself that Bill Harrigan should be cognizant of as he considers what his next steps might be. These include:

- The changing competition for customers: Firms are actively seeking new business and calling on other firms' customers, historically, a "no-no."
- The changing ethos within firms in the industry: Partners are working for partners at some firms, and some firms are actually letting partners go.
- Clients are more widely dispersed geographically and are more likely to expect firms to come to them rather than them coming to New York.
- The culture of the industry is changing, with loyalty increasingly being attached to performance rather than to existing personal relationships.
- Fidelity retains significant strengths in its reputation, in the experience and industry standing of its senior partners, and in key areas such as M&A.

- The partnership culture, with its emphasis on the well-connected generalist who has "apprenticed at the feet of the masters," is changing in the industry and even at Fidelity.

Harrigan must consider all of these factors as he contemplates his strategic agenda and his possible next moves. He must also be aware of the various tactical initiatives (e.g., sales training for partners) that have failed but have raised the levels of anxiety and tension within the firm. Any new initiatives may well be perceived as the next "flavor of the month" in the search for a quick fix. Harrigan clearly needs a comprehensive vision that honors the traditional mission and professional values of the firm and still positions the firm to compete effectively for the business it wants in the changing marketplace. Moreover, he will need a clear personal leadership strategy if he is to "sell" his vision and the strategic actions needed to implement it to his diverse collection of independent, cantankerous, and strong-minded partners.

ANALYSIS

Perhaps the most significant challenge that Fidelity and its competitors have to face is that the nature of the client—the customer—has changed. If, historically, the key relationship with a client firm was with a Treasurer who had been in place for many years, who had a long-standing personal relationship with the Fidelity partner, and who looked to that partner for advice and counsel on industry and market issues and on financial strategies and instruments, today's client contact officer is likely to be younger, more personally mobile, better educated, and more technically savvy. This does not mean that relationships will no longer matter, but it does suggest that they will be built and sustained more on a knowledge/performance/service basis than on a personal one. If one looks at the relationship from a *client* perspective, it is reasonable to assume that the client is looking for several things from its financial services provider. These are shown in the figure on the next page.

```
                    Industry
                   Knowledge
                       |
         Advice        |
           &  ——   Client   ——  Product
         Counsel       |
                       |
                    Sales &
                   Marketing
```

By putting the client at the center, we can see that there are several ports of entry to the client or several functions that the Firm can bring to the client. In terms of the development of a relationship, these would naturally occur in something like the following order:

- Sales & Marketing: the initial and ongoing contacts that seek to open the door and present the Firm to the client; the "new business" getters

- Product: the availability of a portfolio of financial instruments and arrangements that may serve a current or ongoing need of the client

- Industry Knowledge: the competence and information needed to identify financial strategies that are appropriate to the specific circumstances of the client's industry

- Advice & Counsel: the provision of ongoing wisdom, insight, and guidance to the client based on industry/market knowledge and on the unique aspects of the client firm

Notice that, as we move down this list, we go from functions or interactions that are essentially transparent and transactional to ones that are built on intimate knowledge and relationship.

If Harrigan considers the positions of his different partners in light of the above, he can see that each touches wisely and appropriately on some aspects of this client-centered approach—but leaves other aspects unattended. Dedham, for example, is pushing for an aggressive selling organization where deals will be fulfilled by a remote "back office." Such an approach might produce a high volume of transactional sales but is unlikely to build enduring relationships or depth of client knowledge. White, on the other hand, is content to wait for existing clients to come in to be harvested—which will produce a high-quality but shrinking "book of business" as old clients retire out of their firms. Warburg is less concerned with how business is contracted than with winning through having analysts and specialists that are "smarter than the clients."

Harrigan should realize that he cannot choose his core strategy from among these competing viewpoints but must instead develop an integrated approach that draws on the best of all three. Fidelity is, indeed, in a relationship business (White is right) but the nature of the relationships that will sustain the business has changed (White is wrong) and both Dedham and Warburg are partially correct. It would seem that some sort of client team approach, with all of the above functions organized around the client, would best serve Fidelity's values and its clients' needs.

It would also make sense for Harrigan to implement this new vision of a client-centered team strategy in stages; thus, he might:

- Create client-centered teams for all new clients, inviting those senior partners who are willing to do so to join and, perhaps, head such teams

278 TEST YOURSELF "ANSWERS"

- Allow senior partners such as White to continue to serve their clients as they have always done, only moving their clients to the Team approach if and when White et al. retire
- Carefully, with his senior partners, reconsider the evolving nature of the partnership form

Chapters 5 and 6 St. Emily's School
OVERVIEW

Kate Gorham faces seemingly endless challenges and problems—declining enrollment, a decaying physical plant, a persistent and growing deficit, shaky support from her immediate "parent" organization, a competitor on the upswing, a loyal but aging staff, and on and on. She also appears to have a number of attractive but unrealized strengths and opportunities—a growing demand for pre-K care, an excellent reputation and a compelling mission, strong "name recognition" and respect on the street, steady support from the Archdiocese and so on. The problems, however, are tangible and immediate; the strengths abstract and intangible.

St. Emily's is clearly at a crossroad, and Kate must avoid the temptation, on the one hand, to try to fix everything all at once and immediately and, on the other, to apply patches and band aids to the individual problems on a 'squeaky wheel' basis. While an enrollment drive, or an additional fundraiser, or a technology workshop for faculty, or a new roof, may seem urgent and/or quickly doable, taken out of the context of a comprehensive vision for the future of the school, these become merely tactics or holding actions. They are, at best, means to an end. In the absence of a clear sense of the desired future of the school, and in the face of scarce and shrinking resources, Kate lacks a basis for ordering or prioritizing among them. And she certainly lacks the resources, financial and human, and the support, conceptual and substantive, to attack them all at once.

ANALYSIS

Kate's first priority must be to develop a comprehensive vision for St. Emily's that remains true to the school's mission and values—a sense of the school that she intends to bring into being over the next two to three years. Given the current realities and trends, she probably does not have much longer to turn the school around—and she cannot do it overnight either. So it is reasonable for her to begin her strategic thinking in terms of a three-year vision. With such a vision, she would have a basis for attracting resources and support and for ordering initiatives and actions strategically—for *folding back* from the vision to define the "best" sequence or timeline of events to follow in achieving it.

As we have suggested, such a vision would provide a complete description of what one would expect to see if one were to visit St. Emily's three years from now. We offer the following as one possible example of such a statement:

> Three years from now, St. Emily's School, in collaboration with St. Ingrid's School, will be a pre-K–5 school with a minimum of two full classrooms at each age/grade level of average class size of 20. St. Emily's, while still affiliated with St. Emily's Parish, will be separately incorporated with its own Board. It will be fiscally sound and will operate in its refurbished facility, using other community facilities as appropriate for special programming. It will have an active Alumni Association and an active PTO. It will gain revenues from the leasing of its facilities evenings and weekends to community groups.

Note that this hypothetical vision involves a number of significant assumptions and decisions about each of the *vision elements* (Performance, Enrollment, Facilities, and so on) defined in the text. It also makes it clear that these various elements cannot be dealt with separately or independently but must be part of an integrated overall vision and a defined timeline of strategic events and initiatives.

Note also that this example is truly a *vision* in the sense that we have developed the concept. It is a description of a desired future state that would not occur if Kate were to pursue business as usual, trying to fix the various problems as she went along. It represents, instead, a significant potential shift in the nature and direction of the School along a number of dimensions.

The overall vision tells where we are trying to go, and the elements of the vision identify how each of the major functions or components of the organization fits into the overall vision. Further, folding back from the overall vision enables us to choose the initial pathway and to identify the changes that must be made in each of the elements to close the gap between our present reality and our desired future.

Our example above is one possible future direction for the School. In developing an overall vision for St. Emily's, Kate must take into account the following major issues:

- Should St. Emily's continue as a parochial school or as an independent school in the Catholic tradition? "Parochial" means "of the Parish." Does this format best serve either the school or the parish?

- What are the needs of the community and how are they changing? How are today's immigrant families and other residents different from those of St. Emily's past?

- What are the resources of the community and how might they be mobilized to support St. Emily's?

- Who are St. Emily's stakeholders or constituents? Who are the key players—competitors, users, holders of resources, referees, allies?

- What is the educational mission of the Archdiocese and how does this affect St. Emily's?

A thorough examination of these matters in the context of the current and evolving realities of St. Emily's and the community that it serves suggests that the overall vision for the school should incorporate the following consideration or components:

- Community Planning: It makes little sense to plan for St. Emily's as a distinct entity separate from the larger community or neighborhood in which it resides. This suggests that the visioning and planning effort must include, in some way, not only Father Art and the parish finance council, but also St. Ingrid's, the public school, the local business community, the Archdiocese, and the parents. Whether, for example, St. Ingrid's or the Public School are adversaries or allies depends on how and when they are involved in the strategic thought process;
- Core Group: Throughout the case, one gets the sense that Kate is trying to do this all alone and that the other players are pursuing their own agendas, even Father Art. Kate clearly needs to form some sort of core group of advisors and colleagues with whom she can explore ideas and develop strategies and plans. This group needs to be composed of persons who are there primarily to advance the School and not to represent the interests of other parties;
- Revenue Streams: It is apparent that the school will not be able to survive on tuition alone and also that the finance council is reluctant to raise or even continue subsidizing an uncertain deficit [a specific annual grant or percentage of expenses might be another matter]; rather than relying solely on the IPF to make up the gap, the vision should include one or more reliable sources of revenue such as a pre-K program, weekend or evening rentals of classrooms and the gym (once renovated), and so on;
- Renovation of Facilities: The school needs extensive repairs but lacks reserves and easy access to capital; it must seek alternative ways to facilitate renovations such as contributed materials and services from local merchants and tradesmen

(electricians, plumbers, etc.) and through "sweat equity" (contributed or bartered services of parents and others);

- Configuration: While St. Emily's has always been a K–8 school with 16 classrooms, it must now question whether this is the optimal configuration given its strengths and the community's needs. Can demand support two classes per grade at every grade level? Does the school need more special purpose classrooms (Art, Music, etc.)? Would dedicating one or more rooms to a pre-K program make more sense? Are other arrangements available, viable, strategic?

- Management: It is clear from the reactions of Father Art and the Finance Council that the school faces a difficult future in its present status as a program of the Parish. There is no governance body, formal or advisory, providing oversight; funds (revenues and expenses) are commingled; and the school is no longer central to the personal needs of most parishioners. The vision should include an explicit approach for more effective direct overall management of the School.

Finally, in pulling all of these elements and considerations together, Kate must review the final product against the following criteria:

- Is the vision consistent with the mission and values of the School?
- Is the vision feasible? Is it analytically sound?
- Is the vision doable? Is it operationally possible?

Chapter 7 MinuteClinic

1. From a Five Forces perspective, there are several players—large and small, mentioned and not mentioned—in the case:

- Suppliers: CVS, Wal-Mart, and Target are suppliers to MinuteClinic (MC) since customers could be "routed" to MC for help (for example, if CVS customers appear to have colds, allergies, etc. upon entering the store). If MC enters into agreements with insurers, it's possible that these insurance companies—or even employers, directly—could send sick members/employees to MC for help. Other pharmacies/drugstores are likely not to refer patients to MinuteClinic so as to not lose sales.
- New Entrants: At the time of the case, no new entrants are mentioned. However, this model could be copied by a new entrant who could approach other (national) pharmacy chains (like Walgreens), retailers (like Sears, JCPenney, etc.), and other insurers (like BlueCross BlueShield plans). A second entrant may even benefit form MC's business model since MC has already spent a lot of money marketing the idea, allying with partners, making the idea known/accepted (including JCAHO accreditation), etc.
- Substitutes: These include substitute healthcare and "health advice" offerings like Internet-based information sources (like WebMD), self-healthcare (that is, taking care of your aches/pains yourself with over-the-counter medicines), and friend/family care.
- Buyers: These include individual patients, large employers, and health plans.
- Competitors: These include other providers of "basic" or "simple" healthcare including family practice physicians/groups and hospital emergency rooms. Some employers may provide free onsite medical services, but as the case states, some employers have effectively "outsourced" this solution to MC

In terms of customers vs. buyers, in some cases, the customers will be insured individuals, and the buyers will be the health plans (and indirectly the customers' employers) that insure them and thus reimburse for the flat MC fees. In other cases, customers may choose to simply pay, themselves, given the convenience.

Regulation certainly plays a role in this case. The Rhode Island pull-out illustrates that a group of (state) regulators could make market entry difficult. Also, if MC starts treating Medicare patients, the Federal government may be involved since it (the Federal government) may then be reimbursing for some of the cost of MC treatment.

Some players could be in multiple "forces." For example, a health insurer could be a buyer of MC services (for its own employees) as well as a supplier of patients to MC (for insured individuals that it covers). A pharmacy chain could be a direct competitor, if it offers similar MC-like services, or it could be a substitute if it focuses on having its customers ask pharmacists basic health questions about illnesses, etc. In this case, the pharmacy could offer over-the-counter drugs as a substitute for the MC care.

2. Clearly, CVS wants MC to succeed. Hospitals, at some level, would like to see MC succeed too. Hospitals could reduce unnecessary emergency room visits with MCs in place nearby, and MCs could refer more serious cases to the hospital/ER such that better "triage" is accomplished. Insurers like MC because it helps reduce office visit expenses (in some cases).

However, family practices, physician lobby groups (like the American Medical Association), and, to some extent, health insurers don't want MC to be successful. Family practices lose "continuity of care," as do hospitals, at some level, and physician lobby groups want to protect family practice doctors' income. Health insurers have to walk a fine line in terms of helping their (network) doctors get business but at the same time saving money (and cutting costs) for employers and individuals who contract with the insurers

Chapter 8 Minute Clinic

1. In terms of a SWOT analysis, here are some key capabilities to consider from the Family Associates (FA) perspective:

    - Strengths: Long-term and relationship-based family care. FA doctors will likely know a great deal about their patients' histories, medicines, procedures, etc. FA is also a community-based business—not a "big corporate entity" like CVS/MC

    - Weaknesses: MC will likely "steal" some business from FA since patients may enjoy the convenient (and possibly the relatively cheap) services provided by MC. These office visits—and the corresponding continuity of care or medical "full picture"—will be difficult if not impossible to achieve by FA doctors moving forward. Also, with insurers favoring the MC approach for "simple" items, FA may have to depend on more non-insurance business. Lack of FA operational efficiency will continue to be a weakness (including potential lack of sufficient capital to make wholesale changes)

    - Opportunities: FA may be able to rally local (political) support to oppose MC entry. Alternatively, FA may be able to alter its operations to accommodate "basic" medical services differently from other services (although this may require too high of an investment/expense). FA may be able to work with CVS/MC in terms of referrals for more advanced (but non-urgent) cases to FA.

    - Threats: FA faces threats from possible new entrants that may copy MC's business model. Also, if insurers continue to back MC's strategy, then FA may not be able to compete on any other level except quality. If more large employers start recommending MC, this may also hurt FA's core customer/patient base.

286 TEST YOURSELF "ANSWERS"

FA could try to leverage their "quality of care" strength—including the relationship- and family-focused care advantage—to directly market against MC (although this may be expensive). FA could also attempt to improve its operations and "triage" its office visits better. Using its community connections, FA could also rally for local support to keep MC out of its market (or at least try to change local perceptions of it a la anti-Wal-Mart campaigns that some towns have put forward).

In terms of defensive strategies, it's unclear whether FA can prevent and/or protect its customer base in any other way than changing operations and/or pushing the quality-of-care advantage. However, either/both of these require significant investment that FA may not be able to afford given its shrinking family office visit revenues.

2. In terms of a strategy map that compares MC and FA, we propose the following example of how to look at bases of competition and relative investments in them in this market:

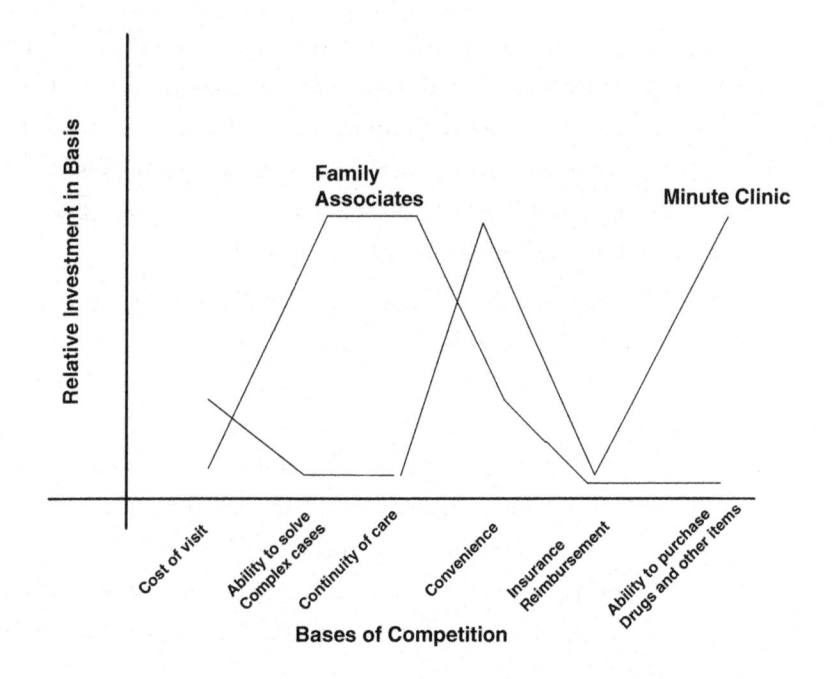

Strategy map showing Relative Investment in Basis (y-axis) vs. Bases of Competition (x-axis): Cost of visit, Ability to solve Complex cases, Continuity of care, Convenience, Insurance Reimbursement, Ability to purchase Drugs and other items. Two lines compare Family Associates and Minute Clinic.

As we can see, FA competes primarily on its MD partners, and their abilities to solve more complex cases and referrals, as well as on the community-, continuity-, and family-focus of its care. MC, on the other hand, competes on convenience, product "tie-ins" by virtue of being in the same space as a pharmacy, and somewhat on cost of the visit, if we consider the opportunity costs of parking, waiting, and then going to the drugstore when a patient visits FA.

Chapter 9 Astral Pharmaceuticals

1. All six of the potential partners have significant pros and cons, and one could argue that there's not one best or "perfect" partner (nor is there ever!). Here are some thoughts with respect to how well each partners "matches" with Astral along conceptual and analytical dimensions:

    a. <u>Agrinetics</u> could take the agribusiness away from Astral at a significant profit, but this would be only a one-time gain. The agricultural business of Astral's portfolio is one of the best in terms of earnings from operations (EFO) and provides solid cash flows for future operations (both within and across Astral business units). Thus, we would *not* recommend this partner since our core business is suffering (i.e., not throwing off much cash), and the agribusiness is a stable (and growing) component.

    b. <u>Humania</u> doesn't have a U.S. operation—great for Astral, which knows the U.S. market well. However, Astral has limited skills in anti-inflammatory drugs, and given the terms of the deal, Astral would take a huge risk in trying to get the drug approved (and delivered) in the U.S. market. Further, Humania is already allied with three large(r) pharmaceutical firms; thus, the deal with Astral would likely not get much attention. Further, Astral would not be in a leading/commanding position, since Humania will control development, distribution, etc., so Astral won't have much control over the relationship once it's formed.

c. <u>Bionamics</u> appears to be a good deal for Astral—it's in a relatively well-understood therapeutic area (but with unproven science). Astral's sales force could be kept busy, but the downside is the risk financing component. Given Astral's current (diminishing) financial picture, this may be a huge bet for Astral. However, given that Astral will control the partnership, and reap huge benefits if the bet pays off, this is an attractive partnership that meets both Astral and Bionamics needs well.

d. <u>Tsujita</u> looks good in the sense that it has no US operation while Astra excels in the United States. However, Astral has limited cardiovascular experience, and the three (small) drugs that Astral has already have plenty of patent life left. The expected instability of the compound is also cause for concern.

e. <u>University Medical Center</u> offers a possible profit stream, but the potential values/mission conflicts between Astral and UMC are causes for concern. The academic medical center focuses on grants and research, not on commercializing a drug. Astral would thus be forced to sell/market the whim of the UMC scientists over time (and would have little say over the basic science being performed at UMC). While complementary in terms of skills and value-added, the fundamental mission and vision of each organization would likely be in conflict long before a drug is launched. However, Astral would certainly have full control over distribution and detailing for this cancer drug (even though Astral has limited/no experience in oncology) assuming the drug could be approved in the United States—and this risk would be entirely Astral's.

f. <u>Micropharma</u>: Although Astral has no experience in diabetes, Micropharma is a good match because they already have a drug that's been *approved,* and the terms of the deal would allow Astral to be the sole U.S. operating entity. Assuming Astral's sales force could learn about this drug, and be able to cross-sell it to physicians and formularies with which they already have long-established relationships, this could be a very beneficial venture for Astral

Thus, we believe that Astral should consider (in order) the following two ventures: Micropharma and Bionamics. Humania, although attractive, would only make sense if Astral were in more of a lead role and if the alliance were at least as large as some of Humania's existing partners. The other potential suitors probably don't make sense to pursue at all. The Agrinetics deal (don't get rid of a money-maker and always exchange an asset for an asset), the Tsujita alliance (risky, unapproved drug), and the University Medical Center partnership (values/mission conflict) should probably be avoided.

2. If we only consider operations and assume that market shares and mission/vision/values are roughly the same and aligned, then we might propose the following ventures be considered strongly by Astral (in order): Micropharma, Bionamics, and Tsujita. In all cases, Astral would spearhead the marketing and sales for the United States for these alliances/partnerships. This would play to Astral's strengths in marketing, detailing, and sales in the United States, and these partners would likely allow a large number of "cross-sells" to existing Astral clients. This would keep the sales force busy, and keep them learning and growing in some new therapeutic categories, while creating limited risks to underlying business operations. Micropharma and Bionamics, however, appear to be the two best fits with Astral's current operations and future directions. They also seem to fit well with Astral's risk profile (Micropharma better than Bionamics given Micropharma's in-hand drug approval), management style, and overall cultural fit.

3. We provided a bit of a head start in the text. In addition to the metrics we outlined, the following may warrant consideration. Note that this list is not intended to be exhaustive:
   a. *Financial*: market share (by therapeutic class) in units and dollars, return on invested capital (if co-investing), sales (both to new customers and to existing)
   b. *Internal*: sales force productivity (sales per account per salesperson), inventories and shipments (especially of new/partner drugs), returns (of new drugs)
   c. *Learning/Growth*: expertise in new therapeutic areas, conference appearances (for marketing department), success in detailer training
   d. *Customer*: new and existing customer satisfaction, attrition, press attention (positive and negative), increased profitability (from existing customers) due to new drug sales, partner company satisfaction (here, thinking of the alliance partner (e.g., Humania) as a customer of Astral)
4. In terms of action plans, we suggest the following (incomplete) list of key activities (noted on the next three pages), in Balance Scorecard format, to support a successful collaboration:
5. A key to Astral's success is retention of its (loyal) customer base. This will require Astral to keep servicing them well in established therapeutic areas while encouraging them to purchase in new areas of interest (due to new partnerships/alliances, etc.). However, there are limits to the costs that Astral can pay to keep these clients in order to achieve its research mission (and to have available cash flow/funding to do so). If other participants ally and try to compete, then Astral should revisit its Five Forces and SWOT analyses and see what the key impacts might be.

Further, Astral will want to consider different end-states, like those mentioned in the problem, and think about what will have

TEST YOURSELF "ANSWERS"

Objective	Measure	Target	Initiative(s)
Financial: generate enough profits to support research agenda	Customer profitability by drug and by therapeutic class	• Increase profitability by 5% for existing customers in existing classes • Become top three seller to new customers (based on new drugs from partners)	• Update training on latest drug developments • Set new sales targets (with increased incentives) • Create "acquisition" team for new drugs • Create "retention" sales team to keep long-term clients and to cross-sell new drugs from partner(s)
Internal: fully utilize the existing sales force and keep them busy full-time	• Visits per account per salesperson • Sales (or profit) per visit • Customer attrition per salesperson	• Increase visits per salesperson by 10% per month • Increase sales by 5% per month (existing customers)	• Revisit scheduling of sales visits; increase daily sales calls • Develop bonus/incentive plan for increased sales • Create new customer

(Continued)

Objective	Measure	Target	Initiative(s)
Learning/Growth: develop expertise in key therapeutic areas	• Training success in new areas (sales force) • New area science hires (and retention) • Conference presentations by Astral scientists	• Achieve 50% success in new customer sales (with new drugs) • Maintain attrition levels at less than 5% • % salespeople trained in new areas per quarter • New area science hires (# competitively hired per quarter); retention of key scientists • Conference presentations per quarter (at leading events; keynote addresses)	• "SWAT Team"—and compensate accordingly—for new sales channels / customers • Rebalance sales force as attrition occurs • Create training bonuses / promotion opp's for salespeople with multiple areas of expertise • Attend / keynote more higher-end conferences • Develop "new science" hiring and retention programs (with dedicated HR resources)

Objective	Measure	Target	Initiative(s)
Customer: Maximize long-term relationships and prevent attrition	• Customer lifetime value • Retention rate • Customer profitability • Customer satisfaction and feedback	• Increase lifetime value by 10% per year • Retain at least 90% of long-term customers per quarter • Increase profitability by 5% for existing customers • Improvement in overall satisfaction (via survey) of at least 5% per year	• Develop analytics around customer lifetime value and set baseline for all current customers • Track retention (reorders, etc.) of key accounts • Report customer profitability (by class and by region) quarterly • Report satisfaction scores—including anecdotal remarks—twice per year

to be true for those end-states to be achieved. In doing so, Astral can determine enablers and other key "levers" that can be used against them in this market. For example, if two firms decide to not work with Astral and to compete directly with Astral, then Astral will have to shift focus to retention and so much on growth/learning and financial metrics. Customer and operational components will become the ones to focus on to ensure retention and flawless execution (but hopefully without too much of a sales or profit impact).

Chapter 10 Graham, Smith & Bendel LLP

OVERVIEW

In the opinion of Aaron Nettles, the relatively new CEO of GSB, the nature of management consulting has changed (you might, for example, want to do a Five-forces analysis of the consulting industry to confirm or challenge Nettles's position) and GSB, if it doesn't change its approach, runs the risk of being left behind. He has, therefore, mandated a new strategic approach for the Firm based on two major initiatives:

1. Marketing/Sales: aggressively pursue and acquire new clients
2. Cross-selling: aggressively pursue additional business across consulting departments with existing clients.

In support of these, he has reorganized the formerly independent consulting departments and newly-acquired groups into two divisions along with a services division, all headed by very senior consultants (old timers?). Finally, he has created the position of Director of Marketing, as a peer to the three division heads, and established a New Business Committee (NBC).

In the three months since these changes were announced, nothing much has happened as the existing consulting groups have continued to pursue business as usual. This may be because (1) the new strategic approach runs sharply counter to the traditional culture and values of the firm as promulgated by its founder, Sir William Graham, and (2) primary responsibility for driving the change has been given to David Stanley, who is both director of marketing and the NBC chair and also a relative newcomer to the firm. Stanley, who formerly worked for a firm noted for its aggressive approach to marketing consulting services, now finds the ball squarely in his court.

Stanley approach to his new tasks, especially to the NBC, has been enthusiastic and seemingly professional, but so far has produced a combination of passive participation and active indifference. Stanley clearly needs to step back and take stock of his situation—to rethink both his strategic responsibilities and his approach—and to develop a coherent "Strategy on a Page."

A brief review of Stanley's strategic situation yields the following observations:

- He has two seemingly compatible responsibilities that may, in fact, be conflicting. His Department is to provide marketing support services to the consulting departments, presumably both when they ask for them and also when Stanley and/or his (junior?) staffers see opportunities. As Chair of the NBC, Stanley is supposed to "foster a greater interchange of ideas within the Firm and to promote new business." On the one hand, he is formally defined as in a support role and, on the other, he is expected to take a leadership role with a committee of middle managers who report to his peers—who are senior to him in service and dubious to resistant about Nettles's strategy. Unfortunately, requests for support have been few and his approach to leadership has consisted mainly of writing memos and calling meetings, with little effort on relationship-building.

- He lacks positional power to drive either of these responsibilities and must develop a strategy based on leadership and performance.

- His principal internal "customers" or "clients," Reldan and Shamtun, have evidenced little "felt need" either to change the firm's traditional approach to business or for Stanley's services.

- While he has been a consultant throughout his career, his image is that of a "marketing whiz" or salesman rather than that of a senior consulting professional.
- Given his relative newness to the Firm and his actions to date, he has developed little by way of either personal or political relationships.
- He apparently has Nettles's support but Nettles appears to be reluctant to intervene or to push too hard on Shamtun and Reldan.

It would seem that Stanley has fallen in to the same trap as Nettles—that of moving directly to tasks and actions without first securing a commitment to the strategy and to the means and measures of implementing it. Nettles announced a new strategic direction and then assumed that the creation of organizational mechanisms, a reorganization, creation of a marketing unit, and naming of a committee, would lead to implementation. Similarly, Stanley has moved directly to traditional tactics and tasks, committee meetings, memos, presentations, without taking the time to rally acceptance of the strategy, or at least agreement to give it a test, or to establish the personal relationships and credibility needed to secure the engagement of the other key players, who are also among his key customers and who, so far, have no incentive to cooperate.

Stanley will have to rethink his approach and to develop strategies for the Marketing Department and the NBC that will provide compelling *value propositions* for his key customers.

ANALYSIS

Let's first look at Stanley's situation in a more organized way. We have said that he has two major responsibilities, to head the

Marketing Department and to chair the NBC, both of which have been created to support the corporate strategy of actively generating new business and aggressively cross-selling current business. To do so, he will both have to work with and to support the existing consulting departments since they will be the actual providers of the services once the business is sold. We can, therefore, map his situations as shown in the following chart.

Stanley's Strategy Matrix

Stanley's Strategy Situation		GSB Services	
		Provided by Single Department	Intergrated across Departments
Client	New	II • Will require more aggressive effort by Marketing Department • Will be seeking to take share from competitors • Internal servicing by consulting departments will not change	III • Will require aggressive full-line promotion with active participation of consulting departments in sales and in servicing
	Old/ Existing	I • Declining market share • Slow Growth	IV • Will require consultants to 'prospect' and to introduce marketing department to 'their' clients • Will require Account Management process to coordinate across projects for given client

Examining the implications of each of the four main boxes, we can see that Stanley will need at least three components in his strategy and that these vary by ease of execution and complexity and provide guidance for Stanley in laying out a timeline and for prioritizing his efforts. To summarize the key aspects of each box, consider the following:

- **Old/Existing Clients—Single Department**: This is the default cell or "business as usual" that is declining and has led to

Nettles's new strategic approach. It is the baseline for assessing and evaluating initiatives in the other boxes;

- **New Clients—Single Department**: This cell represent a classic "new business development" effort. Stanley's group generates new clients and passes them on to the proper consulting departments for servicing. In a more advanced form, Stanley's group works with the consulting departments to "pitch" new business. In both instances, Stanley's group can prove their worth, independently or in partnership, without threatening existing client relationships. This does, however, represent a change in the firm's culture.

- **New Clients—Integrated Across Departments**: This cell would likely to be a second step after Cell II, based on building familiarity with the client and also developing comfort with the consulting departments regarding joint sales efforts. Alternatively, Stanley's group could offer a menu of GSB services to a potential client and then bring the consulting departments in after the client indicates specific interests. In either case, the issues of account management and client ownership begin to emerge.

- **Old Clients—Integrated Across Departments**: This cell represents the greatest degree of change or movement from the traditional GSB approach. It would involve changing (growing, deepening, etc.) the relationship with existing clients and bringing a new party, the Marketing Department, into the relationship. While the ultimate objective of Nettles's strategy, this would probably take the longest to achieve and would require Stanley's group being "invited in" by the existing client account managers.

Pulling all of these considerations together, Stanley should now be able to develop his Strategy on a Page and the Action Plan needed to support it. His strategy should specify:

- Strategic Intent: what, specifically, he intends to achieve in each of the three active cells (II, III, IV), his three market segments, in what order in the next time period;
- Strategic Elements:
    - Product Line—the products and services Stanley and his staff can provide within each of his market segments
    - Marketing—how the Marketing Department will market itself within each of its segments (new external clients (II); internal clients to serve new business (III); internal clients for support in expanding their existing business (IV))
    - Facilities—in the broadest sense, the informational resources that Stanley will assemble in order to support the internal and external marketing efforts
    - Organizational Renewal/R&D—what the Marketing Department can do to make itself professionally valuable to its internal clients
    - Finances—internally, what resources it will take to make the Marketing Department fully operational; externally, the value that Marketing can add to the bottom line of the consulting departments
    - Human Resources—the staff competences that will be needed to (a) sell externally, (b) advise internally, (c) provide technical support to consultant-driven projects and proposals, and (d) lead the creative strategic process at the senior level
    - Management/Organization/Governance—how Marketing will work internally but, more importantly, how it will reach out and build relationships (including mending fences) with the consulting departments at all levels

- <u>Critical Success Factors</u>: demonstrating value to the consulting departments (existing units and new acquisitions) in achieving their objectives; responding effectively to requests for help from consulting departments when asked; gaining acceptance of consulting departments for the business development/cross-selling strategy

Endnotes

CHAPTER 1

1. Carroll, Lewis, *Alice's Adventures In Wonderland,* Avenel Books: New York, p. 89.
2. Ibid. p.182.
3. By Thomas P. Ference. Copyright © 2008 by The Riverside Group. All rights reserved. Used with permission.

CHAPTER 2

1. "The Ant and the Grasshopper," Aesop's Fables, *The Harvard Classics: Folk-Lore and Fable,* Hartford: Grolier 1980, pp. 25–26
2. In chapter 3, we will discuss the factors governing the choice of x, the timeframe for our strategic analysis. While most current practices think in terms of three-year or five-year strategic horizons, we will treat this as a choice variable and will discuss the reasons for making a specific choice for a specific organization.
3. We will discuss "environmental analysis"—the processes of identifying, forecasting, and monitoring all of these potentially changing elements—and its role in formulating and dynamically adapting strategy in greater detail in chapter 7.
4. In the next chapter, we will develop the concept of Vision more fully and will provide detailed guidelines on what constitutes a 'good' or effective vision statement from the perspective of effectiveness in developing and monitoring the strategy.
5. We are not suggesting here a justification for Draconian actions such as wholesale terminations or fire sales of older programs and products.

We are simply pointing out that the strategic perspective allows us to treat as variables, as elements of fresh choice, aspects of any organization that might conventionally have been treated as "givens." We also recognize that existing contracts and commitments must be fulfilled. In later chapters, we will discuss the effective redevelopment and redeployment of human resources and other assets.
6. By Thomas P. Ference. Copyright © 2006. The Riverside Group. Used with permission of The Hay Group.

CHAPTER 3

1. Dr. Seuss, *The Lorax,* Random House: New York, 1971
2. For ease of exposition, we refer here to the "strategist" or the "strategic thinker" as a single individual. In practice, in our complex modern organizations, while such persons clearly exist, it probably makes more sense to speak of the "strategic team" of individuals who, collectively, create and sustain the organization's ongoing strategic perspective. We will refer to the "strategic team" or the "strategist" interchangeably.
3. By Thomas P. Ference. Copyright © 2006 by The Riverside Group. All rights reserved. Used with permission

CHAPTER 4

1. We recognize that one of the difficulties in discussing the Conceptual Level of strategy is that different authors and different organizations use these terms differently and often in conflicting and confusing ways. We will return to the issue of terminology later and will seek to present a jargon- or buzzword-free formulation of the fundamental issues or questions to be dealt with at this level—and then will suggest in a later section a consistent terminology for the purposes of this book.
2. DuPont. The phrase "… through chemistry" was removed in the 1980s. The slogan was replaced by "The miracles of science" in 1999. See *http://heritage.dupont.com/touchpoints/tp_1939/overview.shtml*.
3. Federal Express. Originally, the slogan of Federal Express Overnight. Still in use in modified forms by different divisions of FedEx Corporation, the official name since 2000. The new corporate slogan is "The World on Time."

4. General Electric. Retired in 2003. The new corporate tagline is "imagination at work."
5. What Yogi really wrote was, "Make a firm decision. Make sure it feels right. Learn from the choice you make. Don't second-guess yourself – there's no need to give yourself ulcers." We think that Yogi has a pretty good grasp of strategic thinking and the role of the subjective in guiding the objective. Yogi Berra (with Dave Kaplan), *When You Come to a Fork in the Road, Take It!* Hyperion: New York 2001, p. 5.
6. We will discuss the special meanings of "leader" and "manager" in a strategic context in the next section.
7. While we focus here on organizations, we acknowledge that the strategic process is equally valid and equally important for sole proprietorships and other less complex or formal entities and also for individuals developing career strategies and so on. We will treat these as special cases of the general organizational approach. Our view is, however, that even in these situations, the process will benefit from multiple perspectives or inputs and is best done or driven by those who will be responsible for implementing the results.
8. We fully appreciate the value of expert specialists, be they outside consultants or in-house heads of strategic analysis. These strategic "gurus" in our view—and we aspire at times to be recognized as gurus ourselves—provide value through their mastery of process and concept, and, potentially, through their objectivity, but the members of the organization on the strategic team are the masters of content and substance.
9. We will discuss this further in chapter 10 when we develop the fourth KEY to strategic thinking—the notion of "strategy on a page" or the living strategy committed to and pursued by each strategic unit head.
10. We are indebted Edgar H. Schein, particularly *Organizational Psychology,* Prentice-Hall: Englewood Cliffs, NJ 1965, pp. 7–9, for his seminal development of these ideas. The specific wording and any deficiencies are ours.
11. For the seminal discussion of the differences between leaders and managers, see John P. Kotter, "What Leaders Really Do," *Harvard Business Review*, May-June 1990, pp. 103–111. For a provocative discussion of the different ways leaders can affect an organization, see Jim Collins, "Level 5 Leadership: The Triumph of Humility and Fierce Resolve," *Harvard Business Review*, January 2001, pp. 66–76. For

a discussion of the development of leaders and managers, see Thomas P. Ference, "Becoming an Effective Leader," *Arts & Business Quarterly*, Winter 2003, pp. 1, 10–11.

12. For example, it is unrealistic to expect that a CEO, who had chosen to "lead" the strategic process, would be able to resist setting aside the facilitator's expected neutrality and exercising instead his/her formal authority and power of position in order to resolve an issue on which he/she had a strong opinion.

CHAPTER 5

1. March of Babies [formerly March of Dimes]; *http://www.marchofdimes.com/aboutus/787.asp*
2. Collins & Porras make a persuasive argument for the power of ultimate purpose, which they term BHAGs [*Big, Hairy, Audacious Goals*] in binding organizations together and see the possession of a BHAG as one of the fundamental attributes of organizations that succeed over extended periods of time. We find their insights valuable but are less convinced of the effectiveness of ultimate purposes in providing guides for day-to-day behavior. Thus, we find it more effective to focus our strategic process on more psychologically meaningful 'chunks' of time that we can "get our arms [or our minds] around." These 'chunks' would represent, in Collins & Porras's terms, the next major stage or phase along the path to the BHAG. See J. C. Collins and J. J. Porras, "Building Your Company's Vision," *Harvard Business Review*, September-October 1996, pp. 65–77.
3. We will discuss how to select the value of x below in the section "Defining the Strategic Cycle." In effect, x is the psychologically meaningful chunk for our organization or activity discussed in the previous footnote.
4. We have not included our "So what?" question in this discussion of terminology as the question is intended merely to remind us that intentions and aspirations have no real meaning until they are transformed into actual achievement. Also, there are very few ways to say "So what?" more precisely than "So what?"
5. The literature abounds with guidelines and "rules of thumb" such as "no more than seven words" or "two sentences at most." We do

not find these particularly helpful and often result in sloganizing, perhaps inspiring but not doing the job of providing clear guidance for tough choices. A good mission statement should be as long or as short as necessary to define our basic rationale for existence, attract and inspire our members, and guide decision-making.

6. The fact that our concept of "mission" involves five each of criteria and elements is coincidental. There is no necessary one-to-one correspondence between criteria and elements.
7. In not-for-profit organizations, such as this one, the CEO [often called the Executive Director] and the COO are the senior paid executives; the Board Chairs, past, present, and future, are volunteers, as, typically, are the remaining members of the Board.
8. This is one example of what is often referred to as *mission drift* or the displacement of "ends"—of ultimate purposes—by "means." Thus, we may come to see our function, product, or activity as **the** mission rather than as **a** means to the mission and, consequently, resist any changes to the function, etc., on mission grounds even though other, newer products or activities may be more effective in achieving the core purpose.
9. Google; *http://www.google.com/corporate*
10. USFDA [Food and Drug Administration]; *http://www.fda.gov/opa-com/morechoices/mission.html*
11. Starbucks; *http://www.starbucks.com/aboutus/environment.asp*
12. Novartis; *http://www.novartis.com/about-novartis/our-mission/index.shtml*
13. *http://www.dilbert.com/comics/dilbert/games/career/bin/ms.cgi* Unfortunately, far too many corporate mission statements sound like this intendedly satirical example and leave the reader or listener saying, "Huh?" rather than being moved to action.
14. Note, however, that does not mean to suggest that the mission is simply a listing or catalogue of the organization's current portfolio of programs and services. The mission would be concerned with the attributes and functions that these products and services would provide.
15. The United States Constitution; *http://www.usconstitution.net/const.html#Preamble*
16. By Thomas P. Ference. Copyright © 2000 by The Riverside Group. All rights reserved.

CHAPTER 6

1. *The Godfather;* Paramount Pictures 1972; *http://www.imdb.com/title/tt0068646/synopsis*
2. "Hold dear" is an idiom meaning, in effect, "dear to the heart."
3. This is what Schein has called *the psychological contract*, the implied or explicit relationship between the individual and the organization. See Edgar H. Schein, *Organizational Psychology,* Prentice-Hall: Englewood Cliffs, NJ, 1965, pp. 11–13.
4. IBM; *http://www.ibm.com/ibm/us/en*
5. American Express; *http://home3.americanexpress.com/corp/os/values.asp*
6. Wegman's; *http://www.wegmans.com/webapp/wcs/stores/servlet/AboutUsView*
7. Note that we are not speaking here of simple judgments of success or failure. Referring to our discussion in chapter 1 regarding checkpoints, the issue is to review actual achievement (performance) against aspiration (vision or strategic intent) in order to inform and launch the next round of strategic thinking.
8. We will provide some guidelines for determining how to define what is in "eyesight" in the next section. Recall also that, in a dynamic strategic process, we can extend our eyesight farther into the future at each milestone or checkpoint.
9. Our caution here is in reference to the all-too familiar "output fanatic" who is always pushing for something extra on top of what reason sustains because "it will do you good to try even if you fail."
10. We use the term "chunk" here in the information theoretic or cognitive psychological sense of a meaningful, coherent unit. See William G. Chase, & Herbert A. Simon, "Perception in chess," *Cognitive Psychology*, 1973:4, pp. 55–81.
11. This is not to say that strategists in the toy business should only think in such short terms. Many aspects of this business, as with any other, would involve longer timeframes, such as capital investments in equipment or facilities. These latter examples are, however, tactical and operational, even though they exceed the strategic timeframe. They are not strategic in the sense that they do not speak directly to the intrinsic nature of the business. Buildings could be leased or sold

and equipment could be converted to other uses. The strategic cycle is defined not in terms of the inputs or "means" of the business, but in terms of the core decisions involving the outputs or "ends."
12. This is not a matter of what sort of plant that you might build—nuclear, fossil, hydrodynamic, solar—but of the time it takes to build and bring the new capacity, the new plant, whatever sort it is, on line.
13. This and similar measures of volatility also provide guidance as to how frequently we should introduce checkpoints into our strategic effort. The more volatile or dynamic the industry, the more frequently we should be checking our progress against the plan and making the necessary revisions. We should also be using these checkpoints to extend our vision beyond the initial limits. We should not be waiting for the completion of one cycle to launch the next one but should be renewing the cycle at every major decision or checkpoint.
14. Note that this set of Vision Elements is specific to developing the strategy for a school. The relevant Vision Elements would be different for an organization in another field or industry. The key point is that a comprehensive vision should include elements that touch upon targeted performance or outcomes, internal organization and operations, and external competitive market dynamics.

CHAPTER 7

1. Abbot, Edwin A., *Flatland,* Dover, 1952.
2. The numbering system here follows that begun in Chapter 5 for the key diagnostic questions.
3. Porter, Michael E., *Competitive Strategy,* The Free Press, 1985
4. By Alison Boyle. Copyright © Columbia University, 2007. Used with permission. All rights reserved.

CHAPTER 8

1. Davenport, Thomas H., and Jeanne G. Harris, *Competing on Analytics: The New Science of Winning,* Harvard Business School Press, 2007
2. Lewis, Michael, *Moneyball: The Art of Winning an Unfair Game,* Norton, 2003

CHAPTER 9

1. Bossidy, Larry, and R. Charan, *Execution: The Discipline of Getting Things Done,* Crown Business, 2002
2. Edwin G. Booz, founder of the consultancy (in 1914) that eventually became Booz Allen Hamilton (now Booz & Co.),
3. Ron Boire, former student and senior executive of several major American and global retail and consumer electronics firms.
4. Thomas P. Ference, Copyright © 1996. All rights reserved. Used with permission.

CHAPTER 10

1. Exodus XVIII: 13-24; *The Holy Bible,* The Catholic Press: Chicago, 1950, pp. 62–63.
2. Put simply, the term *synergy* refers to guiding the potential interaction among elements of our strategy such that the whole, the collective output of the units within our organization, is greater than would be the simple sum of their parts *if each were acting independently*. It suggests a situation wherein interaction across units contributes to or leverages the performance of individual units such that the sum of the actual performance of the units exceeds what they could have achieved on their own. See Ansoff, H. Igor, *Strategic Management Classic Edition*, Palgrave Macmillan: New York, 2007, for the seminal discussion of this central concept of strategy.
3. We continue here with the numbering system begun in chapter 5 and carried on in chapter 7 for identifying the "right questions in the right order" that comprise the strategic thought process.
4. See chapter 2 to review our discussion of *milestones* and *checkpoints*.
5. By comparison, in the previous paragraphs, we were discussing those events that are both knowable (expected) and predictable (schedulable) but still function as obstacles to be dealt with. We *know* that we will need a C of O and we *know* that we will have to obtain it before we can open our facility; therefore, we have to include and schedule getting it in our timeline of key milestones.
6. See our more comprehensive discussion of *contingency* and *scenario planning* in Chapter 9.

7. For an excellent discussion of these concepts, see G. Hamel & L. Valikangas, "The Quest for Resilience," *Harvard Business Review*, September 2003. The authors define *resilience* as "a capacity for continuous reconstruction. It requires innovation with respect to those organizational values, processes, and behaviors that systematically favor perpetuation over innovation."
8. It is a *strategic action plan* in the sense that it is the resultant of a strategic thought process.
9. Lest we sound too cynical and dismissive of conventional strategic planning processes and strategic planners, we find both enormously useful as inputs to facilitators of the thought process. Traditional approaches, however, tend to be costly and exhausting and produce documents that are static and inflexible. We much prefer the dynamic process presented here which stresses clarity and simplicity and calls for frequent checkpointing and adjustment to evolving experience. To us, Strategy is a living thing, "shooting at a moving target from a moving platform," that may occasionally be captured on paper for purposes of keeping a record.
10. Refer to chapter 6 for guidelines on determining the length of the *strategic cycle* for a given organization or activity.
11. Recall our discussion of the complexity of "customerness" in chapter 1 where the "customer" is a complex mix of "Who decides," "Who pays," "Who uses," and "Who benefits."
12. Refer to our discussion of The Balanced Scorecard in chapter 9 for more on the critical need to provide for ongoing Learning and Growth.
13. Notice that we very carefully did not speak in terms of "profitability." Our concern here is not whether revenues will exceed costs in the plan period but, instead, what the expected flow of revenues and costs will be. Given sound strategic analysis, we can envision many situations in which we would support a financial plan that runs a deficit in the plan period in anticipation of positive cash flow in future periods, such as most research investments, or in the context of available subsidies from other sources—such as often is the case in not-for-profits.
14. This is not a trivial point. Our experience suggests that most failed strategies run aground on the absence of adequate human resource

planning in support of the strategy. It is often all too easy to rely on "on-the-job training" and to assume that "our people will just have to step up and do more."

15. By E. Kirby Warren, Ian Wilcox, & Thomas P. Ference. Copyright © 2008 b y Columbia University. All rights reserved. Used with permission.

Index

Accounting, 180–81
Achievable visions, 127
Acquisition metrics, 199
Action criterion, 104–5
Action plan
    operational considerations, 188, 191, 202–3, 220
    strategy development, 239–40
Agrinetics, 214
Allies, 11
Allocation, 10
Amazon.com, 147
American Airlines, 198
American Express, 124–25
Analysis, 164
Analytical thinking, 50, 55–56, 68, 76
Analytical tools, 141–42
AOL, 143
Apple iPod, 149
Aspiration, 5
Assessable strategies, 189–91
Assessable visions, 127
Assessment, 10
Astral Pharmaceuticals, 208–18

Balanced Scorecard
    case study, 208–18
    operational considerations, 188, 191–95, 201, 203–4, 219
    strategic thinking and, 57
Beane, Billy, 165
Benchmarking, 57, 203–5
Berra, Yogi, 76
Best Buy, 146, 147, 168
Best practices myth, 204–5
BHAGs, 126, 127, 128, 235

Bionamics, 215–16
Booz, Edwin, 187
British Airways, 150
Burton, Wells & Co., 13–21
Business strategy cases
    Astral Pharmaceuticals, 208–18
    Burton, Wells & Co., 13–21
    Fidelity Corporation, 58–67, 86–87
    Graham, Smith & Bendel, LLP, 240–52
    Ivtak Americas Group, 36–47
    MinuteClinic, 153–63, 181–82
    St. Emily's School, 107–16, 135–36
Business strategy course, 180–81
Buyers, 145, 148–49
Buzzwords, 79–80

Cantor, Eddie, 89
Capacity, lack of, 230
Challenging intent, 126–27
Change, 23–24, 25–26
Checkpoints, 28, 29, 35, 48
Cheshire Cat, 3, 71–72
Circuit City, 146, 147, 168
Collaboration metrics, 199–200
Columbia Records, 198–99
Communicable visions, 127
Competition
    actions of, 142
    analysis of, 56
    macro-market and, 145, 151
    mission and, 132–33, 137
    strategy and, 8–10, 22
Competitive advantage, 176–79
Conceptual level, 96
Conceptual strategy, leadership and, 73–76

Conceptual thinking
   key concepts, 92–97
   launching process, 76–79
   skills, 72
   strategic concept and, 90–91, 117
   strategic perspective, 71–72, 88
   strategic thinking and, 50, 54–55, 68
Concrete visions, 126
Constitution of United States, Preamble, 107
Consumers, 13, 152
Context, setting, 143–44
Continental Airlines, 188
Continental Lite, 188
Contingency plans, 205–8, 220
Contract review, 13–21
Core courses, 180–81, 183
Corleone, Don, 119, 122
Credibility, lack of, 230
Critical success factors (CSFs), 237–38, 240
Customer, 12–13
   analysis, 56
   effectiveness, satisfaction, 188
   metrics, 193, 195–96, 219

Dell, 147, 148
Delta, 25
Delta Airlines, 188
Demand, absence of, 230
Diagnosis, 77–78, 88
Diagnostic approach, 78–79
   buzzwords and, 79–80
Diagnostician, 72, 76
Dilbert, 6
Direction, 10
Distinctive competence, 176–79
Dunkin' Donuts, 174–75
Dynamics, 28

easyJet, 150
Economic criterion, 103–4
Economic values, 123
Effective organization, 81–83
Enablers, 206–7
End-states, 206–8
Environmental scanning, 56, 143–44
Envision, 25
Events
   knowable but unpredictable, 230–31
   unknowable, 231
Excellence, 83–84

Existential criterion, 101–3
Exodus, 224
Experience, use of, 33
Eyesight range, 126, 129

Facilitation, 72
Facilitator, 85–86, 88
Facilities, 236
FDA, 105
Fidelity Corporation, 58–67, 86–87
Finance, 166, 180–81
Financial considerations, 237
Financial metrics, 192, 196–97, 219
Financial services, 58–67
Financial success, 188
Five Forces model, 142, 145–47, 167, 168
   limitations of, 151–52
   strengths of, 147–51
Flatland, 141, 142
Focus, 9–10
Folding back
   fundamental questions, 227–33
   mindmap, 225, 232, 233
   operational issues and, 191
   strategic concept and, 91
   strategic thinking and, 24, 28–29, 33, 36, 48
   strategy development, 225
Forward integration, 148, 198

Gap, 26
Godfather, The, 122
Google, 105
Government, 152
Graham, Smith & Bendel, LLP, 240–52
Growth measurement, 188

Harvard Business School, 191
Holders of resources, 10–11
Horizontal integration, 197–98
Human resources, 36–47, 237
Humania, 214–15

IBM, 124
Identity criterion, 104
Image extension, 33
Implementation, 141
Incremental criterion, 99–101
Individual values, 123
Industrial rhythm, 130–31, 134

Industry analysis, 56
Initiatives, 202
Innovation and growth metrics, 188, 220
INSEAD, 174
Integration, 198–99
Internal process metrics, 192–93, 197–200, 219–20
Intrinsic timeframe, 130–31
Ivtak Americas Group, 36–47

Jethro, 223–25

Kaplan, Robert, 191–92
Kennedy, President, 6
Kim, W. Chan, 174
Krispy Kreme, 188–89

Leadership, 72–76, 83–84, 88
Learning and growth metrics, 193, 200–202
Lewis, Michael, 166
LG, 147

Mac, 148
Macro-market analysis, 141–42, 144, 185, 203
Management, 72, 88
    dashboards, 186–87, 191–95
    organization, governance, 237
Managerial skills, 82–83, 84
Manufacturing metrics, 199
March of Dimes, 89–90
Market analyses, 143–44
Market-driven intervals, 35
Marketing, 166, 180, 236
Market players, 151
Markets, 106
Mauborgne, Renee, 174
Measures, 202
Micro-market analysis, 165–66, 185, 206
    SWOT, 167–71
Micropharma, 217–18
Milestones
    strategic thinking and, 28–29, 34–35, 48
    strategy development and, 225, 240
Mindset, 27–34, 53
MinuteClinic case, 153–63
Mission
    articulating, 99, 106
    strategic concept and, 91, 96–98, 117
    strategic perspective and, 73–75
    strategic thinking and, 55

Mission statement, 91–92, 117
    criteria, 91, 99–105
    elements of, 91, 105–7
    key concepts, 92–97
Moneyball, 166
Moses, 223–25
Motorola, 147

NASA mandate, 6
National Foundation for Infantile Paralysis, 89
Natural flow of events, 26
New entrants, 146, 149–50
Norton, David, 191–92
Novartis, 105

Oakland As, 165–66
Objective, 202
Obstacles, 229–30
Operational metrics, 199
Operational thinking, 185–88
    balanced scorecard, 191–95
    strategic perspective and, 76
    strategic thinking and, 50, 56–57, 68
Operations, 219
Opportunities, 168, 169
Organization, 81
Organizational behavior, 166, 180
Organizational renewal/R&D, 236–37
Outsourcing, 47

PC, 148
Perceptual maps, 171–74
Personal learning process, 33–34
Philosophical values, 123
Players, 10–11
PlayStation, 11, 53
Porter, Michael, 142, 145, 151–52, 164, 168
Primitive, 93
Processes, 106
Producers, 13
Products, 106
Professionalism, 82, 84
Professional values, 123
Program/activity/product mix, 236
Project planning and management, 57

Questions, 78–79, 90
    fundamental, 98

Rationale, 105
Referees, 11
Regulation, 131–32, 137
Resilient strategy, 231
Resources, 8–9, 12, 106
Resource scarcity, 230
Results to date, 33
Robust strategy, 231
Roosevelt, Franklin Delano, 89
RyanAir, 150

Sabin, Dr. Albert, 89
Salk, Dr. Jonas, 89
Sanyo, 147
Scarcity, 8–9, 22
Scenario analysis, 205–8
Segment-specific metrics, 196
Selling metrics, 199
Service metrics, 199
Seuss, Dr., 49–50
Sharp, 147
Smith, Adam, 13
Social values, 123
Song, 188
Sony, 147, 151, 198–99
   Betamax, 189
   Blu-Ray, 189
   Walkman, 149
St. Emily's School, 107–16, 135–36
Starbucks, 105, 174–75, 188
State Department of Education, 5
Statics, 28
Strategic action plan, 225.
   See also Action plan
Strategic analysis, 7, 234
Strategic conceptualization, 7
Strategic cycle, 120, 129–34, 137
Strategic implementation and operation, 7–8
Strategic intent, 96, 126–27, 235–36.
   See also Vision
Strategic leadership, 117
Strategic management, 85
Strategic mapping, 166
Strategic paths, 29
Strategic perspective, 4
Strategic planning, 36, 232
  case study, 240–52
  definition of, 7
Strategic plans, 7

Strategic process, 26, 48
Strategic professionalism, 85
Strategic team, 8
  building, 72, 80–86
Strategic thinking, ix-x, 4, 6, 34–36
  action plan, 254
  business meaning of, 25–27
  definition of, 7
  diagnostic questions, 253–54
  keys to, 253
  leadership function, 84–85, 88
  levels of, 54–57
  phases of, 253
  role of, 90
Strategic thought process, 225
Strategist, 8
  mantra of, 34
  thinking like, 27–34
Strategos, 51–54, 68, 76, 117, 225–26
Strategy, ix, 3, 22, 88, 96, 98
  canvas, 174–75, 181, 183
  definition of, 4, 7
  development, 223–24, 233–35
  importance of, 8–13
  implementation, 228–29
  key concepts, 5–8
  linguistic roots of, 51–52
  operational definition of, 134
  on page, 225, 233–35
  on page components, 235–39
  word origins, 6
Strengths, 168, 169
  -opportunities strategies, 170
  -weaknesses strategies, 170–71
Substitutes, 146, 150
Suppliers, 146, 147–48
SWOT (strengths, weaknesses, opportunities, threats) analysis, 56, 166, 167–71, 181, 183, 185

Tangible outcomes, 126
Target, 146, 202
Ted, 188
Thought process, 30–32
Threats, 168, 169
Tiffany and Company, 173
Time Warner, 143
Timeframe, 91, 130–31, 134, 137
Tsujita Pharmaceuticals, 216–17
TWA, 198

United Airlines, 188
University Medical Center, 217
Users, 10

Value proposition, 4, 12, 22, 166, 176–79
Values
    mission and, 119–20, 137
    strategic concept and, 91, 96–98, 117
    strategic perspective and, 73–75
    strategic thinking and, 55
Values statement, 122–25
Vertical integration, 198
Vision
    defining, 125–29
    factors, 120
    mission and, 119, 120–21, 135–37
    and strategic intent, 201
    strategic concept and, 91, 96, 98, 117
    strategic perspective and, 73–75
    strategic thinking and, 55, 57
Vision statements, 117, 120, 125–29

Wal-Mart, 146, 173, 189
Weaknesses, 168, 169
    -opportunities strategies, 170
    -threats strategies, 171
Wegman's, 125
Wii, 11
Wimpy, 95

Xbox, 11, 53

Zen garden, 71–72, 74, 128

About the Authors

Thomas P. Ference, PhD, has been a member of the faculty of the Columbia Graduate School of Business since 1966 and of the Columbia University Mailman School of Public Health since 1996. He received his BS, MS, and PhD, the latter in Organization Theory, from Carnegie Mellon University (1963, 1966, 1967). His principal interests include strategic management, leadership, the management of professionals, career development and management, and the management of not-for-profit organizations.

Tom was director of the Columbia Business School Executive MBA Program from 1974 through 1994. He is a founding member and first Chair of the Executive MBA Council. He has also taught in the Mailman School's Executive MPH Program since its inception.

Tom has published numerous books, reports, and articles in professional journals. His work on Career Plateauing, in collaboration with E. Kirby Warren and James A. F. Stoner, was instrumental in establishing a research focus on the organizational and individual challenges of effective utilization of managers and professionals over the career stream. His work with Fred Goldner and R. Richard Ritti on the Roman Catholic priesthood during the time of the Second Vatican Council made significant contributions to the study of professions and organizations.

Tom is a founder and Managing Partner of The Riverside Group, a consulting firm that specializes in strategic management and in the design and delivery of executive development programs. Tom has worked with a broad array of firms in the pharmaceutical, financial services, consulting, and communications industries among others. He has also taught in executive programs in the UK, Northern Ireland, China, Japan, Colombia, Malaysia, Brazil, France, and Spain.

Tom is also the founder and past director (1976–1993) of the Columbia Business School Institute for Not-for-Profit Management. He has consulted with numerous prominent not-for-profit and public sector institutions in the criminal justice, human services, health and hospital, education, and philanthropic sectors among others. His clients have included national and local agencies, all levels of government, and non-US NGOs. He has also chaired and served on several not-for-profit boards. Tom and his wife, Ellie, live in Haworth, New Jersey. Tom can be contacted at tompf@prodigy.net.

Paul W. Thurman, a Columbia MBA valedictorian, service award winner, and multiple teaching-awards recipient, has extensive management consulting and line management experience helping a variety of start-ups and Fortune 500 companies realize value from innovative and coordinated business, operations, and technology strategies. He has held senior positions at Booz Allen Hamilton and American Express, and he has served public and private sector clients on five continents. Paul is also the author of Kaplan's best-selling text, *MBA Fundamentals Statistics,* (January 2008), and his *Pocket Guide to Statistics,* also from Kaplan Publishing, will be available in selected Asian markets in the coming months.

Paul has been a consultant to several global financial services, health care, retail, and consumer products firms across a broad set of business disciplines. His consulting work has focused mostly on analytical modeling to support strategic planning and decision-making, corporate cost management, and technology and business integration. He has also developed analytical solutions around customer segmentation, demand modeling, profitability, and experience mapping. Paul currently leads his general management and executive education consultancy, Thurman and Associates, and is a frequent academic and business conference presenter.

Since 2003, Paul has taught strategic management and data analysis courses at Columbia University's School of International and Public Affairs and at its Mailman School of Public Health. He also serves as executive director of the Columbia University Alliance for Healthcare Management, where he coordinates research, academic, and industry programs among Columbia's graduate schools of Public Health, Medicine, and Business. From 1998–2003, Paul taught courses in decision, risk, and operations in the full-time and Executive MBA Programs at the Columbia, London, and University of California, Berkeley business schools.

In addition to his full-time faculty appointments, Paul serves as a clinical professor and affiliated researcher at the US National Cancer Institute's Center for Cancer Research at the National Institutes of Health. His recent peer-reviewed, published research has focused on scientific collaboration and its effect on research quality, cancer drug prices and FDA regulation, and on optimal cancer center organizational structures and management disciplines. He is also a visiting professor and senior research fellow at the Hellenic American University (HAU) in Athens, Greece, where he teaches a variety of MBA courses, conducts research, and has coauthored several published papers and conference presentations on immigrant entrepreneurship in emerging markets. In 2009, he and two of his HAU colleagues will publish a research compendium on female immigrant entrepreneurship, comprising research collected and analyzed across 20+ countries.

Paul sits on the boards of the Greenburgh (New York) Nature Center, the Scarsdale (New York) Teen Center, and a New York City-based charity. He also serves on the advisory boards of a number of entrepreneurial ventures, including a cancer drug development and marketing alliance, a Web security software company, and a regional sports marketing and advertising firm.

Paul received his BS in mathematics from Stanford University and his MBA from Columbia University (with highest honors). He is currently pursuing a doctorate in business (DBA) from the Ecole des Ponts Business School in Paris, France. He and his family live in Glen Ridge, New Jersey. Paul can be reached at Paul.Thurman@Columbia.edu.

Made in the USA
Middletown, DE
11 March 2020